S0-BBZ-533

Newt Gingrich

Capitol Crimes and Misdemeanors

John K. Wilson

Common Courage Press
Monroe, Maine

Copyright © John K. Wilson 1996
All Rights Reserved
Cover design by Matt Wuerker
Photo by Impact Visuals

Library of Congress Cataloging-in-Publication Data
Wilson, John K., 1969—
Newt Gingrich: capitol crimes and misdemeanors/John K. Wilson
p. cm.
Includes bibliographical references and index.
ISBN 1-56751-097-3 (cloth)
1. Gingrich, Newt. 2. Political corruption—United States. 3. United States—Politics and government—1993- I. Title
E840.8.G5W55 1996 96-27363
328.73'092—dc20 CIP

Common Courage Press
P.O. Box 702
Monroe ME 04951
207-525-0900
Fax: 207-525-3068

First Printing

Contents

Part IV: The Pseudo-Intellectual

Acknowledgments

Several people assisted me in this project. Greg Bates, my editor at Common Courage Press, was extraordinary in his encouragement for the book, his help in editing it, and his patience in awaiting its finish. Thomas Wilson, Amy Traub, Elizabeth Seger, Sarah Rose, and Dave Aftandilian read drafts of the book and made helpful comments. Some of my earlier writing on Newt Gingrich appeared in the *University of Chicago Free Press*, *Democratic Culture*, the *Chicago Sun-Times*, and *In These Times*.

This study was not supported in any way by any foundation or by the Democratic Party. It is entirely a work of independent journalism. Because I did not have access to political leaders or the resources to mount a full-scale investigation, I depended on the reporting of several journalists as sources of information. The stories in *Roll Call* (especially by Glenn Simpson) proved invaluable, as did several articles in *Mother Jones*, most notably those by David Osborne and David Beers. The Federal Election Commission's lawsuit against GOPAC revealed important information about Gingrich's empire which I was able to examine.

Several websites--most notably those of Newtwatch, Mother Jones, and Frontline--provided valuable data on Gingrich and his friends. Links to these sites, along with further updates on Gingrich, can be found on my world wide web page at http://student-www.uchicago.edu/users/jkw3 .

I encourage readers to contact me through Common Courage Press or by email at jkw3@midway.uchicago.edu .

John K. Wilson
Chicago
July 1996

Acknowledgments

Introduction

The End of Democracy

> "Is it any wonder this country is leaderless when we are literally governed by criminals?"
>
> —Newt Gingrich, October 14, 1976

Corruption and Newt Gingrich are almost synonymous. Gingrich is the most powerful Speaker of the House in the history of Congress. He is also the most corrupt Speaker ever, with a litany of crimes marking his rise to power: numerous violations of federal election law, fraudulent use of nonprofit groups, and shameless influence peddling.

Gingrich has not only turned over the government to corporate America, he has also modeled his rise to power on the worst of the corporate raiders. Like the CEO downsizing a company, Gingrich is downsizing government: shredding the social safety net, widening the gap between rich and poor, and destroying the concept of a compassionate country. Gingrich's downsizing of America means the destruction of the principles of social responsibility, the annihilation of the idea of a common good, and the unrestrained pursuit of wealth and power.

Newt Gingrich's crimes are serious enough to justify not only an independent counsel, but several indictments for violating federal election, tax, fraud, and bribery laws. Gingrich should be serving a term in prison, not as Speaker of the House. But his worst crime of all is the betrayal of democracy by a public servant. In his rise to power, Gingrich sacrificed the integrity of the democratic system. Instead of serving the public interest, he sold his influence to the corporations and wealthy donors who financed his rise to power. And that, much more than all of his violations of the law, was the most destructive influence Gingrich has had on American democracy.

The people who have suffered most from Gingrich's selling out of democracy to the rich are the marginal members of our society. They are the single mothers who are struggling to get off welfare, the homeless who are seeking help, the unemployed workers who search fruitlessly for a decent job, the working poor who are trying to keep their balance in an unsteady world with a shrinking safety net, the young people who want an adequate, affordable education. These are the victims of Gingrich's betrayal. They don't have high-priced lobbyists who press their views in Washington. They don't have the money to make large contributions to his front groups. They don't have influential jobs in the Washington establishment. They don't get to put their spin on the latest news. In the world of American politics, they don't matter.

These Americans have the right to vote, but it is a right eviscerated by the power of money. Even though they can cast their ballots, they are disenfranchised because dollars determine so much in every election. Politicians like Gingrich care more about a few big donors than they do about the majority of Americans. Instead of having representatives in Congress, poor and middle class Americans can only vote for two different degrees of the same evil. For decades, both Democrats and Republicans have sold out to the corporate donors who financed their elections. The result has been a growing chasm between the attitudes of the American people and the ideas which get heard in the mainstream media and the offices of Congress.

Although Gingrich is only the latest politician to serve business interests over the public interest, his rise to Speaker of the House represents a radical extension of their influence over Congress. Gingrich is a corporate lobbyist's wet dream.

But just who *is* Newt Gingrich? And more importantly, how did he become Speaker of the House and one of the most powerful men in the world?

Scenes from the "Revolution"

On January 4, 1995, Newt Gingrich stood as the Speaker of the House of Representatives, reveling in the chants of "Newt! Newt! Newt!" from the Congresspeople who had promised their loyalty to him. This moment was the culmination of the Republican Revolution, the long-dreamt-of takeover of Congress that Gingrich had been plotting for two decades.

Yet behind all of his revolutionary rhetoric was a political movement deeply entrenched in the status quo. Gingrich's reactionary agenda fundamentally alters the rules of politics to permanently enhance corporate power. By cutting taxes on wealthy investors, destroying programs to help the poor, and making lawsuits against corporations harder to win, the Republican Revolution is devoted to serving big business.

If Ronald Reagan was the Teflon president, Gingrich is the Teflon ethicist. When it comes to ethics, Gingrich displays a hypocrisy of incredible proportions. Gingrich is obsessed with poor people's sex lives, but he is reluctant to say anything about his own womanizing. He condemns men who fail to support the women they use, yet overlooks the fact that he was a deadbeat dad—a member of Congress who had to be hauled into court and ordered to pay alimony and child support to the ex-wife he had dumped for having cancer and being unattractive.

Gingrich has used ethics rules to destroy Democrats in the pursuit of partisan politics without receiving serious scrutiny for his own ethical lapses, which are far more serious than any of the Democratic crooks who have been forced out of office and imprisoned for their crimes.

In April 1996, Dan Rostenkowski, former chairman of the House Ways and Means Committee, pled guilty to corruption charges, accepting a jail sentence of 17 months and a $100,000 fine. Rostenkowski's crimes, however, were minor compared to what Gingrich has done. Rostenkowski admitted to giving taxpayer-financed gifts from the House Stationery Store to constituents and politicians, and also confessed to having people on his office payroll who would "on occasion perform limited ... political errands for me." U.S. District Judge Norma Holloway Johnson condemned Rostenkowski for "shamelessly abusing your position." Johnson declared to Rostenkowski, "You have brought a measure of disgrace on the institution you have had the privilege of serving a number of years."[1]

Although Rostenkowski's abuse of power was severe and his guilt clear-cut, several other members of Congress—currently in good standing—have committed similar crimes, and Gingrich is the most noteworthy among them for both the power he currently holds and the extent of the crimes he has committed. Unlike Rostenkowski, Gingrich's crimes were political as well, as he illegally used taxpayer money to finance his campaign to take over the House, rather than just to pay off his friends.

Like Rostenkowski, Gingrich frequently did campaign work from his office, in violation of House rules. His former district administrator, Dolores Adamson, notes, "It always would amaze me how insignificant Newt thought all of that was." Dorothy Crews, another former staffer, reports that after Adamson resigned, Gingrich and his staff would "blur the line of separation between congressional and campaign work." Gingrich also used taxpayer-financed staffers to help line his own pockets, ordering them to work on his 1984 book, *Window of Opportunity*, from which he earned all the royalties. Gingrich never paid the staffers personally for their work, illegally relying on taxpayers to subsidize his efforts at self-promotion.

While Rostenkowski used leftover Congressional office funds to pay off a friend, Gingrich did exactly the same thing to pay off his top campaign workers. Gingrich had two top staffers take a leave of absence from the office to work on his campaign in 1986 and 1988. When they returned to his office in the fall, Gingrich gave them an end-of-the-year bonus. Because such bonuses are not allowed under House rules, Gingrich simply evaded the rules by temporarily doubling their salaries. This violated House guidelines which declare that "year-end increases should be made only on a permanent basis, and only when the services of the individual(s) warrant."[2]

Gingrich, who condemns Democratic congresspeople as "spendaholics," defended this wasteful and illegal spending by saying, "It's a fairly common practice if you have money at the end of the year." However, it was not common—and certainly not legal—for members of Congress to use excess money exclusively for bonuses to the staffers who had worked on their campaigns. House rules prohibit using office funds for campaigns, although staffers can volunteer in their spare time. But Gingrich was not allowed to reward them for the campaign work, since that would be a taxpayer subsidy of a re-election campaign. Throughout his political career, Gingrich repeatedly broke the law, using any money from any source he could find—taxpayer dollars, wealthy business leaders, Republican organizations like GOPAC, and even nonprofit groups—to support his campaigns and his plan to become Speaker of the House. But unlike Rostenkowski, Gingrich is still too powerful to face prosecution.

The Rise of America's Most Hated Speaker

The ascension of Newt Gingrich to Speaker of the House of Representatives is one of the most important events in American political history. The story of how it happened reveals the darker side of our political system, where power and influence triumph over principles and ethics. Although Gingrich presents himself as the ultimate revolutionary overthrowing the establishment, he is truly the consummate politician, in the worst sense of the word.

Gingrich would have everyone believe that he is the leader of a mass revolution. However, all of the evidence supports the conclusion that there was not a shift to the right among the American people during the 1994 elections, but only a small group of Republican voters prevailing due to low voter turnout. Gingrich swiftly became the most hated politician in the country when he attempted to pass the Contract with America.

His negative ratings jumped from 16% in October 1994 to 32% in December 1994 and 42% by July 1995. A December 1995 survey by *Time* found that only 34% of Americans felt that Gingrich was bringing needed change to government.[3] Sixty percent said Gingrich was not "someone you can trust," while 49% called him "scary."[4] The fact that the leader of America's legislature frightens half of the population is astonishing. No American politician in recent memory has managed to maintain his power in the face of such overwhelming unpopularity.

By March 1996, Gingrich had a 51% unfavorable rating, and only a 22% favorable rating. Pollster Peter Hart observed, "I can't find a group—Democrats, Republicans, Buchanan supporters, independents—that has much good to say about Gingrich."[5] But Gingrich's unpopularity did not affect his influence.

How, in a democratic nation, could someone so reviled become Speaker? The rise of Newt Gingrich is also the story of the decline of democracy, and its systematic destruction in a government where money triumphs over morality. Pandering to wealthy donors, Gingrich built an empire which recruited and trained his loyal supporters, and funneled money to his campaigns. He is important to examine because of the ruthless ambition which drove him to seek power, and how he succeeded in getting it. He is a master of propaganda, and probably the most skilled politician in Washington.

Republicans took over Congress in 1994 not because Americans were voting for the Contract with America, but because of the failure of the Democratic Party to mobilize its supporters. The Republicans won because they appealed to the sense of cynicism and disgust with politics that pervades America today and because they were able to discourage a large part of the electorate (especially the poorest Americans) from participating in the 1994 elections.

The Republican Revolution was revolutionary only in the sense of a dramatic shift of power to the right in Congress. It was neither a revolution demanded by the American people nor one that overturned the Washington establishment. On the contrary, it was a coup d'etat by the rich and powerful special interests who now control Congress to an extent that makes the old corruption seem trivial by comparison. On Capitol Hill, where the sport of influence peddling is played every day, Newt Gingrich is its superstar.

Gingrich constantly talks about "renewing American civilization," but his focus as a politician has always been on renewing campaign contributions. His pretentious intellectualizing is just a cover for his skill at playing the Washington game of quasi-legalized bribery: seeking out wealthy businessmen, writing letters to federal agencies on their behalf, promoting them in his college course, and voting for their pro-business agenda. However, not all of the bribery was legal.

Gingrich did favors for businessmen who gave him money to help him write and publicize his books. He did favors for contributors to GOPAC, the Republican political action committee he controlled, which in turn illegally funneled some of the money for "Newt support." He did favors for contributors who donated to his "Renewing American Civilization" course—via a non-profit foundation created to illicitly finance Gingrich's political ambitions. As one GOPAC memo to Gingrich admitted, "Remember what Ollie North said to Mr. President, you don't want to know about this. We are protecting you, Newt."[6]

Gingrich's dirty money formed the building blocks for an empire of political influence unmatched in American history. The Gingrich empire covers a vast area of the US political landscape. It starts with his Congressional district in Georgia and the Conservative Opportunity Society he formed during the

1980s, and stretches across the country, to the state and local Republican candidates he recruited to run for Congress while he was chair of GOPAC. It extends via satellite and cable TV, through GOPAC's non-profit Abraham Lincoln Opportunity Foundation and the Progress and Freedom Foundation, which funded Gingrich's college course and his cable TV show on National Empowerment Television.

It was through these organizations that Gingrich organized the Republican Revolution and anointed himself as its leader. With a combination of fierce partisan resistance to the Democrats in Congress, patient cultivation of alliances with moderate Republicans and the Far Right, and the use of money and influence to assist up-and-coming candidates, Gingrich established himself as the energetic leader of a Republican movement to take back Congress—and put it under the control of his corporate supporters.

It's Not the Principle—It's the Cash

The Contract with America was Gingrich's crowning political achievement of deceit and misdirection. The metaphor of a contract is the perfect expression of Gingrich's narrow view of government. Worshipping the free market as the model of individual liberty and opportunity, he treats politics as just another business with contractual agreements and mutually beneficial deals. To build his majority in the House, Gingrich became the master of deal-making, exchanging political influence for money on a scale never before attempted. The Contract with America was just a larger version of all the smaller contracts he made with business leaders who wanted favors done, a promise to follow the orders of corporate America.

In Gingrich's mind, the government does not serve a larger public good; instead, it is an instrument of power, designed to be used by those who can control it. Gingrich often talks about an "opportunity society," but he sees this as a natural result of the free market, not something that government is involved in creating. Ultimately, Gingrich supports a libertarian model to eliminate government, apart from basic functions such as national defense and law enforcement.

But Gingrich is a politician, not an ideologue. This enables him to live with the contradictions created by his promises to the Religious Right and political contracts with the Friends of Gingrich, those wealthy businessmen who have bankrolled the Republican Revolution. While crying out against welfare, and promising but never acting to target corporate welfare as well, he invariably defends the interests of big business.

An example of how Gingrich shifts his philosophy based on bribery is offered by Paul Weyrich, a longtime Gingrich supporter who runs the right-wing Free Congress Foundation and National Empowerment Television

(NET), a conservative cable network that showed Gingrich's television show. In 1995, Gingrich was the main attraction for a $50,000-a-plate tax-deductible fundraising dinner held for NET.

Yet even a strong ally like Weyrich calls Gingrich an "experiential conservative," meaning that Gingrich changes his views to follow whatever serves his current financial interests. According to Weyrich, "initially he was ambiguous on trade. Then Roger Milliken got hold of him, and he became protectionist and voted for the textile industry. But the big money is with the free-traders, not the protectionists, and he changed his position, given his ambition—where he wanted to go."[7]

Milliken is the co-owner of Milliken and Co., and he gave $345,000 to GOPAC and $15,400 to Gingrich's campaigns. In 1990, Gingrich supported a protectionist bill on Milliken's behalf that was vetoed by George Bush. The bill would have put a quota on imports of textiles, apparel, and shoes. Gingrich devoted 20 minutes to Milliken's company in a 1993 seminar, and showed a three-minute promotional video in his college course about Milliken's company: "In carpeting, Milliken offers a choice of over 1,000 colors and patterns delivered in just seven days."[8] But Gingrich eventually supported NAFTA and GATT despite Milliken's opposition because of the greater money to be raised from free trade advocates.

Milliken was only one of several dozen Friends of Gingrich who has donated large amounts of money to Newt in exchange for political influence. The money came to Gingrich illegally via GOPAC and the non-profit Progress and Freedom Foundation run by Gingrich to circumvent federal laws which limit campaign contributions to $1,000.

Perhaps the most explicit example of Gingrich's influence-peddling came in a letter from Miller Nichols, a Kansas City commercial real estate developer who exchanged at least 14 letters with Gingrich in a span of 18 months. Nichols's company owned old buildings constructed with asbestos, and he objected to federal health regulations. In a January 19, 1990 letter, Nichols reminded Gingrich of his donations to GOPAC: "replying to your letter of Dec. 19, 1989, in which you solicited our continued support," he wrote, "I am pleased to respond favorably and enclose my check to GOPAC in the amount of $10,000. For your information, I list below my record of giving since 1985. My total support...equals $59,000." After explicitly listing all the money he had given on Newt's behalf, Miller had a favor to ask: "The federal government is causing the J.C. Nichols Co. ...a great deal of financial distress. This is in connection with the asbestos regulations....It may be that I will call you for an appointment to come back to Washington to discuss this issue....It is costing my company millions and millions of dollars to comply with federal regulations."

Gingrich took the demands of a major donor very seriously. GOPAC chairman Bo Callaway wrote on a copy of Nichols's letter on January 24, "Please put in folder to discuss with Newt—emphasize that it is very important for Miller to get a quick answer." The next day, Gingrich bracketed the request and scrawled, "Laura wrote and asked him to send me a copy of the research when finished." The letter sent back to Nichols that same day had more exclamation marks than periods, virtually promising a quid pro quo deal to Nichols: "Your continued support of GOPAC is very important to me! I want you to know how very much I appreciate your generous contribution!....Regarding the problematic asbestos regulations—please send me a copy of your research when you are finished and I will look into it."

Gingrich then acted on Nichols's behalf. On April 24, 1991, Gingrich contacted EPA administrator William K. Reilly: "I am writing you with concern over the crisis that is arising in our courts from asbestos litigation....I would appreciate any help you could lend to this matter." Nichols' name was on the "cc" of the letter, so that the EPA would know what influential donor was pulling Gingrich's strings and Nichols would know that the favor had been accomplished. As a Republican appointee, Reilly would not ignore a letter from his party's House minority whip, and he assigned an EPA asbestos specialist to talk with Gingrich's staff. As for Nichols, he has continued as a GOPAC charter member giving $10,000 a year to Gingrich's pet projects—the admission fee to the corridors of power in Washington.

Nichols clearly regarded Gingrich as "his" personal congressman, even though he lived a thousand miles away from Gingrich's district. Nichols's wife reported, "One year he wrote to Newt, he was vexed...you've got a congressman back there—you're going to tell him." As columnist Robert Scheer observes, "This is a blatant violation of the Ethics in Government Act of 1989, which states, 'No member of Congress shall solicit or accept anything of value from a person...whose interests may be substantially affected by the performance or nonperformance of the individual's official duties.'"[9]

Nichols also exerted influence over GOPAC; at his request, GOPAC met with a candidate running for the office of executive in Jackson County (Mo.) and gave him $1,000.[10] Only in the corrupt world of Congress could such influence peddling be considered acceptable behavior, and even by Washington standards this was extraordinary. Gingrich was violating all of the ethical standards he publicly espoused, along with federal bribery laws. But then, ethics aren't for the powerful.

Setting Congress's Standards for Selling Out: The Gingrich Fundraising Technique

Miller Nichols represents a pattern, and he was not the only wealthy business executive who received favors from Gingrich. The *Wall Street Journal* reported that Gingrich "has used his position, in a series of noteworthy intercessions, to help his own friends with special connections." To take one example, Newt and Marianne Gingrich spent Thanksgiving of 1993 and 1994 on Little St. Simon's Island, the private 10,000-acre $500-a-night island resort of timber CEO Michael Berolzheimer, head of P & M Cedar Products. On August 16, 1994, after their first free luxury vacation, Newt wrote the U.S. International Trade Commission at the request of P & M to urge anti-dumping duties against Thai and Chinese pencilmakers. P & M supplies the wood for a large number of American pencils, which may explain why Gingrich suddenly discarded his free-trade views in favor of protectionism.

Spokesperson Tony Blankley's weak defense of Gingrich's action reveals the depth of political corruption in America: "This story and others like it could be written on any member of Congress." Blankley argued Gingrich's lobbying was "the standard appropriate pattern for congressmen and senators in our form of government." But Berolzheimer (and his company, and the incense cedar used for pencil wood) aren't even in Gingrich's district; his only connection to Gingrich was the free vacation he gave to Newt and Marianne again in 1994, as a reward for Newt's help. Blankley reported that Gingrich had "a vague recollection that someone brought up something about forest issues" over the holiday. Indeed, Gingrich did seem to remember something about it: he gave his personal support in 1995 to a lucrative timber industry measure allowing companies to "salvage" so-called "damaged" trees on federal land at a discount.[11]

Gingrich regularly asked federal regulators to help out those making big contributions to his Progress and Freedom Foundation. On July 22, 1994, Gingrich wrote to FDA Commissioner David Kessler on behalf of Luvox, a drug for obsessive-compulsive disorder made by Solvay Pharmaceuticals, a subsidiary of the Belgian company Solvay SA—and a donor of $30,000 to Newt's foundation earlier that year. According to Gingrich, "Time delays of months or even weeks are critical to a small company in this industry." The drug was approved in December 1994.[12]

On September 2, 1994, Gingrich wrote White House chief of staff Leon Panetta on behalf of a home AIDS test made by Johnson & Johnson subsidiary Direct Access Diagnostics. Gingrich demanded that "the delay must end immediately" for FDA approval. Johnson & Johnson, Direct Access Diagnostics, and its president Elliott Millenson are all contributors to the Progress and Freedom Foundation, and soon after the intervention on their behalf, Direct Access donated about $30,000 for Gingrich's services.[13]

For Gingrich, this was business as usual. Giving special treatment to a major donor has helped make him the largest recipient of corporate donations in Congress, and the biggest fundraiser in the history of American politics.

Gingrich also introduced legislation to reduce tariffs on lactulose, a liquid laxative sold by Marion Merrell Dow. Its vice president, William Hoskins, is a major donor who gave $41,690 to GOPAC through 1993, along with $7,000 to Gingrich's campaigns. Richard Krieble, a major GOPAC donor who has given a total of at least $172,624, understands clearly what he gets for his money. Krieble once told reporters about his contributions to Gingrich, "I'm buying the man."[14]

The Republican Revolution did not bring a new style of government to Washington; instead, it only accelerated the amount of influence being bought by major corporations.

When Can a Contract Be a Lie?

Whatever Gingrich's venality, his legislative agenda represents a more serious and permanent threat in his efforts to sell out the very core of democracy. The Contract with America is a quintessential example of his skill: provide cover for an attack on democracy by spouting false claims to be loyal servants of the polity.

The Republicans presented the Contract during the 1994 campaign as if it were the direct will of the American people. At the signing ceremony on September 27, 1994, Dick Armey declared that Republicans were "listening to the concerns of the American people and responding with specific legislation" and proclaimed that "the people's House must be wrested from the grip of special interest groups and handed back to 'the people.'" Republican pollster Frank Luntz, who came up with the specific provisions in the Contract, claimed that it arose from the ideas most popular with the American public. Although it hurt the Republicans to appear to be mindlessly following the polls, it also helped by allowing them to seem more in touch with what the people wanted.

But other poll results showed that the Contract with America was not a popular document. Most of the American public had never heard of it by election day. An early October poll (taken right after the big event on the steps of the Capitol) found that only 24% of Americans had ever even heard about the Contract, and only 4% said they would be more likely to support a Republican candidate because of the Contract.[15] Even these numbers greatly overstate the public awareness of the Contract, because respondents were never tested to see if they actually knew what the Contract with America was, nor were they asked to volunteer information about its particular provisions.

Gingrich blamed "totally dishonest" questions for the negative poll results. But despite his complaints, it was Gingrich's pollster who had been asking biased questions. After discrepancies between Republican pollster Frank

Luntz's data and later polls appeared, Luntz was asked about his methodology and his questions. Luntz evaded the inquiries, claiming that only the Republican National Committee—his client—could release the data. But the RNC had never seen or commissioned the survey. Luntz then claimed that it was his own personal survey, and "private information" which he refused to release. Eventually, Luntz admitted what had already become obvious: the poll showing the popularity of the Republican agenda was a farce. Luntz had only tested campaign slogans which were designed to manipulate results, a tactic that any legitimate pollster would have dismissed immediately. The Contract with America was, from the start, built on a lie.[16]

Beneath Gingrich's propaganda, the Republican Revolution is a deeply anti-democratic and unpopular movement. The public favors balancing the budget rather than cutting middle-class taxes by a margin of 56% to 37%; it wants to maintain Medicare rather than reduce the deficit by 70% to 24%. Clearly, the American people favor keeping Medicare, balancing the budget, and then cutting taxes, in that order—the exact opposite of the Republican priorities. Furthermore, 79% favor a large increase in the minimum wage, while 82% think "there need to be stricter laws and regulations to protect the environment."[17]

The Contract with America was even less popular than most polls indicated because polls are unable to address the complex issues involved in the legislation proposed by the Republicans. For example, a Gallup Poll shortly after the 1994 election found that 58% of the public favored (and 27% opposed) "changing the rules under which individuals can sue companies and each other." Of course, a large number of Americans want legal reform. But that doesn't mean people support the Republican plans to restrict consumer rights and give special advantages to big business. While 88% of Americans in the poll are in favor of "tougher anti-crime legislation," that doesn't mean we need destructive anti-crime laws that rely on symbolism rather than substantive reform, or legislation that overturns the Fourth Amendment in the name of battling criminals.[18]

It is hardly surprising that 83% of Americans support "a cut in taxes for most Americans." But the real effect of the Republican laws will be to cut taxes for the rich, not for most Americans. The more people learned about Newt Gingrich and the Contract with America, the more suspicious they became of a "revolution" that actually increased the power of big business and the right-wing elite.

Destroying the "Welfare State"

As with other issues, the ideology behind the Contract's stance on welfare is fundamentally at odds with what Americans believe. Gingrich promises "the death of the liberal welfare state" and the birth of "a conservative opportunity society." In truth, Gingrich wants to discard the social safety net and valuable government programs, offering nothing but a future of increasing poverty and hopelessness in their place.

Gingrich's favorite line, repeated over and over again in almost every speech he gives, is: "No civilization can survive with 12-year-olds having babies, with 15-year-olds killing each other, with 17-year-olds dying of AIDS, with 18-year-olds getting diplomas they can't read."[19]

Gingrich thinks that if we lower the capital gains tax and cut welfare, the 12-year-old will decide to become an entrepreneur rather than a mother; if we execute underage killers in electric chairs and ban death-penalty appeals, the 15-year-old will decide not to join a gang; if we stop teaching young people about sex in public schools, the 17-year-old will never have sex and get AIDS; if we decimate federal funding for education programs and libraries, and instead let private charities pay kids $2 to read a book, we will solve the literacy problem for every 18-year-old.

But Gingrich hasn't even defined the problems accurately. Young adolescents having children is tragic, but the number of 12-year-olds who have children is insignificant—only 1.4 out of every 1,000 girls aged 10 to 14 gave birth in 1991, most of whom were 13 or 14. The birth rates for women in their 20's are more than 80 times higher.[20] Although sexual transmission of AIDS is a serious health crisis and the spread of HIV among youth is a major concern, teenagers are actually the demographic group least likely to be dying of AIDS. Through September 1993, only 1,415 teenagers had been diagnosed with AIDS—far less than the 4,903 infants and young children diagnosed with AIDS. Compared with the 154,934 adults who had been diagnosed with AIDS in their thirties, the number of teenage AIDS deaths is very small. [21]

Regardless of their size, Gingrich's policies will exacerbate, not solve, these social problems that he understands so little. Gingrich has joined the Religious Right's attack on making sex education and birth control readily available, claiming that eliminating welfare will stop teen (and pre-teen) pregnancy—despite the complete absence of any proof for this assertion. Gingrich has led the attack on effective gun control and crime prevention programs, claiming that executions and more prisons will stop teenagers from murdering each other. Gingrich has accepted the far right's anti-gay agenda to stop AIDS education, end programs for drug addicts, and eliminate counseling for gay youth. Gingrich has proposed sharply cutting federal funding for education from Head Start to graduate school (programs which helped him and his children), ensuring that another generation of Americans will be deprived of adequate schooling.

Gingrich cannot solve any social problems because he lives under the delusion that government causes all of the evils in the world. Believing that the "welfare state" is the root of every problem, he wants to slash the only social programs that are ameliorating these serious troubles. At a time when we should be expanding and improving these programs to address serious problems, Gingrich wants to destroy them and let the "free market" deal with teen pregnancy, ignorance, and crime.

Gingrich's solutions are deceptive as well as morally bankrupt. He masks the politics of cruelty with the slogan of "effective compassion." He undermines government (and cuts taxes for his rich contributors) under the guise of helping the poor escape the welfare state. Gingrich's entire career in Congress has been devoted to gaining power by fundraising, often providing special favors to his wealthy donors. He has not created or improved one federal program to help the average American in nearly two decades as a member of Congress.

The Contract We Never Signed and the General in the Class War

Gingrich presents himself as the leader of "a conservative Congress elected to do the people's work."[22] But what people elected this Congress? It was Democrats, not Republicans, who mentioned the Contract in TV ads, and virtually no Republican candidates for Congress emphasized the Contract during their campaigns.[23] There was no popular mandate in 1994 to undermine government, only a frustration with the failure of Democrats to take action. Less than one-fifth of Americans voted for Republicans, and none of them—not even the people in his own district—voted to make Gingrich the Speaker of the House.

Among the 1994 voters, 51.3% cast a ballot for Republicans, 46.6% for Democrats. But this ignores the great majority of Americans who, disillusioned and apathetic about the political system, did not vote. Out of all American adults, only 17% voted Republican, compared to 16% who voted Democratic. But what's remarkable are the views of the non-voters who form two-thirds of the American people. According to a *Times Mirror* survey, these non-voters shared attitudes that were almost identical to those of the Democratic voters. Both Democrats and non-voters were twice as likely as the Republican voters to agree that "Government often does a better job than people give it credit for." Both Democrats and non-voters were twice as likely as the Republicans to say that "Poor people have hard lives because government benefits don't go far enough."[24] The Republicans won the 1994 election not because their ideas were accepted by the public, but because a large proportion of adults, disgusted with the state of politics and the Democratic Party, stayed home on election day.

Newt Gingrich is Speaker of the House only because the people who vote are not representative of the electorate. The 1994 elections revealed an enormous and growing class gap among voters. The Census Bureau reported that voting among Americans who earn $50,000 a year or more rose from 59.2% in 1990 to 60.1% in 1994. But only 19.9% of those making less than $5,000 voted in 1994—a one-third drop from the 32.2% who voted in 1990. For people making between $5,000 and $10,000, the proportion voting fell from 30.9% to 23.3%.[25] If the poor voted as often the rich in America, the Republicans would never win another election.

The gap in political influence between the wealthy and the poor is intensified by the importance of money. When both Democrats and Republicans can get the money they need by servicing the rich, neither party bothers to formulate a message that appeals to the poor or working class in this country. As a result, poorer Americans, who are the most opposed to the Republican attacks on them, did not vote because they never felt that Democrats would represent their interests.

Whenever anyone presents the truth that we have an unjust political system that favors the rich over the poor, Gingrich and the other conservative Republicans inevitably will complain that this is "class warfare." But the real class warfare is played by Gingrich and the other servants of corporate America, Democratic and Republican, who give special treatment to their major contributors. There is already a class war going on, with Gingrich as its commander-in-chief leading his troops to take from the poor and give to the rich.

The Republicans know that an increased electorate reflecting the American public's views would destroy their political power. In 1993, Gingrich attacked the "motor voter" bill designed to increase voting registration by allowing people to register when they renew their driver's license. He claimed that "the bill would create a nationwide Chicago, where the dead can vote, illegal aliens can vote and the political machine can pressure people to vote for their candidate."[26] These arguments are silly—can the dead get a driver's license? But their entertainment value aside, they masked the real fear of Gingrich and the Republicans: if the nation's voters began to resemble the entire American public, it would threaten Gingrich's power, which has always been based on attracting the financial support of powerful, conservative business leaders, not on a populist appeal. No one can look at Gingrich's rise to power and imagine that his reign is of, by, and for the people.

What Newt Gingrich brings to the House of Representatives is not a new way of running government. Rather, Gingrich's reign is a caricature of the old adage about absolute power. Where lobbyists for major corporations once exercised considerable indirect influence on legislation, today they are writing the legislation themselves and delivering it to Republicans for passage into law. Where political deals once were made in the backrooms of Congress, today the Republicans (and Democrats) openly sell political power to the highest bidder.

By exercising authoritarian control over the new Congress, and manipulating the political process, Gingrich was able to push through the Contract with America in the face of public opposition and internal resistance. But as the most powerful politician in Washington, Gingrich does not merely seek control over the House; he uses that power to enforce the agenda of the wealthy corporate donors who gave him the money to launch the Republican Revolution.

Part I
The Crimes of Newt Gingrich

Chapter 1

The Hypocrite of the House

Throughout his career in Congress, Gingrich has been the House thug. He has never written any significant legislation. Instead, he made his reputation with one significant talent: smearing his opponents. Taking the role as the attack dog of the far right, Gingrich went after Democrats with a viciousness rarely seen before in the House. Gingrich has attacked Democrats as "traitors," the party of "total bizarreness, total weirdness," and the "enemy of normal Americans."[1] A 1985 *Washington Post* article about Gingrich even referred to him as "the House brat."[2]

Gingrich began his ethics attacks immediately after entering Congress in 1979, when he went after Congressman Charles Diggs (D-MI), who had been convicted of mail fraud. Next, Gingrich led the fight in the early 1980s to expel Gerry Studds (D-MA) and Daniel Crane (R-IL) from the House for having sex with underage Congressional pages. Gingrich said, "There is no high school or college in America where exploiting, seducing, or sleeping with students, boy or girl, would be punished with a reprimand."[3] This was a particularly odd statement from a man who seduced his high school geometry teacher, married her, and became legendary for repeatedly cheating on her.

But as Fred Wertheimer of the watchdog group Common Cause observes, Gingrich "has always worked both sides of the street on the corruption ethics issues." While Gingrich made his reputation going after Democrats on ethics charges, Wertheimer says, "he built a financial empire based on special interest and private influence money. He did everything he could to block the reforms."[4]

Gingrich also participated in many of the same scandals he blamed on the Democrats. In 1989, Gingrich was a leader in exposing the House banking "scandal" even though Gingrich himself had made 22 overdrafts, including a $9,463 check to the IRS. The scandal itself was insignificant by Congressional standards: it amounted to a highly generous bank policy allowing overdrafts without penalty. The net cost to the taxpayer was negligible, but it was a politically volatile issue because it exposed the different standards that applied to members of Congress, who did not have to pay bank penalties for their financial mismanagement. While the media focused on the evils of free banking, larger political issues—like the multi-billion-dollar bailout of failed savings and loans—disappeared from the political map. Gingrich, in his zeal for the free market, had supported the S & L legislation that may go down in history as the worst and most expensive law ever passed by Congress, as well as the massive bailout designed to prop up the financial institutions that failed.

Although both parties were guilty in the S & L scandal, and both sides of Congress took bribes in the process, it was primarily a Republican scandal pursuing a conservative philosophy about the inevitable brilliance of the free market. By contrast, the House bank scandal was primarily a Democratic scandal, since they were the incumbents.

Gingrich is the kind of politician who can condemn the Democrats for doing exactly what he did. He attacked the bank overdraft scandal as evidence of "a Democratic machine political scandal," yet he made overdrafts himself and rode around in a government-funded chauffeured car. But for Gingrich's political goals, it scarcely mattered that he himself was corrupt. Exposing the arrogance and corruption of Congress, the overdraft issue helped to undermine the incumbent Democrats more than any other scandal.

It was almost a disastrous decision for Gingrich, who was nearly destroyed in the resulting backlash against Congress (fueled in part by a $44,000 pay raise for members of Congress that Gingrich strongly supported). He had to fight for his political life in the 1990 election, winning by less than a thousand votes. He won a 1992 primary by a similarly close margin.[5] His friend Vin Weber decided to resign and become a lobbyist rather than face a tough re-election campaign with a 125-check overdraft target painted on his back. But Gingrich survived, knowing that every scandal destroyed the credibility of Congress a little more, and made his dream of becoming Speaker that much closer to reality.

Gingrich's support of a congressional pay raise despite political risk reflects his top priority: to constantly seek money regardless of the danger courted. According to Gingrich, he and his wife live on a "limited income"—even though Gingrich alone makes $171,500 and has been earning a large salary as a member of Congress for nearly two decades, with a generous pension. And this doesn't take into account the substantial money his wife has earned.[6] But in the world of the super-rich where Gingrich spends his time fundraising for the Republican Revolution, he is impoverished by comparison.

"I Am Now a Famous Person"

While Gingrich took on the Democrats over ethics issues, he tried to raise his profile within the Republican Party, whose leaders regarded him as an extremist. His drive to take over the Republican Party began in late 1982, when he organized the Conservative Opportunity Society (COS). Meeting at Paul Weyrich's right-wing Free Congress Foundation were a handful of conservative colleagues, including Connie Mack, Vin Weber, and Robert Walker. COS was Gingrich's mechanism to organize like-minded Republicans and play the role of leader. The main job for COS members was to give speeches on C-

SPAN when no one else was in the House, attacking Democratic policies.

Explaining the idea behind COS in a November 3, 1983, speech to an empty House, he noted that "while Ronald Reagan has slowed down the liberal welfare state, he has not fundamentally changed it." Gingrich warned that "the Republican Party is clearly trapped within its minority status" and declared that "only a long-term mass movement" could solve its problems. Gingrich pointed to "the liberal welfare state" as the enemy and proclaimed that "we need to change from the triangle of the Republican minority to the circle of the Republican majority."[7]

Conservatives in Congress used COS to assault the Democratic Party, arranging tag-team attacks on the House floor. In speeches before empty House chambers in 1984, Gingrich pushed the Democratic leadership to the edge. Directed at the C-SPAN television audience, Gingrich and company viciously attacked Democratic foreign policy, reading a paper written by Gingrich chief of staff Frank Gregorsky quoting decade-old comments by Democrats out of context. Calling the Democrats "blind to communism," Gingrich accused them of disloyalty, un-Americanism, and treason.[8] He threatened to "file charges" against ten Democrats who wrote a letter to Nicaraguan leader Daniel Ortega, accusing them of using "Communist propaganda," which turned out to be a listing of 2,000 Nicaraguan mothers who had family members killed by the Contras in Nicaragua.[9] According to Gingrich, the Democrats "invite the Nicaraguan Communists to establish their policy with an eye to weakening conservative forces in America" and were plotting to "bring Third World Soviet colonies into the process of manipulating American politics and politicians."[10]

An angry Tip O'Neill, Speaker of the House at the time, expressed "total disgust" at the far right's tactics, accusing Gingrich of having "pointed a finger at an empty chair and accused a man of being un-American."[11] O'Neill said to Gingrich, "You deliberately stood in that well before an empty House, and challenged these people, and challenged their Americanism, and it is the lowest thing that I have ever seen in my 32 years in Congress."[12] In response, then-minority whip Trent Lott asked to have O'Neill's remarks stricken under a House rule banning personal attacks on members of Congress. Although O'Neill's statement was fairly mild compared to some of Gingrich's previous remarks (such as in 1979 during the Iranian hostage crisis, when he referred to the Democratic leader as "Ayatollah O'Neill"), the chair ruled in Lott's favor, the first time since 1798 that a Speaker had been silenced.[13]

Gingrich pretended to be greatly offended by O'Neill's comment, declaring that "it is my patriotism being impugned." But in reality, he was ecstatic. Gingrich felt he had finally prevailed at gaining media attention by staging fights. "I am now a famous person," he told the press after his confrontation with Tip O'Neill, which was obviously his primary goal.[14] The night of O'Neill's criticism, Gingrich took to the House floor to proclaim that the fight on the floor was a "historic process" in which "formerly dominant people see the traditional establishment and the formerly dominant power structure decay, they become nervous, uncertain and uneasy." Gingrich declared that "we are entering a new era" and predicted that "the House will never again be quite the same when we are done with this process. It may take 6 months. It may take 1 year. It may take 5 years."[15] In fact, it took 10 years, but the revolution Gingrich foresaw did happen. No one, not even Gingrich himself, could imagine in 1984 that Gingrich would bring down O'Neill's successor, Jim Wright, and eventually seize the office of Speaker himself.

Taking Down Jim Wright

Embarrassing Tip O'Neill was an audacious act, but it was mild in comparison with what was to come.

In 1987, Gingrich took on Speaker of the House Jim Wright, and after a long war waged in the media and on the House floor, eventually forced Wright to resign in 1989. By standing up to the Democratic leadership, Gingrich gained the respect, if not always the admiration, of the Republican Congresspeople who were tired of being in the minority. By undermining Wright, Gingrich also took out one of the strongest Democratic leaders who might have been able to oppose him, and left the Democratic Party in disarray.

Wright upset the Republicans partly because he was an effective Speaker, determined to shift the balance of power away from the Republican president. Wright pursued a strong domestic agenda, and even became a foreign policy leader, negotiating the Central America peace agreement in 1987. But Wright also angered Republicans because he violated the spirit of partisan friendliness that had dominated the House in the past. When Wright took power in 1987, he imposed his will on the House with little restraint. On October 29, 1987, Wright, having lost a vote on a tax bill, adjourned the House and then reconvened for another legislative day ten minutes later in order to evade House rules against two votes on the same day. The second time, Republicans lost by one vote, and minority whip Richard Cheney was one of many Republicans who condemned Wright's maneuver as "the most arrogant, heavy-handed abuse of power I've ever seen." Cheney declared, "There's no comity left. Why should you, if you are a Republican, think of a Democrat as a colleague? They aren't colleagues."[16]

It was a perfect environment for someone like Newt Gingrich to thrive in, since his confrontational approach was exactly the opposite of minority leader Bob Michel. Gingrich's political specialty was ethics charges. He liked to use Democratic scandals because they generated much more publicity than everyday legislation, allowing him to condemn the Democratic establishment as corrupt. After several months of indecision about whether he wanted to take on the Speaker in the face of skepticism from his colleagues, he filed an ethics complaint against Wright. His staffer, Karen Van Brocklin, worked full-time digging up incriminating information and feeding it to reporters.

Gingrich decided, "I'll just keep pounding and pounding on his ethics. There comes a point where it comes together and the media takes off on it or it dies."[17] On September 24, 1987, the media took off. The *Washington Post* revealed another ethical blunder by Wright. Wright's book, *Reflections of a Public Man*, had been sold in bulk with a 55% royalty rate pocketed by the author in a scheme designed to avoid Congressional limits on speaking fees. Although Wright didn't get an advance, his steep royalty rate was unusually high. His take: $62,000 on bulk orders to groups he was speaking to for "free."

Adding to the appearance of corruption, the book's publisher had spent time in prison for illegal campaign contributions and was paid $250,000 by Wright to print campaign literature.[18] In 1984, when Wright made $3,000 for a speech at Southwest Texas State University, he had already earned the House limit on outside income, so he had the school buy $3,000 worth of books, on which Wright made $1,650.[19] These revelations were particularly important because it was a clear violation of the spirit, if not the letter, of House ethics rules, and Wright was undeniably guilty.

Gingrich continued to pour on the pressure, creating a confrontation to give the press an opportunity to write negative stories about Wright and providing the most extreme soundbites himself. He compared Wright to Mussolini and called him "a genuinely bad man...a genuinely corrupt man."

Gingrich and the media spread several false rumors about Wright, such as claiming that federal grants he got for Fort Worth went to his personal business partners. Perhaps the greatest irony was that Gingrich used the S & L crisis to bring the downfall of the Speaker, declaring that because of the S & L bribes to the Democrats, "It makes it possible to create in Jim Wright a symbol of a political machine."[20] Gingrich's own votes for the disastrous de-regulation and the multi-hundred-billion-dollar bailout by the government went unmentioned. He pinned the blame for it on the Democrats.

A false report printed in the magazine *Regardie's* and repeated in the *Wall Street Journal* accused Wright of conspiring with Donald Dixon, a thrift operator, to "corrupt the thrift industry."[21] But journalist John Barry found that Wright had only met Dixon at a fundraiser for a colleague, spoken once on the phone, and made a call on Dixon's behalf; nothing more corrupt was ever proven, as the editor of *Regardie's* later admitted. By this standard, Gingrich and many others in Congress were guilty of far greater corruption.

But Gingrich's own corruption was ignored as he levelled his accusations.

The pressure from Gingrich for an ethics investigation was powerful enough that the House Ethics Committee decided on June 10, 1988, to appoint an independent counsel, Richard Phelan, who went after Wright with prosecutorial zeal. In addition to Wright's book deal, Phelan focused on an allegation involving Mallighto, a company formed by Wright, his wife, and their friends, George and Marlene Mallick. The key question was whether Wright's wife, who had been hired to run the company, had actually earned her $72,000 in salary and benefits and use of a Cadillac. If she hadn't really worked at the company, then it was an illegal gift to the Wrights. Despite Phelan's allegations to the contrary, it seems clear from John Barry's investigatory research that Wright's wife did at least work part-time for the company. However, Phelan charged Wright with 116 violations of House rules, and the Ethics Committee found "reason to believe" that Wright was guilty of 69 violations.[22]

Wright's position in 1989 was fatally weakened; his whip, Tony Coelho, had just resigned over ethics questions. And Wright had alienated many of his colleagues who disliked his management style. Ambitious Democrats saw a chance to move up the leadership ladder with Wright out of the way. None of them ever imagined that losing Wright would threaten their seemingly unassailable majority in the House. With his power undermined, and his supporters unwilling to stand up for him, Wright resigned.

The parallels between Gingrich and Wright are dramatic; neither was satisfied with merely being Speaker; both wanted to expand the office to become the leader of the country and dominate the public debate. Both Gingrich and Wright imposed tight control over the House, and successfully pushed through their agendas by enforcing party discipline and ignoring the minority party. But when Gingrich started telling every reporter he saw in the fall of 1987, "Jim Wright is the least ethical speaker of the twentieth century," he spoke too soon.[23] Gingrich himself would snare that honor before the close of the millennium.

With self-serving morality, Gingrich claims that the difference between his ethics violations and Jim Wright's is that "Jim Wright was a crook! When they investigated Jim Wright, he had to resign." By these standards, if you get away with it, you are not a crook.

But Gingrich's crimes are far worse than anything Wright ever did. While Wright evaded House rules on outside income, Gingrich not only violated many House rules on outside funding, he evaded several federal election laws and laws covering IRS nonprofit organization status. He profited personally and financed his campaign to take over the House from these illicit funds.

But as long as he denies every violation forcefully enough, and attacks the rare journalist who brings up the issue, Gingrich knows he can stay in power. Unlike Jim Wright, Gingrich is seen as essential to the leadership of his party, and unlike the House Democrats in the 1980s, many of whom felt invincible and wanted to see Wright resign for their own political gain, the Republicans are desperate to keep Gingrich in charge despite his illegal and unethical activity. Without Gingrich's power to push through all the legislation that the American people oppose, the Republican Revolution, already in dire trouble, would fade away.

While the media have so far failed to put the same kind of pressure on Gingrich that they applied to the Wright case, Gingrich's illegal and unethical activities go far beyond anything Wright did, with a much larger political impact.

Gingrich and Wright: Felons of a Feather

Despite being fierce political opponents, both Wright and Gingrich have pursued power in the House ruthlessly, running over the rules along the way. The House Ethics Committee warned Gingrich about the Progress and Freedom Foundation (PFF) and its "Renewing American Civilization" course, telling him to "avoid using congressional resources to solicit for the group." Yet Gingrich spoke on the House floor, repeatedly urging his colleagues and C-SPAN viewers and *Congressional Record* readers to call his 1-800-TO-RENEW phone number to buy video and audio tapes for hundreds of dollars. Ironically, one of the ethics violations that brought down Jim Wright was Wright's endorsement in the *Congressional Record* for a home video program by the company that employed his wife.[24]

Gingrich, like Wright, also faces questions about the favoritism shown toward his wife, Marianne Gingrich. She was given a job with the Israel Export Development Company (IEDC) because of her connections with its lobbyist, Vin Weber, a former representative and Newt's close friend. Needless to say, Marianne's experience in selling cosmetics, whatever her talents, normally would not lead to a $2,500-a-month job (plus commissions) in international trade, convincing American companies to join a business park in Israel. Weber himself violated the law by lobbying for IEDC in 1993, disobeying a moratorium on former Congress members lobbying the year after they leave office. Weber convinced six senators and thirteen representatives to write letters to the Israeli government in favor of a free-trade zone, and lobbied his friend Newt, who contacted prime minister Yitzhak Rabin. Marianne was hired soon after Newt told Israeli officials that he was in favor of the free trade zone. Gingrich spokesperson Tony Blankley claimed that Newt "was giving advice to a friendly Government about what their policy should be" and not "acting in an official capacity." But Weber reported, "I lobbied him."[25]

Marianne was also involved in some suspect stock deals. In January 1992, she bought more than $1,000 of Boeing stock; three weeks later, Newt helped kill amendments to the NASA Authorization Act that would have cut funding for the space station program. Boeing later became the prime contractor for the space station.[26] Although Newt has always been a strong supporter of the space program, the Gingriches bought Boeing stock only after Newt may have had inside information about whether Congress was likely to kill funding for the space station. As programs were being cut by the House in the 1996 budget, Gingrich staved off all but a small decline in NASA's budget, while other agencies were decimated.

How to Succeed as a Writer Without Really Trying

By far the most remarkable similarity between Gingrich and Wright is their use of book deals to evade House rules and pad their bank accounts. Wright's book deal was clumsy and corrupt, but Gingrich has been involved in several book deals that were far more unethical, albeit more cleverly concealed. Gingrich the politician used his pretensions as a writer as a front to raise money from his campaign contributors for his personal use.

When Newt Gingrich first ran for Congress in 1974, he observed: "Congressmen are not bribed anymore. They simply have a lot of friends who are willing to help them out whenever they find it necessary."[27] Although he initially said it sarcastically, Gingrich learned that lesson about Congressional corruption all too well. Even before he won his election for the first time in 1978, Gingrich relied on "friends" to help him out.

In 1977, a consortium of business leaders paid him $15,000 to take a vacation in Europe in what may have been the most unusual book deal in the history of publishing. Wealthy donor and local businessman Chester Roush led the formation of Nomohan, Ltd., a limited partnership created in 1977 to funnel money to Gingrich under the pretense of "investing" in a futuristic novel he was writing. The money paid for Gingrich to bring his family to Europe for the summer on vacation (or "research," as Gingrich termed it). Roush gave Gingrich $2,000 and convinced a dozen other Republican businessmen to donate $1,000 to the partnership. In the publishing industry, a deal to "invest" in an unproven writer is completely unknown. Even publishers are highly unlikely to pay an advance to a first-time novelist.[28]

Tom Glanton, a Carrollton real estate developer, jointly co-signed a loan for Gingrich's first campaign and was one of the partners in Nomohan, Ltd. Glanton said: "You have to remember that in 1977 Chester and his friends believed they had hitched their wagon to a rising star. They had supported Gingrich in both 1974 and 1976. They were, for the most part, staunch Republicans who had long been represented by an entrenched Democrat. Frankly, they were looking for a young Republican savior who they thought represented their values. So the book partnership is really a logical extension of that support, an opportunity for these same political supporters to have their personal values vicariously fulfilled through the political servant they'd been supporting."[29]

The only fiction that got written was the contract for Nomohan, Ltd., this imaginary partnership that everyone knew was just a covert way to pay off Gingrich. Gingrich friend Steve Hanser reports that Gingrich finished a draft of the novel in 1978, but he never tried to finish it. According to Hanser, "The book is not bad, it's just not good." Another friend, futurist Alvin Toffler, read it and told Gingrich that, fortunately, he was better at shaking hands than writing books. Gingrich said he wrote the novel "to increase the public's awareness of military preparedness" and the threat posed by the Soviet Union. The novel features lines like "the budgetary squeeze tightened like an economic python squeezing the vitality out of the U.S. forces in Europe."[30] Gingrich did not finish the novel nor did he ever contact an editor and try to have it published. The investors lost all of their money (a fully deductible tax loss), but they got something much better than a best-selling science fiction novel. They had a Congressman in their control, a debt owed by the type of politician who didn't turn his back on the people whose money got him where he was.

At the time, Gingrich was desperately short of cash. His job as an assistant professor at West Georgia College never paid more than $15,400 a year, and he frequently took unpaid leaves to run for office. Gingrich was on the verge of losing his job, since colleges are required to make a decision after seven years to either promote and give tenure to faculty members, or dismiss them. Gingrich had failed to publish anything and showed little interest in an academic life, and he didn't even bother applying for tenure. But with the help of the "book" deal and his wife's teaching salary, Gingrich was able to stay afloat financially. He also survived with the help of Southwire Co. head Roy Richards (for whom Gingrich later did many favors), who owned the People's Bank, which in 1977 paid Gingrich several thousand dollars to speak to employees about the future.[31]

Another beneficiary of the novel deal was Gingrich's friend Chester Roush, who was the guiding force behind Nomohan, Ltd. Roush was head of a real estate development company called The Dorchester Corp., which obtained at least nine low-interest loans from the Farmers Home Administration and received $12.6 million in federal subsidies during Gingrich's first decade in office. A 1989 article in the *Atlanta Business Chronicle* noted that "Gingrich has taken a far more personal interest in federal public policy matters affecting Roush's business interests than he has previously indicated in interviews with reporters."

Gingrich owed a lot to Roush, who is one of the most powerful businessmen in Carrollton, Georgia. Roush contributed to Gingrich's 1974 and 1976 campaigns and was an important early fundraiser. By 1989, Roush and members of his family had contributed almost $5,000 to Gingrich campaigns, and Roush co-signed two loans to Gingrich campaigns. Roush's daughter helped sponsor a $250-a-person appreciation dinner for Gingrich.[32]

Although Gingrich denied ever helping Roush in any way, he once appealed for him to the Farmers Home Administration, and in 1986 wrote a personal appeal to Department of Housing and Urban Development Secretary Samuel Pierce, asking for Roush's rejected application to be reconsidered. Gingrich requested copies of the report and wrote, "I believe there is cause for reconsideration of this project. If there is a reallocation of recaptured grant funds, I'd like you to take another look at this application to see if it qualifies." Pierce promised him that "staff is looking into the matter and we will provide you a full response as soon as possible."

However, Gingrich wasn't quite so responsive when the constituent concerned about housing wasn't a wealthy contributor. Gingrich was contacted by the administrator of a low-income housing development for the elderly, asking him to support an override of a veto by President Reagan, who deferred $2.3 billion in housing funds appropriated by Congress. Gingrich refused, writing that "I think the best way to help preserve the American dream of owning a home in this country is to reduce government spending." But in 1988 and 1989, Roush's daughter, who was CEO of The Dorchester Corp., asked him to support the low-income housing tax credit. In response, Gingrich co-sponsored the bill.[33]

Gingrich once declared that he was "absolutely appalled at what we are learning about how HUD was run. This fits exactly the model I was describing all spring of the corrupt liberal welfare state." Yet Gingrich was part of the same system of favoritism and corruption that he was shocked to learn about. When HUD secretary Jack Kemp was scheduled to testify in front of a House panel investigating how political favoritism affected HUD grants during the Reagan years, Gingrich wrote him a letter on July 6, 1989: "I understand you will be testifying before the Government Operations Subcommittee on Employment and Housing on July 11, 1989. The hearings to date have concentrated on the Reagan years in an attempt to both politicize the issue against Republicans and avoid a discussion of the real problems. You must take the offensive and explain why the existing HUD bureaucracy has not, and indeed cannot, succeed in helping Americans meet their housing needs."[34] Gingrich wanted Kemp to make an attack on government bureaucracy, not a critique of Republican corruption—one which might implicate Gingrich if his earlier attempts to influence HUD were revealed.

Real Books for Real Money

Nomohan Ltd. was merely the first suspect book deal that Gingrich was involved in. In 1984, twenty-one major business leaders and campaign contributors each gave $5,000 to provide a $105,000 fund to pay for advertising and an author's tour to promote Gingrich's first book, *Window of Opportunity*. Marianne Gingrich herself pocketed $11,500 of the money from the private partnership, COS Limited (named after Gingrich's congressional group, the Conservative Opportunity Society), for administrative duties in promoting the book. Despite this massive investment, Gingrich's book only made enough for Gingrich and his wife to take in $24,000 in royalties. The "investors" lost all their money as a tax writeoff, a common theme in Gingrich's literary endeavors.[35] In his first decade in Congress, these investors (none of whom had ever invested in a book before) and their families contributed $60,000 to Gingrich's campaign, and several were involved in federal contracts. Gingrich admitted his book deal was "as weird as Wright's," but claimed it was "a real book."[36] However, the House rules do not distinguish between real and phony books, and Gingrich's book—like Wright's—was mostly composed of recycled speeches he had given.

Gingrich also violated House rules by using his Congressional staff to work on *Window of Opportunity*. According to his district administrator at the time, Dolores Adamson, Gingrich used his House office staff to edit, copy, and mail drafts of *Window of Opportunity*. Adamson says, "Newt's attitude was: 'The rules don't apply to me.' He became angry whenever things got in the way of what he wanted to do." Dorothy Crews, who served as Gingrich's executive assistant from 1979 to 1984, confirms this: "I did not think it was appropriate for us to work on the book." She was told that the book (for which the Gingriches received a hefty advance) was a government "policy statement." Adamson reports, "I told [Gingrich] he couldn't do it. His response was that he didn't talk to me at all." It was not until years later, when the $105,000 publicity deal was revealed and sparked controversy, that Gingrich claimed the book was "strictly a business venture."[37]

By far the most media scrutiny about Gingrich's ethical problems has focused on the $4.5 million book contract he signed in 1994, which ironically was probably the most legitimate book deal Gingrich has ever been involved in. The book contract was certainly a crass effort by Gingrich to cash in on his political office, but it is doubtful that Rupert Murdoch ordered the HarperCollins publishing arm of his mega-corporation to bid high for Gingrich's book, or that its editors would agree to offer Gingrich an extraordinary bribe from Murdoch. However, Murdoch's editors must have known that their owner was fond of losing money on right-wing political ventures, and that he would be pleased by their signing of a conservative like Gingrich (and more willing to overlook the millions of dollars they were risking on his book *To Renew America*).

Gingrich violated several House ethics rules in the process of getting his book contract. Although he argued that the scrutiny given to his deal showed a double standard, since Democratic politicians like Al Gore have received large advances for their books, the truth is that Gingrich has never followed the same rules. Gore's book, *Earth in the Balance*, earned him a $100,000 advance and about $850,000 in royalties; however, Gore requested a review of his contract and got clearance from the Senate Ethics Committee before doing the book, and he was asked questions about whether his publisher, Houghton Mifflin, was lobbying him or had any business involving the committees he served on.[38]

By contrast, Gingrich defied the Ethics Committee by signing his contract even though the committee was deadlocked about approving it.[39] Gingrich's lawyer had written to them, saying that he would assume the deal was acceptable unless he heard otherwise. The day before Gingrich signed the contract, the bipartisan House ethics panel wrote back to his lawyer, "You should make no such assumption."[40]

Gingrich claimed that the opposition to the book deal was due to "jealousy." Although no evidence came up proving that there was any kind of quid pro quo deal between Gingrich and Murdoch, there was certainly reason for suspicion. Gingrich met secretly with Murdoch on November 28, 1994, shortly before the heavy bidding on his book contract. Gingrich kept this fact concealed during the initial controversy over his book deal, hoping that it would go unnoticed. On December 30, 1994, trying to defuse the criticism about his $4.5 million advance, and perhaps hoping to keep his meeting with Murdoch a secret, Gingrich announced that he would only accept a $1 advance, and earn his money via royalties. The fact that Gingrich only made $1.2 million in royalties (most of which went to his agent, ghostwriter, fact checker, and book tour expenses) shows how inflated the initial book deal was.[41]

Gingrich's attempt to keep the Murdoch connection hidden failed. After the press revealed it, Gingrich spokesperson Tony Blankley tried on January 12, 1995, to claim that Gingrich and Murdoch "passed the time of day," meeting for only a few minutes.[42] Gingrich's office said that the meeting with Murdoch was merely a "courtesy call" and "nothing serious was discussed." Only after pressed by the media did Gingrich's spokesperson admit that it was a 15-minute meeting with Murdoch and his lobbyist, and that the controversy over Murdoch's efforts to avoid regulation of the Fox television network was indeed discussed.[43] It was not until several months later that the Ethics Committee investigation revealed that Greg Wright, Gingrich's congressional office chief of staff, was also at the meeting and may have prepared a memo for Gingrich about what Murdoch wanted from him.[44]

Murdoch is well known for using his money to promote the Republican Party. He also has a track record of influencing the media he owns in a conservative direction. Murdoch took over the *New York Post* in 1993 and conservative columnists and investigative reporters were hired at Murdoch's request.[45] In 1995, Murdoch provided several million dollars to William Kristol and his Project for the Republican Future to start the *Weekly Standard*, a right-wing opinion magazine which is virtually certain to lose money.[46]

After the meeting and the book deal, Gingrich was actively involved in helping Murdoch. In 1995, the House passed a bill to repeal tax benefits for minority broadcasters and the companies that sell them stations. But a special provision hidden in the conference report saved Rupert Murdoch tens of millions of dollars. The *New York Daily News* reported that "Republicans dropped their opposition to the tax break after learning Murdoch was the beneficiary of the legislation and consulting Gingrich, according to six sources involved in the negotiations."[47]

What few people realized was that Gingrich never needed a $4.5 million bribe to be influenced by Murdoch. He was already happy to support Murdoch, knowing that Murdoch's political donations and media influence would benefit the Republicans. Gingrich noted that Murdoch "is a leading right-wing conservative who was very close to the Reagan Administration" and "in the Reagan years he was very helpful editorially."[48] Peggy Binzel, Murdoch's lobbyist, said that promoting her client's agenda to Gingrich was like "pushing on an open door."[49] Gingrich himself admitted, "I've been on Rupert's side ideologically from day one."[50] And financially, too: in June 1995, Murdoch was one of the co-chairmen who raised at least $100,000 for the Republican Party in a "Salute to Newt Gingrich" held aboard the USS *Intrepid* in New York.[51]

Republican Censorship and Democratic Fumblings

Rather than confront Gingrich's unethical behavior, Republicans have tried to silence his critics. When Rep. Carrie Meek (D-Florida) declared that because of Gingrich's book deal, "now more than ever before the perception of impropriety, not to mention the potential conflict of interest, still exists," Gingrich's friend Bob Walker interrupted and demanded that her words be "taken down"—stricken from the record, in Orwellian fashion, as if they had never been said. The chair, Cliff Stearns (R-Florida), declared that "references to personal improprieties is not within the decorum of the House," and a party-line vote upheld the censorship.[52] Republicans also voted 231-173 to bar the November 16, 1995, issue of the *New York Daily News* from the floor because it showed Gingrich in diapers with the headline: "Cry Baby: Newt's Tantrum: He closed down the government because Clinton made him sit at back of plane."[53]

The Republicans in the House see a severe threat to their power if Gingrich's illegal and ethically questionable activities are made public, and they are determined to silence the opposition.

With all of these ethical violations, it is surprising that Gingrich has been able to avoid serious scrutiny. Unfortunately, the Democrats made the mistake of trying to use Gingrich's book deals as a form of partisan revenge. They held back an early ethics complaint about Gingrich until after he had decided to go after Speaker Wright publicly. Because the Democrats were not nearly as skillful as Gingrich at pushing ethical issues in the House and in the media, they were unable to hold Gingrich accountable to the same ethical standards he imposed on others.

Chapter 2

Newt, Inc.: The Gingrich Empire

Newt Gingrich has always understood the fundamental importance of money to a member of Congress, and he has never hesitated to bend the rules to get what he needs. According to one story, as a professor of history at West Georgia College, Gingrich asked his students to donate five dollars a week to his campaign "in the interest of good government."[1] It is commonly accepted that teachers who ask their students for dates are engaging in inappropriate harassment and abuse of power. The request that students contribute to a teacher's campaign should also be abhorred. Back then, as today, Gingrich ignored the ethical obligations of an individual in power, since any request by a professor for money suggests that student grades may depend on their generosity.

Gingrich has not changed his unethical fundraising tactics of the early days. But today, he is reaching into deeper pockets. The political and monetary fortunes he has amassed throughout his two-decade political career by violating ethics rules, nonprofit tax laws, and federal election laws have been spent on promoting himself with untiring zeal. Although Congress has always been a corrupt place, no politician of our time has used corruption more effectively to his advantage than Newt Gingrich.

Gingrich Meets GOPAC

While Gingrich's book deals were his primary means of covertly pocketing money from corporate donors, they didn't give him the power he needed to rise to the top of the Republican Party in the House. After the confrontation with O'Neill in 1984, Gingrich finally got some respect for standing up to the Speaker of the House: journalist David Broder called him a future leader, right-wing activist Richard Viguerie described him as "the single most important conservative in the House of Representatives," and *Mother Jones* had featured a critical article about this "shining knight of the post-Reagan right."[2] However, no one could figure out what he had accomplished beyond his own self-aggrandizement. Nor did Gingrich improve his own situation in the House, where he was even more of a pariah than before.

The Conservative Opportunity Society enabled Gingrich to create a small group of activists within Congress, but it hadn't done enough for Gingrich's grand ambitions. Gingrich had irritated the Democrats running the House, but this meant little in the broader political context. After his infamous confrontation with O'Neill, the Democrats realized that the best way to deal with Gingrich was to ignore him, and they did. The Republican leadership had never been happy with this young upstart and his angry rhetoric, and minority leader Bob Michel distrusted him. If he wanted to take control of the Republican Party and make himself a historic figure, Gingrich needed to reach the next generation of Republican political activists. He needed a position of power and he needed money to finance his revolution from within. GOPAC was the answer.

In 1978, Pierre "Pete" duPont IV and a dozen Republican governors founded the GOP Action Committee (GOPAC) to help create a "farm team" of state and local Republican candidates. It was a low-profile group, primarily devoted to funneling small amounts of money to low-level Republican candidates that were often ignored by the more prominent Republican National Campaign Committee. But in 1986, when duPont planned a run for president, he decided that GOPAC needed a new leader because if he stayed on, "people would say that's part of Pete duPont's presidential campaign."[3] This might have raised legal issues since GOPAC was focusing solely on state and local races, and wasn't registered as a national PAC.

When duPont asked himself, "Who's got the energy? Who's got the ideas?" he turned to his friend of five years: "Newt Gingrich stood out." Gingrich was an easy choice: he was power-hungry, but because he was reviled by Democrats and disliked by the Republican leadership, he had been excluded from any position of power in the House. His lack of legislative and oratorical skills made it difficult for him to influence policy on the floor. Gingrich had both ambition and talent, but nothing to do in the House. His leadership skills would prove invaluable in making GOPAC the most active Republican group in Congress.

Under Gingrich, GOPAC grew in power and influence while the national Republican committee floundered due to financial problems and poor leadership. Instead of giving money to candidates, Gingrich gave them advice—in the form of audio and video tapes of himself discussing how to win. GOPAC held seminars, conducted polls and focus groups, and gave out training manuals, motivational tapes, and "Newt Gingrich Wants You" posters. Gingrich shifted GOPAC away from direct contributions to state and local candidates, and toward serving Gingrich's own agenda, training candidates to promote his ideas—and making sure an entire new generation of Republican candidates would be personally indebted to Gingrich and give him control over the Republican Party in the House.

duPont explains that Gingrich turned a "narrowly-focused campaign vehicle" into "a broader vehicle to explain the Republican ideology and philosophy and he expanded it enormously."[4] But GOPAC had little connection to policy matters or an ideological revolution. Instead, GOPAC spread information about Gingrich's specialty: how to demonize your political opponents. Early in his career, he told a group of College Republicans to "do things that may be wrong, but do something," and warned them that one of the "great problems" within the Republican Party is that "we don't encourage you to be nasty."[5]

Dale Carnegie—With JAWS

Perhaps no document better embodies Gingrich's approach to politics than the GOPAC guide entitled "Language: A Key Mechanism of Control." Distributed to Republican activists across the country, it declared, "we have heard a plaintive plea: 'I wish I could speak like Newt.'" According to GOPAC, "That takes years of practice." But it promised "a significant impact on your campaign" if the Newt wannabes would use the right rhetoric: "The words and phrases are powerful. Read them. Memorize as many as possible."[6]

The "Control" memo admits that things like morality and fairness may make some candidates reluctant to smear their opponents: "Sometimes we are hesitant to use contrast." But victory justifies any means: "Remember that creating a difference helps you." Among the "contrasting words" urged were such notable adjectives as "radical," "pathetic," "destructive," "ideological," "insecure," "anti-flag," "anti-family," "anti-child," "anti-jobs," "pessimistic," and "self-serving." Other words and phrases for use in demonizing opponents were such classics as "liberal," "failure," "unionized bureaucracy," "criminal rights," "welfare," "mandates," "taxes," "cheat," "steal," "disgrace," and, ironically enough, "abuse of power."[7] For Gingrich, it is simply routine to attack your opponents as "sick" and accuse them of being "traitors." In truth, most of the contrasting words can be applied to Gingrich himself (particularly "shallow," "destructive," "corruption," "hypocrisy," "intolerant," "status quo," and "patronage"). But the "Control" memo showed Gingrich's mastery of empty political rhetoric which he would use effectively to push the Contract with America in the face of popular resistance.

The Secret Federal Machine

Under Gingrich, GOPAC wasn't just a conservative propaganda-training institute. It also served as the Republican clearinghouse for his efforts to influence Congressional elections. Although GOPAC's charter limited it solely to state and local races, Gingrich ignored GOPAC's by-laws and federal election laws. The purpose of GOPAC was no longer to create a "farm team" by helping state and local candidates; instead, efforts were re-directed—illegally—towards Gingrich's ultimate goal of a Republican-controlled House of Representatives.

Gingrich admitted in a secret 1989 GOPAC meeting: "I am interested in causing changes as a consequence of which we will win control of the House and the country. Now, the GOPAC segment of that is to normally focus its resources on state, legislative, and local races, but in fact we also focus a lot of our resources on the first half of that question."[8] He was saying in a private meeting what GOPAC and Gingrich would later deny: that GOPAC spent large amounts of money to gain control of Congress, money separate from its support for state and local races.

Because federal election laws required disclosure of all donors and limited the amount that could be given to a federal political action committee, Gingrich used GOPAC to illegally take secret, unlimited donations. In 1988, GOPAC counsel Daniel Swillinger explained all the advantages of being a political action committee for state and local races with no involvement in federal elections: "Because GOPAC is not a federal committee, it may legally accept corporate contributions. There is no limit to the amount either an individual or a corporation may contribute. Likewise, contributions to GOPAC do not count against federal giving limits."[9] If Gingrich's goal of using GOPAC to take over the House of Representatives were revealed, GOPAC would be subject to the more severe federal regulations on contributions and public disclosure of donors that govern federal elections.

On September 18, 1990, the Democratic Congressional Campaign Committee filed a complaint with the Federal Election Commission (FEC) accusing GOPAC of illegally contributing money to candidates running for federal office. Federal election laws prohibit any group from using their resources to help federal campaigns without registering as a federal PAC and revealing their donors. GOPAC kept its financial information, and its influence on various elections—especially Gingrich's own re-election campaigns—a secret, in direct violation of the law. The FEC determined on May 7, 1991, that the complaint was valid and began an investigation of GOPAC. One day later, GOPAC finally registered as a federal political action committee. After that time, GOPAC legally became what it had been surreptitiously for years: Newt Gingrich's instrument for achieving power and starting the Republican Revolution.

Guilty as Charged: The FEC Investigation

Late in 1993, the FEC completed its investigation, which determined that GOPAC had violated several federal election laws. To FEC investigators, the evidence of guilt was overwhelming. The internal documents turned over by GOPAC revealed a long history of GOPAC's plans to help Gingrich take over the House.

The FEC estimated that "the vast majority, approximately 85 percent, of

GOPAC's 1989-90 expenditures were for the purpose of electing Republican candidates to the United States House of Representatives." One major expenditure was a GOPAC direct mail piece sent in 1989 and 1990 asking the public to contribute to GOPAC's "Campaign for Fair Elections," which clearly aimed at raising money for federal races. "Let me ask you a disturbing question," Gingrich wrote. "How would you feel if I told you that every penny you have ever paid in federal taxes was spent to pay the postage on your Congressman's unsolicited junk mail?" In keeping with his pattern of accusing opponents of his own shortcomings, in his 1988 re-election campaign he was one of Congress's highest junk mail spenders.[10]

In the memo, Newt Gingrich told the direct mail recipients, "The only way to clean up the mess and restore honesty and decency to Congress is to break the Democrats' stranglehold on power." Gingrich described GOPAC as "the Republican committee dedicated to building a Republican majority at all levels of government"—even though GOPAC's charter prohibited it from any involvement in Congressional elections. He concluded, "With your help, we can break the liberal Democrats' iron-grip on the House of Representatives and build a new Republican majority."[11]

A July 1989 direct mail plea again underlined GOPAC's focus on Congressional elections: "GOPAC also wants to assist the national Party Committees in educating the voters in 'swing' Congressional districts about their Democratic Congressmen's voting records." GOPAC's "National Activist Network," according to another memo, was created to "design federal legislation" and help give Gingrich "a means to activate our community all across the country on specific issues and legislation."

The evidence of GOPAC's efforts to influence federal elections in violation of disclosure laws is overwhelming. The direct mail letters explicitly promised to "defeat or seriously weaken a large number of Democrats in 1990. And that will give us the momentum we need to sweep in a majority of Republicans in 1992." Obviously, Gingrich's letters were directed at helping Republican candidates for Congress in the next election, not creating a state-based "farm team" for the distant future.

GOPAC chairman Howard "Bo" Callaway wrote to Roger Milliken, a major Gingrich and GOPAC supporter, inviting him to a meeting and declaring that "We will be looking at plans to recruit and support candidates in 210 congressional districts across the country."[12] GOPAC also used federal officials in fundraisers, holding regular meetings for Charter Members where they met cabinet members, members of Congress, and other Republican officials.

GOPAC donors knew that this was an organization to influence federal elections, and that their money gave them influence over Republicans in Congress. And they expected a return on their investment. Wisconsin businessman Philip Gelatt, who had given $230,000 to GOPAC, refused to show up at a GOPAC retreat in Colorado after learning that Gingrich would not appear. A GOPAC staffer warned in a memo that Gelatt was ready to give "in the six figures" but noted that Gelatt had said "something to the effect that he doesn't mind paying the piper if the piper plays."[13]

Years before the FEC investigation forced it to register as a PAC, a 1988 GOPAC fundraising letter to 800,000 potential donors declared its national political aims: "It is vital that House Republicans recognize that only an all-out effort to arouse, mobilize and lead the American people will produce enough candidates, energy and votes to break the left-wing machine's illegitimate grip on the House of Representatives."[14] It would be illegal to promote GOPAC influence on federal elections without registering as a federal PAC. GOPAC's counsel was clearly worried, warning Gingrich about his letters urging donors to give in order to strengthen the Republican Party in federal congressional districts: "GOPAC is prohibited by its charter and by-laws from contributing to candidates for Federal office, or to committees supporting candidates for Federal office."[15] Gingrich was fully informed about federal laws as early as February 1988, yet he knowingly continued to violate them.

In addition to breaking federal election laws, GOPAC also violated various state election laws. In order to evade disclosure requirements in Texas, Gingrich sent a letter with campaign contributions to two Texas candidates in 1989 and 1990, claiming that "GOPAC received no contribution in excess of $100 during the past 12 months."[16] This was an obvious lie—GOPAC had numerous donors who had given at least $10,000 each. Texas law also required that any group which gave more than 20% of its contributions to Texas candidates needed to register with the state. In 1989, GOPAC gave 42% of its contributions to Texans, and in 1990 that proportion increased to 54%. GOPAC avoided the law by asserting that it collected enough money from small contributors to cover the donation to state candidates, even though all of its donations went into the same account. Another illegal GOPAC accounting trick was to recycle reporting of contributions to various states. The same eight businessmen who each gave $5,000 were listed in reports to New Mexico, Mississippi, Arizona, Michigan, Indiana, and Georgia. This allowed GOPAC to keep the identities of most of its donors secret.[17]

Republicans regularly used these tricks to avoid following the law. In 1995, House Majority Whip Tom DeLay (R-Texas) raised over $175,000 in corporate "soft money" for his leadership PAC called "Americans for a Republican Majority". To evade Texas law, DeLay registered the PAC in Virginia.[18] GOPAC and similar "state and local" groups allowed Republicans to launch a covert attack on the Democratic Congress, much like Oliver North's illegal plot to funnel money to the Contras in Nicaragua. For the

Republicans, it was a morally justifiable evasion of the law in order to undermine the Democratic Party. Gingrich knew all along exactly what GOPAC was doing; it was an organization that he controlled completely and which served his goal of becoming Speaker. As the Capitol Hill newspaper *Roll Call* observed, GOPAC was "not an arm of Newt, Inc., but the corporate headquarters."[19]

Not Guilty, But Not Innocent: the Dismissal of the FEC Suit

In the GOPAC case, the FEC tried for several months to reach a settlement with Gingrich and his staff—who refused, fearing that any admission about GOPAC's activities would prompt further inquiries into Gingrich's ethics. The FEC filed suit against GOPAC in federal court on February 1, 1994. Two years later, on February 28, 1996, U.S. District Judge Oberdorfer ruled that GOPAC was not guilty of violating federal election law. Although Gingrich quickly claimed vindication, Judge Oberdorfer's opinion revealed something quite different. Oberdorfer found that GOPAC had, without question, violated the law. But he ruled that the law itself was unconstitutional because it unfairly restricted the First Amendment right of political organizations to influence federal elections.

Judge Oberdorfer came to this conclusion by a wild misreading of the Supreme Court case *Buckley v. Valeo*, a 1976 decision which found that although federal law could regulate federal elections, it could not limit the amount an individual spent on his or her own campaign. The result has been a huge loophole allowing the super-rich (Ross Perot and Steve Forbes among them) to outspend all other candidates. But a lesser-known part of the Buckley case warned about overly broad definitions of political committees which might infringe on their First Amendment rights. Oberdorfer interpreted this to mean that any organization—even GOPAC, the main planning group for the national Republican Party—was not "political" even if it devoted millions of dollars to the Republican takeover of Congress. Federal election law prohibited "anything of value made by any person for the purpose of influencing any election for Federal office" to be given secretly if it was worth more than $1,000. GOPAC's polling data, election advice, mailing lists, and fundraising assistance amounted to millions of dollars being devoted to Gingrich's goal of becoming Speaker of the House. But Oberdorfer ruled that as long as GOPAC never directly contributed money to a candidate's campaign fund, it could assist Republicans running for Congress in any way it wanted, and spend unlimited amounts of money to fund the Republican Revolution. As Christina Jeffrey, the House historian appointed—and then dismissed—by Gingrich, observed, "If I understand GOPAC, it's a way of getting around campaign finance law."[20]

GOPAC's Direct Support for Newt

Much of GOPAC's illegal intervention in federal elections was focused on one candidate: Newt Gingrich. In 1988, GOPAC's mailing list was used to send direct mail which solicited contributions to Gingrich's campaign. As with its help provided to other congressional candidates, this was a clear violation of its charter and federal law to help Gingrich get re-elected and finance his personal expenses.

In 1990, Gingrich faced the fight of his political life, and he needed GOPAC's help to get re-elected. Despite running in a heavily conservative district (it voted 75% for Bush in 1988 against Dukakis), Democrat David Worley mounted a strong campaign against Gingrich, pointing out his hypocrisy in accepting a $30,000 Congressional pay raise and his failure to help local striking Eastern Airlines workers. The district had one of the largest groups of aviation workers in the country, and more than a third were on strike against Eastern Airlines. As ranking minority member of the House Public Works and Transportation Committee's aviation subcommittee, Gingrich was too busy building his own power structure to worry much about the strikers. He failed to support a House bill asking the president to have an emergency board arbitrate the strike, perhaps because Eastern Airlines owner Frank Lorenzo was one of Gingrich's contributors.[21] In the end, Gingrich beat Worley by 974 votes despite outspending him by $1.5 million to $330,000.[22]

But to win, Gingrich had to cheat. GOPAC help was desperately needed for his campaign, and GOPAC officials—who were Gingrich's friends and personally appointed associates—saw his potential loss as a threat to all their organizing efforts. So GOPAC provided $250,000 in secret "Newt Support" to re-elect Gingrich, including paying the salaries and travel expenses of political consultants who devoted most of their time to helping Gingrich.[23]

GOPAC officials at a 1989 planning meeting are quoted in internal documents as stressing that "Newt must be re-elected," and that steps were needed "to inoculate Newt Gingrich from Democratic attacks." A 1990 memo emphasizes that "GOPAC has a deep interest in Georgia." In 1989 and 1990, when GOPAC did research with focus groups, it chose voters in or near Gingrich's district and gave the results to him; one GOPAC employee reported that Gingrich used the research in "countless speeches." Another letter to GOPAC donors explained that Georgia was targeted during the election with more GOPAC seminars than any other state "to protect Newt Gingrich" during the state's redistricting.[24]

At a 1989 GOPAC retreat, charter members were told by GOPAC executive director Jeff Eisenach, "as long as you charter members understand that we're putting funds to help Newt think, and we don't show them it's hard to explain, when you get down there, how many dollars went out, you know, you just gave dollars to help Newt. As long as our charter members understand that's probably the most single high priority we've got in dollars."[25] Buried in this confusing statement was an essential point: charter members were being told that donations to GOPAC end up supporting Gingrich's political ambitions. Both GOPAC leaders and its donors understood that GOPAC was an entity of, by, and for Newt Gingrich. A GOPAC official observed in an August 6, 1990 meeting, "Newt is the only unique product we have." GOPAC had to walk a delicate line, privately assuring charter members that their donations would be funneled to Gingrich—but publicly concealing this fact.

At the 1989 planning meeting, a GOPAC official declared: "I mean we're supplying, my guess would be, a quarter of a million dollars in 'Newt Support' per year." The transcript gives an example of "Newt Support" as follows: "If Newt decides he's got a Saturday free in Georgia, he wants people [around] him. And GOPAC pays those bills." Another GOPAC staffer said, "Newt needs interplay. Newt needs to talk with all of us. Newt needs people like Jeff [Eisenach] here, and Lutzback and Steve [Hanser] and others. GOPAC is able to provide all of that to Newt. It's able to provide it in a way that most of you understand. So we're able to provide that to Newt and that's happened." Eisenach's full salary and travel expenses were paid by GOPAC even though most of his time was spent helping Gingrich's campaign. Gingrich's close friend and political advisor Joe Gaylord was paid $132,000 by GOPAC as a consultant. The research provided for free to Gingrich and other congressional candidates cost about $50,000.[26] GOPAC also paid for Gingrich's travel expenses and his American Express card membership fee.

GOPAC head Bo Callaway wrote an August 13, 1990 memo to Gingrich, promising him that GOPAC leaders decided "unanimously" that "the regular funding for GOPAC, to include charter and direct mail, should be spent for Traditional GOPAC and Newt support."[27] The fact that "Newt support" was seen as something outside of "Traditional GOPAC" activities is clear evidence of the massive GOPAC efforts to help Gingrich win his 1990 election.

Protecting the Boss

Within GOPAC, staffers worried about the laws and ethics rules they were violating. One memo noted, "There is concern among some that we could be criticized" by the media with the accusation that donors who gave large gifts "are doing so to gain special treatment from you or the Whip office."[28] A special 1990 memo to Gingrich noted that secret GOPAC projects had illegally aided Gingrich and his ambitions: "Remember what Ollie North said to Mr. President, you don't want to know about this. We are protecting you Newt."[29]

The expenses paid for advisors and consultants also do not account for all the national fundraising done on Gingrich's behalf via GOPAC. GOPAC mailed its major supporters asking them to donate to the Republican Congressional Campaign Committee and individual campaigns in order "to keep the current team," a direct violation of the law prohibiting GOPAC from helping in federal campaigns without registering. GOPAC's large donors contributed $124,503 to Mr. Gingrich's personal campaign committee during the 1990 elections, more than seven times the amount they gave to any other candidate.[30]

Even Gingrich's staffers couldn't separate GOPAC and the re-election campaign. Minutes of a June 9, 1990 planning meeting included a note at the top that asked, "Is this a GOPAC planning meeting or a Congressman Gingrich planning meeting?"[31] One internal memo proposed creating a special account for Gingrich at GOPAC: "this should stop all of the Joe Barton-type criticism that money that he is raising is going to Newt support rather than candidates, and two, it would be an answer to allegations that Newt is taking advantage of GOPAC by getting some kind of perks that are not intended by donors."[32]

A Bribe By Any Other Name... Friends in Monied Places

House rules prohibit "unofficial support" of a member of Congress or a candidate via a slush fund like Newt Support. Federal election law forbids a political action committee from giving anything like this amount of money to any candidate and then concealing the donors. Yet GOPAC explicitly tied donations to Gingrich and the "opportunity" to "influence" him. "One of the things that makes GOPAC so unique is the opportunity for our Charter Members to work with Newt Gingrich and to influence his issues and direction," GOPAC chairman Bo Callaway wrote in a letter to several donors that practically begged for a *quid pro quo* exchange.[33] Gingrich himself offered donors "an hour of uninterrupted conversation" with him during early morning walks.[34] It is not unusual for corporate leaders to influence politicians with their donations. But it is unusual—and illegal—for anyone to offer Congressional influence in exchange for money. It's called bribery, and it's exactly what GOPAC was doing.

By offering political donors a place to pour large amounts of money and buy influence with Gingrich, GOPAC increased its power and importance. In essence, Gingrich became a national congressman, representing conservative businessmen donating money from all around the country. And GOPAC became another Gingrich money-laundering scheme, a way for these donors to exceed the federal election limits of $1,000. Of course, GOPAC wasn't the only way to evade the law. Wealthy contributors who wanted to get around the limits could also give money to the party national committee in the form of so-called "soft money." This loophole in federal election law allowed the wealthy to continue buying influence in Congress, and enhanced the power of the parties to control elections.

But unlike the legal "soft money" route, GOPAC's evasion of federal election laws allowed the donors to remain secret. The public would not know who was giving money to Gingrich, nor could journalists easily draw connections between GOPAC's contributors and the favors Gingrich did for them. Even after GOPAC filed as a federal political action committee, it continued to illegally support Gingrich and illegally conceal the names of most donors. Between 1991 and 1994, GOPAC spent $5.8 million. Only $76,000 went to either candidates other than Gingrich or the training tapes that Gingrich made for candidates. GOPAC spent $810,000 on travel and $1.4 million on consultants, and it became a private source of funds for Gingrich. Gingrich also used GOPAC to pay for personal travel without revealing all of the trips in his financial disclosure statement. GOPAC paid for Gingrich and his wife to take a two-day vacation to Bermuda, covering both a $250-a-night hotel and travel expenses. When Gingrich failed to disclose the GOPAC payment on his financial disclosure statement, he blamed the omission on a "staff slip-up."[35] Gingrich also concealed an 18-day vacation with his wife at Bo Callaway's ski resort in Colorado, where he met with advisors to plan the Republican takeover of Congress. Only after the media revealed the story did Gingrich amend his financial statement to include the gift from GOPAC.[36]

Gingrich frequently intervened with government officials to help major GOPAC donors from around the country. Emil E. Ogden, a Texas oil entrepreneur who contributed over $51,260 to GOPAC, asked Gingrich for assistance in contacting a Bush Energy Department official. In a January 1989 letter, Gingrich reported his success to Ogden: "I have also written to [the official] on our behalf. Please let me know if there is anything more I can do to help."[37]

Throughout his political career, Gingrich has always applied two standards for influence. One was for the average voter in his district, who got ignored between elections while Gingrich pursued his self-aggrandizing schemes. But for the wealthy contributors to his campaigns and the Gingrich empire, he has a different standard. The largest donors regularly bought close contact with Newt and a remarkable level of influence. These men, the Friends Of Gingrich, latched on to a rising politician and took him to the top with the help of their money.

On June 4, 1990, a GOPAC staffer wrote a memo to Gingrich telling him that GOPAC charter member James Lightner was "very angry at your vote" in favor of the Americans With Disabilities Act and "will think long and hard before renewing his membership." The aide informed Gingrich that Lightner "felt hurt and slighted by not having his call returned more promptly. I placated him somewhat, but he would like to hear from you."[38] Lightner fully expected his GOPAC donations to buy him direct influence with Gingrich.

Southdown, Inc., the largest American-owned cement company, used GOPAC to complain about a Mexican cement maker, CMEX, that they accused of dumping cement in Southern states. One Southdown employee reported, "We reached out because we thought we needed help. We wanted some letters written to the International Trade Commission." Giving money to GOPAC was their way to buy influence.

Southdown contacted Rep. Joe Barton (R-TX), the Texas GOPAC chair and the congressman who was second to Gingrich in fundraising from GOPAC charter members in 1990. In a September 27, 1989 letter, Southdown executive vice president and general counsel, Edgar J. Marston III wrote to Barton, "Thank you for interrupting your busy schedule yesterday and visiting with me and my associates regarding our dumping case against Mexican cement producers. I also appreciate your offer of assistance in that matter." Marston added, "As we discussed several months ago, I am enclosing a check for $10,000 payable to GOPAC."

In response, Barton sought signatures to support the American cement firm, and got Gingrich and 15 other Republican House members (along with 19 Democrats) to sign two letters on October 20, 1989. The letters urged the federal International Trade Commission (ITC) and Commerce Secretary Robert A. Mosbacher to support the American cement companies. Within weeks, the ITC determined that there was a "reasonable indication" that American cement makers were harmed by the Mexican sales, and the Commerce Department also ruled that dumping had occurred. On August 23, 1990, the International Trade Commission voted 2-1 that cement dumping had caused the U.S. companies "material injury" and imposed duties on Mexican producers.

In 1989 and 1990, Southdown paid GOPAC a total of $25,000 for its services. On December 13, 1990, Gingrich wrote to Southdown executive Edgar Marston, thanking him for "staying on board as a charter member." However, Southdown stopped donating to GOPAC after the favor was done.[39] Small deals like this one marked business as usual inside GOPAC. Because federal election laws limited how much an individual could contribute to a candidate and prohibited corporate donations, companies with money who wanted to buy influence had to find other outlets. The Republican Party offered the most obvious target, but companies found that giving to GOPAC was a superior form of bribery because the contributions were kept secret and the influence on members of Congress like Newt Gingrich was more direct.

Making Welfare a Secret Virtue for the Rich

The biggest welfare beneficiary in America is Dwayne Andreas, chair of

Archer Daniels Midland. His company produces 60% of the country's ethanol and benefits from an annual federal subsidy that may reach $1 billion by the year 2000, in addition to hundreds of millions from state governments. When Rep. Bill Archer, chair of the House Ways and Means Committee, proposed reducing ethanol subsidies to save $2 billion over seven years, Gingrich intervened to stop any limits on the subsidies. As James Bovard observed in the *Wall Street Journal*, "Gingrich's action made a mockery of his fervent promises to slash wasteful federal spending."[40] But for Gingrich, a corporate executive like Andreas (who has given more than $70,000 to GOPAC) is too powerful to offend.

Gingrich's largest supporters have been Wisconsin entrepreneurs Terry and Mary Kohler, who have given nearly a million dollars to GOPAC. In 1990, GOPAC spent $123,100 for a Wisconsin independent expenditure project to support three state candidates. "Unfortunately," the Wisconsin GOPAC group observed in 1990, "Wisconsin has very restrictive laws" which "made it nearly impossible for GOPAC to have any real impact on elections if we operated in a traditional manner." The state required political organizations to disclose any donors who contributed $100 or more. GOPAC avoided the law by lying, claiming that it only used small donations to fund the Wisconsin program. In fact, as a 1990 GOPAC report noted, "With the leadership of charter members Mary and Terry Kohler special funds were raised to help fund an independent expenditure campaign in Wisconsin."[41]

The Wisconsin GOPAC group was a personal project of the Kohlers. From 1988 to 1995 they gave $784,500 to GOPAC ($273,000 in 1990 alone), along with unknown amounts contributed to the Progress & Freedom Foundation and $9,000 directly to Gingrich's campaign committee. Shortly before the 1990 election, Kohler advised Wisconsin GOPAC members to keep quiet: "Your membership in GOPAC should not become known to anyone as a result of this effort, but if you get any phone calls on the subject, you should remain 'mum.'"[42] For Kohler, GOPAC provided a way to influence the political system while keeping his involvement secret, and he advised friends to join GOPAC to become "Gingrich guerrilla[s]."[43] Kohler has his reasons to remain behind the scenes. Despite his wealth, he was rejected for the University of Wisconsin board of regents because of his offensive remarks about blacks in South Africa.[44] Kohler calls GOPAC a "multi-faceted political engine difficult to describe, but enormously gratifying to its members."

On January 7, 1991, Terry Kohler's secretary wrote to GOPAC (including a $100,000 check), "My understanding is that the money is to be divided evenly between the GOPAC 92 Plan and Newt Gingrich projects." For Kohler and other charter members, GOPAC functioned as a scheme for laundering illegal donations to Newt Gingrich.

The law limits Kohler to a $1,000-a-year donation to Gingrich's campaign, a sum that was too small to make a dramatic impact on a candidate. This was exactly how the law was intended to operate since it discouraged favoritism toward wealthy contributors. But GOPAC gave Kohler an opportunity to purchase influence with Gingrich, since he was obviously informed about the "Newt Support" scheme and knew that GOPAC was partly a covert Gingrich re-election campaign organization.

Kohler's massive GOPAC donations led to enormous influence over Gingrich. In December 1994, while Gingrich was planning his takeover as Speaker, Kohler summoned him to his home for a meeting of the "Sheboygan Economic Club." It is a sign of how much Gingrich panders to his wealthy clients that he would immediately obey a request to go to Wisconsin in the midst of his plans to take over Congress.[45]

But GOPAC was always too limited an organization for Gingrich's ambitions. It gave him access and power over Republican political activists and potential candidates for Congress, creating a loyal cadre of supporters who he envisioned making into a Republican majority with himself as its leader. However, Gingrich was still not a household name. Outside of his district, Washington, and Republican political circles, no one had ever heard of him. GOPAC would fuel his ambition for power, but it couldn't satisfy Gingrich's desire for fame—or provide the name recognition he would need if he wanted to run for President. To achieve these larger goals, Gingrich started nonprofit organizations for political purposes, adding a violation of tax laws to the crimes he was willing to commit in his drive for power.

Chapter 3

Politics for Profit: The GOPAC Files

In addition to using GOPAC as a fundraising tool, Gingrich turned GOPAC into his personal public relations machine. His years of using C-SPAN to promote his ideas had convinced him of the political importance of television and new technology. In 1990, GOPAC sponsored a major event called the "American Opportunity Workshop" (AOW) that was broadcast via satellite at a cost of more than $500,000; it was hosted by Gingrich from a restaurant in his district. Gingrich made a series of speeches on the House floor to promote the broadcast, again breaking House rules against making commercial endorsements. But this violation of the rules was minor compared to Gingrich's next step: illegally creating nonprofit, non-political groups for the purpose of spreading his political ideas and influence.

In 1990, GOPAC took over a tax-exempt organization, the Abraham Lincoln Opportunity Foundation (ALOF), which had been started by Colorado Republicans and GOPAC chair Bo Callaway in 1984 to help inner-city youth. By 1989, ALOF was a defunct group with no money.[1] But in 1990, Callaway revived the nonprofit organization, using the GOPAC network of donors to raise $97,750 for ALOF to broadcast a series called American Citizens Television (ACTV) on cable TV. Gingrich wrote to a major GOPAC donor, stating that ACTV "will carry the torch of citizen activism begun by our American Opportunity Workshop on May 19. We mobilized thousands of people across the nation at the grass roots level, who, as a result of AOW, are now dedicated GOPAC activists. We are making great strides in continuing to recruit activists all across America to become involved with the Republican Party."

Using a nonprofit group to create GOPAC activists for the Republican Party was illegal; but GOPAC never informed the IRS of the sudden change in ALOF's purposes. In this case, GOPAC could not pretend that it was staying within the law by promoting state and local candidates, rather than federal ones. Using a tax-exempt organization to support any political activism is forbidden. The IRS requires that nonprofit organizations must "not participate in, or intervene in (including the publishing or distribution of statements) any political campaign." Political parties and their political action committees (like

GOPAC) are prohibited from creating nonprofit organizations.

But, as the *Washington Post* discovered, "GOPAC's financial records show that the cable television project was viewed as a GOPAC project on the organization's books."[2] Financial records for GOPAC and ALOF were kept together on the same page.[3] The president of ALOF was chair of GOPAC; the secretary-treasurer of ALOF was GOPAC's executive director; the ALOF executive director was GOPAC's executive political director; and ALOF's checks were signed by GOPAC's financial director. GOPAC rented office space to ALOF, and loaned the group $45,000 in 1990 (but failed to disclose this fact in tax records).

ALOF, which supposedly existed to help inner-city youth (but did nothing for them), actually was used to launder GOPAC donations so that donors could get a tax deduction. As a GOPAC staffer noted about ACTV in one meeting, "we've been doing it 501(c)(3) so it's deductible."[4] In the early 1990s, ALOF raised $226,000, almost entirely from GOPAC and right-wing donors: Pat Robertson's Family Channel gave $47,750, Callaway's own foundation gave $80,000, RJR Nabisco, Inc. gave $5,000, Alan Keyes's Citizens Against Government Waste gave $37,000, and GOPAC donor and 1994 Colorado gubernatorial candidate Bruce Benson gave $10,000.

GOPAC and ALOF were virtually identical. GOPAC staffers treated ACTV money as part of the GOPAC empire, according to the transcript of a GOPAC meeting: "charter money comes primarily from individuals. Deductible money comes primarily from corporations and foundations." Because ALOF had 501(c)(3) nonprofit status, GOPAC could get money from charitable foundations, which are prohibited by law from donating to campaigns or political action committees. On January 16, 1990, Gingrich wrote a thank-you letter to Wall Street executive Tucker Andersen "for your commitment to GOPAC and to ALOF."[5] A 1990 memo by Bo Callaway to Newt Gingrich referred to ACTV as one of the "three broad things that GOPAC does."[6] Twice in 1990, GOPAC's lawyers warned about this illegal use of a nonprofit group. One wrote, "A very controversial program is being undertaken by a (c)(3), indicating that it may have involvement in the electoral process, not withstanding the express prohibition on it."[7] Yet Gingrich didn't stop the illegal use of ALOF by GOPAC.

In December 1993, GOPAC gave $43,785 to ALOF in order to keep it alive. But by 1994, the donations reduced to a trickle, and ALOF was disbanded in early 1995. By this time, Gingrich and GOPAC had moved their energy and fundraising to Gingrich's next venture, another nonprofit group called the Progress and Freedom Foundation (PFF), which focused on promoting Gingrich's college course. In 1993, PFF head Jeffrey Eisenach pointed to "significant similarities" between ALOF's programs and the planned course. Callers to ALOF got a recorded message referring them to the Progress and Freedom Foundation.[8]

Since no one had investigated GOPAC for the misuse of ALOF, Gingrich and his staff decided that the coast was clear. The opportunity for tax-subsidized political donations was too tempting to pass up, particularly since the nonprofit designation was essential to convince schools that Gingrich's course was not a political program. ALOF's television shows and the Progress and Freedom Foundation course originated at a 1989 GOPAC meeting, when Gingrich proposed a "Saturday morning television program that's by satellite, but basically says anyone in the country to anybody who wants to get involved...or your local college, or your high school, or a neighbor of yours who owns a dish receiver, and then you make it available to everybody, because it really is broadcasting."[9]

Gingrich decided to expand on the cable TV show idea by establishing a college course that would be broadcast around the country. But to do that, he needed more than $250,000 to put the class on satellite, and a location to teach the class. And because he knew that any college would be reluctant to allow a course to be sponsored by an explicitly Republican political action committee like GOPAC, Gingrich and his GOPAC staffers decided to create another nonprofit organization. In typical Gingrich style, they gave a positive-sounding name to a Gingrich self-promotion campaign: the Progress and Freedom Foundation.

Newt 101: The Professor from Corporate America

According to Gingrich's lawyer, Jan Baran, Gingrich did not have "any involvement in founding" the Progress and Freedom Foundation. This is an outright lie. In the foundation's first newsletter, GOPAC executive director Jeff Eisenach (who took charge of PFF) wrote, "the Progress and Freedom Foundation emerged from a series of conversations with my friend Newt Gingrich about the current state and future prospects of American Civilization."[10] Even Eisenach's comment was a deception designed to disguise the depth of Gingrich's connection.

The truth is that the Progress and Freedom Foundation was created for the sole purpose of generating money to support Gingrich's course, "Renewing American Civilization." It was only after Gingrich began to gain more notoriety and bring in more money that PFF expanded its aims. Realizing that it needed to diversify in order to avoid the allegations that it was an illegal offshoot of Gingrich's political campaign, and having the good fortune to accumulate large donations from people who wanted to influence Gingrich, PFF expanded its mission beyond the narrow promotion of Newt Gingrich's course to become a conservative think tank promoting various aspects of Gingrich's agenda. Today it includes the Orwellian-titled Center for Effective Compassion, run by Gingrich friend Arianna Huffington, along with programs that focus on attacking government regulation and expanding conservative influence on the Internet.

The Progress and Freedom Foundation spent $460,471 in its first year; $291,536 was allocated to broadcasting Gingrich's college course, and an additional $94,712 was earmarked for Gingrich's TV show on the right-wing cable network, National Empowerment Television, called the "Progress Report With Newt Gingrich." Another report found that in the first 21 months up to December 31, 1994, the foundation raised $1.7 million and spent $1.26 million, half of it for Gingrich's class and TV show. As a report in *Business Week* noted, "PFF appears to have almost single-mindedly promoted the Speaker."[11]

Gingrich saw his course as a platform for promoting his political message. In a 1993 draft summarizing the "Renewing American Civilization" course, Gingrich noted that Democrats had the advantage of a clear message, a system for training candidates, and a network of powerful supporters. Gingrich wrote, "Despite the American people's consistent rejections of liberalism, the Republicans were unable to duplicate or overcome the advantages of a decaying but entrenched establishment...It is these advantages we will have to overcome to truly renew American civilization." The draft was faxed from Gingrich's congressional office, with a handwritten note asking for copies to be sent to his Georgia district office and GOPAC.[12]

Gingrich saw "Renewing American Civilization" as a way to establish the Republican Party as the new power broker (and himself as its leader) in Washington. His course would be an extension of his tapes for GOPAC. But instead of giving practical advice and campaign techniques, Gingrich envisioned himself as the ideological foundation for a new Republican revolution. Instead of merely reaching potential Congressional candidates, Gingrich would be able to influence a large number of potential activists, hoping to (in the words of a fundraising letter sent out by GOPAC) "train, by April 1996, 200,000+ citizens into a model for replacing the welfare state and reforming our government."[13]

A draft outline for Gingrich's course identified "three great advantages" that Democrats had over Republicans, including the Democrats' "system for training and developing professionals" and "a network of powerful institutions such as the big-city machines, the labor unions, and the left-wing activist groups (including trial lawyers and gays)." Gingrich wrote to College Republicans across the country, declaring that the goal of the course was to define the future and "to explain that future to the American people in a way that captures first their imagination and then their votes."[14]

Despite Gingrich's pivotal role as the Foundation's controlling influence, when the Progress and Freedom Foundation applied for tax-exempt status, it called itself "independent" and deliberately concealed information about Gingrich's close connections to the course. Although it outlined in detail the college course and the TV show it planned to fund, the founding documents omit the fact that Gingrich would be the teacher of the class and the host of the show.[15] Nor was Gingrich's plan to recruit new activists and voters to his party disclosed.

William Safire defended Gingrich in a *New York Times* column, condemning what he called "a guerrilla campaign to discredit and besmear the Speaker." Safire wondered "did Professor Gingrich's course have an 'overt' political purpose"? He answers, "Of course it did, and what's unethical about that?"[16] But Safire apparently doesn't understand that the IRS prohibits nonprofit groups from having a political purpose—precisely in order to prevent politicians from using nonprofit organizations to solicit secret tax-deductible contributions.

The connections between Gingrich, GOPAC, and "Renewing American Civilization" are numerous. The Progress and Freedom Foundation's offices are located in Washington and in Marietta, Georgia, which is in Gingrich's district. Frank Gregorsky, one of the founders of PFF and one of its fellows, was Gingrich's chief of staff from 1981 to 1983. Jeffrey Eisenach, the head of PFF, is a close friend of Gingrich, his "closest intellectual advisor," and was the director of GOPAC. Perhaps the most damning evidence is that Eisenach did early fundraising and promotional work for Gingrich's course and PFF from GOPAC's office. GOPAC faxed solicitations for the course on GOPAC letterhead. In April 1993, GOPAC held a spring charter meeting titled "Renewing American Civilization," and at the same time as the conference, GOPAC's senior staffers were raising tax-deductible funds from GOPAC donors for Gingrich's course and the Progress and Freedom Foundation.[17]

Many of the Progress and Freedom Foundation donors—including Johnson & Johnson, Health South, Solvay, Searle, Glaxo, Genzyme, Burroughs Wellcome, AT&T, Turner Broadcasting, and Lockheed—are subject to federal regulations or have contracts with the government, and so they are prohibited from directly donating to Newt's campaign.[18] The Progress and Freedom Foundation offered them a way to evade the law (and its limits on donations) and buy influence with Newt, with a tax deduction to boot. Gingrich and his staff regarded the course—and the PFF—as merely an extension of GOPAC, which in turn was merely an extension of Gingrich himself.

Sometimes even Gingrich couldn't keep the story straight and admitted to GOPAC's heavy involvement in PFF. Gingrich wrote to the ethics committee on October 4, 1994 that "those who were paid for course preparation were paid by either the Kennesaw State Foundation, the Progress and Freedom

Foundation, or GOPAC." But in a December 8, 1994 letter, Gingrich changed his story about GOPAC's role: "Where employees of GOPAC simultaneously assisted the project, they did so as private, civic-minded individuals contributing time and effort to a 501 (c)(3) organization."[19]

Gingrich's lawyer Jan Baran claims, "GOPAC has had absolutely no role in funding, promoting, or administering it. GOPAC did not become involved in the Speaker's academic affairs because it is a political organization whose interests are not advanced by this non-partisan educational endeavor."[20] However, GOPAC was directly involved in "Renewing American Civilization" precisely because it wasn't a non-partisan educational endeavor, but a top political priority in Gingrich's campaign to make himself a nationwide figure in preparation for a presidential run that GOPAC officials were discussing as early as 1989.

Lies, Lies, and ... Higher Learning?

To get required approval from the House Ethics Committee for his college course in 1993—and keep his PR machine rolling—Gingrich lied to them and concealed important information. In letters to the committee on May 12 and July 21 of that year, Gingrich omitted any mention of GOPAC's role. And in an August 3, 1993 letter, he promised that GOPAC would "do no mass mailings" to Republican supporters on behalf of the class. However, a July 7, 1993 report on the course indicated that 19,000 registration forms were being sent to the GOPAC "farmteam."

GOPAC sought out contributors and Eisenach sent out a letter from Gingrich to more than a thousand College Republican groups around the country, telling them that "the recent tribulations of the Clinton Administration have made all of us feel a little better for our short-term prospects," and going on to explain the need for a long-term Republican vision which would be provided by the "Renewing American Civilization" course.

Fred Grandy and James McDermott, the Republican and Democratic leaders of the Ethics Committee at the time, wrote a bipartisan letter to Gingrich about these lies on October 31, 1994, noting that "GOPAC's role in seeking funding for the course was not disclosed to the committee in your letters." They found that GOPAC documents "raise questions as to whether the course was...partisan political activity intended to benefit Republican candidates."[21]

Yet Gingrich continued to deceive the Ethics Committee regularly with misinformation. In a March 27, 1995 letter to the Ethics Committee, Gingrich lawyer Jan Baran claimed that, "In a March 1993 speech, Mr. Gingrich stated that he wanted to resume teaching while serving in Congress out of the belief that an intellectual renewal of core American values was critical to solving the nation's major domestic challenges. Dr. Tim Mescon, an acquaintance of the Speaker and dean of the Kennesaw State College School of Business Administration, heard Mr. Gingrich speak and invited him to teach a course at the college."

The truth was that Gingrich contacted the Agency for International Development (AID) to help Mescon solicit them for consulting contracts. In a September 17, 1992 letter, Mescon had asked Gingrich to introduce him to the director of the Bureau of Private Enterprise, a federal foreign-aid agency, to help promote interests that he and colleagues at the Mescon Group had in Ghana and other West African countries. In an October 12, 1992 letter, Gingrich notified Mescon that he had contacted AID on his behalf, and wrote at the bottom, "I am very interested in working with you after the election. We should block out an hour or two and you should brief me on the school and your activities." (Gingrich underlined "very" twice.) After Newt's re-election in November, Mescon wrote to congratulate Gingrich and thank him for contacting Ronald Roskens, the head of AID. Mescon told Gingrich that his firm had been given the names of agency officials who dealt with Ghana. In February 1993, Mescon wrote a letter to Gingrich staffer Krister Holladay, saying that he would "submit a proposal soon regarding [Gingrich's] teaching on campus in the fall quarter." Mescon (who did not live in Gingrich's district) also asked for more "assistance" that "you might be able to provide in assisting with our attempt to expand our many activities both in Ghana and domestically."

One week later, Gingrich sent Mescon a three-page memo outlining the course. In another memo, Newt invited Mescon to co-author the course's books: "Together we are going to make history as well as teach it." Long before March 1993, Gingrich and Mescon had met in Washington, D.C., and Gingrich had illegally assigned his Congressional staff and GOPAC consultants to work on the course.[22]

It was a remarkable deal, even for Gingrich. Instead of doing his usual favors for wealthy donors who had already given money to him and GOPAC, Gingrich directly targeted a university official and used political influence on his behalf in order to aggressively pursue his attempt at self-promotion. Gingrich was planning to teach the "Renewing American Civilization" course, and he needed a local college to let him do it, in order to give it credibility and make it convenient to teach; otherwise, critics would dismiss it as merely another GOPAC satellite promotion. Mescon's connections at Kennesaw State were an ideal opportunity, and Gingrich was never above doing a favor for someone willing to help him out.

Gingrich taught the class at Kennesaw for free because House members are prohibited from receiving compensation for teaching positions and state law prohibited elected officials from serving as state employees. However, the money that would have normally been used to pay the instructor was instead used to hire a marketing staffer to help promote the class. So, the state of Georgia was still subsidizing Gingrich's class.

A New Theory of Relativity: Advertising = Education

The political nature of Gingrich's course was evident from the beginning. When asked by a campus newspaper if the class would "have a balance of liberal ideas," Gingrich replied, "No. I'm going to allow Democrats but not liberal ideas." A Gingrich spokesperson, Allan Lipsett, explained that "liberal ideas" would not be allowed in the course because "liberal ideas have failed." According to Lipsett, if "you're teaching a cooking course, you teach how to produce a good dinner. You don't teach your students how to produce a bad dinner." Chef Gingrich explained: "People who disagree with me have every right to teach their own course...I have no obligation to clutter the course with people who I regard as explicitly wrong."[23] The *St. Louis Post-Dispatch* called the one-sided class "a new low in political cynicism" and editorialized, "These statements, plus Mr. Gingrich's reputation for the bitterest kind of partisanship, make clear that his course will be an exercise in propaganda, not education. But it will be paid for in part by all taxpayers—liberals and conservatives—who bear the burden of the tax deduction his political supporters receive for defraying the course's expenses."[24]

Much of the money needed to support the $291,000 cost of putting the course over satellite came from businesses who contributed to Gingrich's political campaigns, including Cracker Barrel, HealthSouth Corporation, Southwire Corporation, Golden Rule Insurance, Scientific Atlanta, Associated Builders and Contractors, and textile magnate Roger Milliken—most of whom were heralded by Gingrich in his class, where he showed their promotional videos.

For the corporations, Newt 101 offered a tax-deductible form of political lobbying. Companies got the same lobbying influence by giving money directly to Gingrich's foundation, but at a cut-rate price because they could deduct the "charitable donation" and escape disclosure requirements along with contribution limits.

Gingrich and his GOPAC staffers frequently asked corporations to donate money and in return gave them what amounted to commercials during the class when Gingrich used them as examples of his ideals. Hewlett-Packard ($5,800) is called "one of the great companies in American history." Health South ($11,000) does "a remarkable job in helping people with rehabilitation." Scientific Atlanta ($2,500) is a "model of the spirit of invention and discovery." Milliken & Co. is praised as "the most effective, most productive textile company in the world" (Roger Milliken gave $300,000 to GOPAC). Course donors were told that if they gave $50,000 or more they could be "sponsors" of the course and have the chance to "work directly with the leadership of the Renewing American Civilization project in the course development process." ($25,000 and $10,000 donors would have only the opportunity to "influence" the course's development.) When Gingrich planned to discuss a company that hadn't given money, they would be directly solicited: Ford Motor Company was asked to donate because "we'll be talking about your-all's experience."[25]

Gingrich upheld this promise to let corporations design his course and script the words coming out of his mouth. Richard Berman, a lobbyist with the Employment Policies Institute—a restaurant trade group which crusades against minimum wage laws—was just one donor who affected Gingrich's course. Pamela Prochnow, GOPAC's finance director and a staffer for Gingrich's course, reported in a May 10, 1993 memo about a meeting with Berman, who said he might make a contribution of $20,000 to $25,000 "if the course can incorporate some of the ideas" that "entry level positions are not necessarily dead end"—obviously an important concept for fast food restaurants to promote, especially if they wanted Gingrich to resist efforts to increase the minimum wage.

Later, along with the $25,000 check for Gingrich's course, was a note from Berman reporting that he had "spoken with Jeff Eisenach (who has been very helpful) about making available to you anecdotes, stories, and general information that you can use for program material. I know this information will be very useful. I'm delighted that it will be part of your lecture series." Perhaps it's no coincidence, then, that Gingrich's introductory essay in the readings for "Renewing American Civilization" features this statement: "Entrepreneurial free enterprise is not only a source of personal success and economic prosperity. It is central to our success as a civilization. How many people consider that McDonald's has the most powerful job training system in the world? More young people get more entry level training in McDonald's than anywhere else."[26] Without Gingrich (and the suggestions of his wealthy donors), few college students would have the opportunity to learn that flipping burgers at McDonald's is the essence of American civilization.

Gingrich also praised one of Berman's biggest clients, Chili's and Steak & Ale founder (and Gingrich donor) Norman Brinker. The promotional video made by his company and shown to the class declares, "Whether it's his beloved game of polo or his magical success in business, Norman Brinker simply does not know how to lose."[27]

But Berman's $25,000 bought more than just collegiate influence. Berman added a handwritten note at the bottom of his letter donating the $25,000, saying: "Newt, Thanks again for the help on today's committee hearing."[28] Berman, an old friend of Gingrich, had asked for help to get an appearance at a

Congressional committee hearing on drunken driving, which Gingrich apparently provided obligingly. Both Berman and Gingrich deny that the donation was a payment for his assistance. "It was a dumb thing to write on the note," Gingrich admitted, saying that he immediately called Berman because "I wanted him to understand there were no circumstances involving any *quid pro quo*. If he had any confusion about that, I told him I'd send the check back."[29] Perhaps Gingrich was afraid that close scrutiny of Berman's note might lead to dangerous questions about the offers to influence the course, and other *quid pro quo* deals Gingrich made with major contributors.

In return for donations to the Progress and Freedom Foundation, Gingrich did special favors for corporations just as he did for the contributors to his campaigns and GOPAC. Ten days after the Georgia Power Co. gave a $7,500 donation to the Progress and Freedom Foundation in 1994, Gingrich wrote a letter to the Securities and Exchange Commission Chairman, Arthur Levitt, on behalf of Georgia Power's parent company, Southern Co., which had been waiting 10 months for a ruling on its application to create a wireless communications subsidiary. Gingrich told Levitt, "I would, therefore, urge the Commission to act expeditiously." Later that year the application was approved.[30]

This link between political lobbyists and a college course can be explained by the involvement of GOPAC, Gingrich's political action committee. According to Gingrich, GOPAC had "the most incidental involvement." But Gingrich admits, "I took all the help I could get...I wanted people near me, helping me, who I know and trust." Gingrich adds, "they're the best fund-raisers I know."[31] Gingrich has never addressed the ethical and legal problems of having a Republican political action committee raise funds for a supposedly nonpartisan nonprofit foundation.

Galileo, Copernicus, Socrates—and Newt?

Gingrich's openly political course was supported by Kennesaw State administrators who owed Gingrich a political favor, but the faculty were more critical of Gingrich's attempt to package his musings about civilization as a college course. In July 1993, nine professors wrote to administrators, "We are disappointed and outraged to hear that the college is permitting, in fact promoting, use of college time, equipment and personnel for the advancement of the political ideas of an elected official." Dozens more faculty spoke out against the course and signed petitions protesting it.

Still, some came to Gingrich's defense. Republican pollster Frank Luntz (who would later invent the phony polling for the Contract with America discussed earlier) called Newt a victim of political correctness and added, "just as the Greeks attempted to stifle Socrates (by killing him), the academic establishment continues to repress those who challenge conventional wisdom. Galileo, Copernicus, and countless others were censured and persecuted for their ideas, only to be proven right in the end." In response to complaints, the Georgia Board of Regents amended its policies to tighten the loophole and prohibit elected officials from teaching at state colleges or universities, regardless of whether or not they are paid. In 1994, Gingrich moved the class to Reinhardt College, a small private school in Waleska, Georgia, that had been a two-year college until it recently started a four-year business program.

In the end, Mescon regretted allowing Gingrich to teach the class at Kennesaw State College, saying that he never realized how "embarrassing" the project would become. He says that he "naively thought it would bring stature to this institution." Mescon now says, "If it ever arose again, we would systematically avoid individuals participating in an academic exercise who see politics as a vocation."[32] Mescon never realized that Gingrich would use the course merely to promote himself and his corporate donors, disguising his political goals behind a nonprofit foundation.

When Education is Campaigning

Creating tax-free "charitable" foundations to promote political goals has been a common Republican scam in recent years. Republicans realized that the IRS rarely cracks down on foundations when they serve blatantly partisan purposes in violation of federal law. Even when a foundation is shut down, there is almost never any prosecution for tax fraud or retroactive taxation of donors.

Gingrich's first illegal nonprofit group for political purposes was the American Opportunity Foundation (AOF), which he founded in 1984, serving as chairman and director. AOF's secretary-treasurer was GOPAC lawyer Dan Swillinger, who was also the treasurer of Gingrich's Abraham Lincoln Opportunity Foundation. The AOF board of directors included GOPAC advisor Eddie Mahe and GOPAC charter member James C. Richards. AOF's only significant activity was sponsoring a celebration of the one-year anniversary of the US invasion of Grenada. In conjunction with the College Republicans, AOF staged "Student Liberation Day" rallies at over 100 college campuses in October 1984. As one College Republican official explained about the political purpose of the event, "I am confident that an impartial study of the contrasts between the Carter/Mondale failure in Iran and the Reagan victory in Grenada will be most enlightening to voters 12 days before the general election." By 1990, when the foundation disbanded, it was using GOPAC's headquarters in Washington as its official address.[33]

Joe Gaylord, a Republican activist and Friend of Gingrich who helped organize "Renewing American Civilization" and earned $130,000 in consulting fees from the Progress and Freedom Foundation, tried to found another tax-exempt program, the American Campaign Academy (ACA), that the IRS ruled (and US Tax Court upheld) to be an illegal training school for Republican Party campaign managers. The entire $972,000 budget for ACA was provided by the National Republican Congressional Committee, and the Academy taught topics like "How some Republicans have won black votes" and "Use of GOP allies."[34] The IRS declared that the Academy would "benefit Republican Party entities and candidates more than incidentally. Also, your activities serve the private interests of Republican Party entities rather than public interests exclusively."[35] Jan Baran, currently Gingrich's lawyer in the ethics proceedings, filed the incorporation papers for the Academy.[36] Gingrich and his friends learned to be more subtle in their future attempts to create nonprofit groups for the Republican Party which served the same private interests that the IRS found illegitimate in 1987.

The IRS is currently trying to revoke the nonprofit status of an abortion rights organization for its political activities, declaring that "intervention in a political campaign may be subtle or blatant. It may seem to be justified by the press of events. It may even be inadvertent. [But] the law prohibits all forms of participation or intervention in any political campaign." *Roll Call* reported that the IRS objected to a sentence in one fundraising letter: "Together, we can change the shape of American politics." According to the IRS, "When this happens...voter education becomes voter direction."[37]

The IRS noted that the abortion rights groups "would have us believe that providing politically oriented statements to [its] intended audience had no meaning except for giving a sense of urgency to fundraising appeals." The IRS observed that "The tax laws specifically reject this contention," and that such fundraising letters were "equivalent to a pastor preaching to the choir."

The Progress and Freedom Foundation was far more guilty of political activities than the abortion rights group that is losing its nonprofit status. However, PFF and similar direct tools of politicians like Gingrich have escaped scrutiny because the people who run them are too powerful politically. The movement to crack down on nonprofit groups advocating political views was started by the Republican Congress, and it is no surprise that the first victim is a liberal abortion-rights group. The right knows that if liberal nonprofit groups are intimidated from expressing their views on legislation, it will increase the power of corporations who favor Republican policies and who face no limits on their political activity. Marcus Owens, director of the IRS Exempt Organizations Division, told *Roll Call* that Congress had directed a "zero tolerance" policy for politically active charitable groups. Obviously, this "zero tolerance" is intended to apply only to left-wing critics of the Republican Revolution, not the conservative politicians who have violated the law far more blatantly.

Gingrich was not the only leading Republican to run an illegal nonprofit foundation: Lamar Alexander started the Republican Exchange Satellite Network to promote himself. Pat Buchanan used American Cause, a tax-exempt nonprofit formed in 1993 after his previous presidential bid and headed by Angela Bay Buchanan, his sister and campaign manager. Buchanan created both a tax-exempt educational group and a political/lobbying arm, which got donations from conservative businessmen like Roger Milliken, one of the major GOPAC donors. American Cause was shut down in March 1995 when Buchanan again began his run for president.[38]

Bob Dole's Better America Foundation raised $4 million in 1994 and spent $1.5 million on polls, issue papers, and TV commercials; right before the 1994 elections, this nonprofit, non-political foundation ran commercials featuring Dole and Gingrich and asking viewers to "help turn Congress around."[39] In June 1995, Dole announced that the foundation would be shut down to avoid the embarrassing questions about his benefactors and the foundation's ties to his campaign.[40] But unlike Dole or Buchanan, Gingrich has continued to keep his nonprofit foundation in operation, refusing to admit the ethical and legal violations involved with it, and continuing to conceal its donors.

The Secret Donors to GOPAC

GOPAC has repeatedly refused to reveal the full extent of its financial support. Since it claims to primarily support state and local candidates (even though GOPAC's explicit goal is to create a Republican majority in Congress), GOPAC only discloses a small percentage of its donors. Donors who want to remain secret in order to disguise their influence on Gingrich need only request to be left out of the reports and GOPAC happily obliges. GOPAC also uses its support for state and local candidates as an excuse to violate federal election law limits. GOPAC chair Gay Hart Gaines claimed in the *Washington Times* that "we play by the rules"—a day before the *Washington Post* reported that GOPAC took $10,000 each from 35 people and $25,000 each from four donors, when the law limits individuals to $2,000 per election cycle in donations to a campaign committee.[41]

In November 1994, Gingrich promised to disclose future donors to GOPAC, while keeping old donors secret. However, the grudging disclosure concealed a great deal of information required by the Federal Election Commission, including how the money was spent, and the full addresses and business affiliations of donors. GOPAC released the names of 36 donors who contributed $415,000 in the first quarter of 1995, but it kept the business affiliations secret. The listing of a $10,000 contribution from Rick Rodgers failed to reveal that he was a lobbyist donating a corporate contribution from Federal Express. Reporters must make an appointment to come to GOPAC's

Washington headquarters and copy the information by hand, because GOPAC prohibited any photocopies of the information, claiming that it is protecting donors from being "harassed" by reporters or fundraisers. Meanwhile, the Progress and Freedom Foundation still refuses to say how much each donor contributed.[42] Gingrich told the *Washington Post* about GOPAC's concealment, "They were clumsy," shifting blame to an organization that he has had total control over for a decade.[43] Gingrich is well aware of the serious violations at GOPAC under his control, and he is already distancing himself from the group, having resigned as its head: "I just kept wandering into rooms that are interesting, wandering off and giving speeches. So there was an immense amount that happened that I don't know about."[44]

In reality, Gingrich knew exactly what was happening at GOPAC, and probably ordered many of the illegal activities. He was intimately involved in fundraising for GOPAC, and regularly did favors for its major donors. To Gingrich, GOPAC mattered far more than his part-time job as a member of Congress. It was GOPAC that gave him a vehicle for self-promotion and the organization of a Republican majority with himself at the helm.

Gingrich is also guilty of violating House rules by using C-SPAN and the *Congressional Record* to push his ideas for profit. Five times in the 1993-94 sessions of Congress, Gingrich stood on the House floor, promoting his college course, giving his 800 number, and urging listeners to call and order the $160 set of audiotapes and $200 set of videotapes. In 1990, Gingrich was specifically warned against doing commercial promotions by the House Ethics Committee because it violates House rules. But Gingrich continued to knowingly disobey the rule, claiming that the Constitution entitles him to say anything he wants on the House floor.[45] Although this was a minor incident, it illustrates Gingrich's belief that he is a Congressman who is above the law.

Gingrich is deeply frightened by the ethics investigation. Continuing his tactics of denial and intimidation, Gingrich even urged the House Ethics Committee to consider disciplinary action against the members who filed the ethics complaints because they were "baseless and malicious."[46] He knows better than anyone else the power of ethics charges to ruin a political career—he played the ethics game from the other side like a master. But Gingrich never imagined that he would be the target of a sustained ethics attack. Like many other members of Congress, he was always too insignificant and he never made a gross ethical error or committed a sexual crime, so he was able to avoid scrutiny.

Now his power as Speaker makes him a target for Democratic minority whip David Bonior and others, and Gingrich understands that an ethics violation in Washington is like a sudden hurricane—you never know when, (or if) it will appear, and how powerful it might be. Anyone can look into Gingrich's past and see a trail of unethical and illegal activity littering his record. The only question is whether the press and the public are so cynical and apathetic that they will shrug their shoulders at Gingrich's crimes.

The Ethics Committee: Newt's Hand-Picked Investigators

Although the House Ethics Committee received several complaints in the last part of 1994 and throughout 1995, it was slow to investigate the charges and appoint an independent counsel to investigate them. As *Wall Street Journal* columnist Albert Hunt noted, "For the first time in its history, the House Ethics Committee has been stalemated on a major case."[47] Richard Phelan, the Special Outside Counsel who investigated Jim Wright, urged that "if Mr. Gingrich intends to practice in office what he preached on the campaign trail, he has no choice but to ask the Ethics Committee to name an independent counsel to investigate his own case." As Phelan observed, since 1980 "every significant House Ethics Committee investigation has begun with the appointment of an independent counsel."[48]

As Newt himself observed during the investigation of Speaker Jim Wright, the rules "normally applied by the Ethics Committee to an investigation of a typical member are insufficient in an investigation of the speaker of the House, a position which is third in the line of succession to the presidency and the second most powerful elevated position in America. Clearly, this investigation has to meet a higher standard of public accountability and integrity."[49]

But that was Wright, and the standards for Gingrich are different. For months, while Gingrich pushed the Contract With America, Republicans in the Ethics Committee held up the investigation. This was hardly surprising, since Gingrich personally appointed all of the Republicans to the Ethics Committee, knowing that they would be investigating him. All of the Republicans had ties to Gingrich or GOPAC.

The chair of the Ethics Committee, Nancy Johnson, is a friend who contributed to Gingrich's campaign committee and helped Gingrich win his post as minority whip in 1989, seconding his nomination and praising him as "a leader who has the vision to build a majority party and the strength and charisma to do it."[50] Johnson's influence was essential for Gingrich's narrow 87-85 vote for whip over Edward Madigan. Perhaps suspecting that he might need a friend in charge of the Ethics Committee, Gingrich selected Johnson as chair, and when Johnson submitted her resignation from the Ethics Committee, Gingrich convinced her to stay on the job.[51] Johnson owes Gingrich a favor because in 1992 he supported her run for a junior leadership post against a more conservative candidate. Gingrich also pushed Johnson's Medicare bill through the House, despite his promise to put Medicare reform on hold until after his first 100 days in office were up and a task force had offered recommendations.[52] It is difficult to believe that Johnson will make a serious examination of charges against her party's leader whom she regards as "the most visionary thinker in politics."

The fact that virtually all of the Republicans on the Ethics Committee had some link to Gingrich and GOPAC shows how far Gingrich's empire reached. In 1994, Rep. Porter Goss (R-Fla.) gave $5,000 to GOPAC. Rep. Jim Bunning (R-Ky.) accepted campaign money from GOPAC and was mentioned as a possible replacement for Gingrich as chair of GOPAC. In 1994, Gingrich campaigned for Rep. David Hobson (R-Ohio), GOPAC assisted him as a state candidate, and Hobson solicited a letter for Gingrich's defense from a former Ethics Committee staffer. The Republicans are unlikely to make an objective evaluation of Gingrich's violation of the ethics code, particularly when the future of the Republican majority in Congress depends on him.

Gingrich pressured Johnson and the rest of the Ethics Committee not to appoint a special prosecutor. According to Gingrich, "If there is any unethical behavior going on, it is on the part of Democrats who have filed totally false charges." He claimed that all the charges are "a joke."[53] Gingrich declared that the ethics charges were invented by "a bunch of very bitter left-wing Democrats." He added, "So the Ethics Committee, I think, agrees with me. They've not appointed a counsel."[54] Gingrich also said, "It's an insult to consider an independent counsel."[55] Gingrich knew that an independent prosecutor would be taken as a sign that he was guilty of something, and he obviously wanted the Republicans to dismiss the case.

Conservative allies of Gingrich also didn't want an independent counsel investigating the Republican regime. After Johnson told reporters that the charges against Gingrich could not be dismissed as "frivolous," National Empowerment Television founder and Gingrich friend Paul Weyrich warned in an op-ed piece: "If she makes the wrong decision she will weaken the speaker of her own party and may well affect her chances of continuing to be a committee chairman beyond this Congress." A month earlier, Gingrich had held a $50,000 per person tax-deductible fundraising dinner for Weyrich's network.[56]

At a March 1995 meeting with representatives of right-wing think tanks, Gingrich amazed one participant with "how obsessed he is with his ethics problems. He thinks they are going to be used to destroy him." According to an observer, "He started talking about how his ability to get his agenda done depends on whether the ethics charges against him take hold. He was clearly worried." A witness to the proceedings said, "He wanted us to think of ways to deal with the allegations. He urged us to help any way we could."[57]

Delays, Denials and More Delays...

The Republicans decided that delay and denial was the best approach. While Gingrich pushed through the Contract with America, the Republican-controlled Ethics Committee stalled. Not until July 1995 did the Ethics Committee hear from Gingrich, and ranking minority member Rep. Jim McDermott (D-Wash.) declared that the Committee had been "totally unprepared to question" witnesses.[58] The *Hartford Courant* noted that the investigation of Gingrich has been much slower than the investigation of former Speaker Jim Wright: "What is taking so long?"[59] Congressional watchdog Ralph Nader added, "These proceedings are irreparably compromised by a long list of incompetencies, violations of precedent, and other extraordinary irregularities. By a strange coincidence, all of these seem to work to the advantage of the speaker."[60] Nancy Johnson herself admitted: "We didn't allow enough time for analysis. In the beginning, we didn't think we needed it."[61] The Republicans had hoped that the ethics investigation of Gingrich could be silenced without analyzing his crimes.

In the end, the charges were far too serious for the Ethics Committee to simply dismiss all of them. But at the same time, the Republicans knew that Gingrich would retaliate against them if they gave an independent counsel carte blanche to investigate him. A compromise was reached, criticizing Gingrich for three minor violations, dismissing 64 out of 65 charges, and appointing a counsel to look at only one charge, a narrow examination of whether Gingrich had violated tax laws. In fact, the Ethics Committee never heard any evidence that most of the charges were untrue; it was simply a political decision to declare Gingrich innocent. The Democrats went along with the cover-up only because it ended the deadlock and gave them what they wanted most: an independent counsel investigation.

When Gingrich was pressing for an investigation of Jim Wright, he favored Common Cause's guidelines for an independent counsel to have full authority to issue subpoenas and review all evidence available from any source.[62] He declared that the counsel "has to be able to follow leads where they lead" and "can't be on a short leash."[63] But it's not clear if the independent counsel will go beyond the very narrow mandate established by the Republicans on the Ethics Committee. There is certainly good reason to do so: virtually every ethics charge against him revolves around his illegal use of non-profit foundations, from the Abraham Lincoln Opportunity Foundation to the Progress and Freedom Foundation.

For the Republicans, Gingrich creates a dilemma. Many of them dislike his tactics and his leadership, but they want him to continue with the power and energy that he has brought to the job. Today, the Republicans depend on Newt to provide the leadership and discipline to run his agenda through

Congress. They will never investigate him, or discipline him for his crimes, because to do so would weaken the party.

The agreement between Republicans and Democrats on the ethics committee to appoint a special prosecutor was a deal forged in order to save face on both sides. For the Democrats, it allowed them to embarrass Gingrich by claiming that there was substance behind the ethics charges. For the Republicans, it allowed them to delay the issue once again by having a special prosecutor investigate it, with the hope that the narrow bounds of the investigation would prevent any serious examination of Gingrich's violations of the law and House ethics rules.

As of this writing, Gingrich has been lucky: the IRS has been reluctant to pursue any investigation of the Progress and Freedom Foundation, perhaps fearing the same retaliation via budget cuts that the FEC suffered. Political power also prevented the FEC from appealing Judge Oberdorfer's ruling for GOPAC, which they would have probably won in an appeals court. Although the FEC board voted 3-2 on March 19, 1996—along strictly partisan lines—in favor of appealing the lawsuit, four votes are needed to pursue an appeal. Because Republicans control two slots in the FEC, they could not stop the investigation of Gingrich, but they were able to prevent an appeal that would threaten Gingrich's power in Washington.[64]

But the independent counsel, attorney James Coles, is the wild card. If the counsel decides to pursue Gingrich and make a legitimate investigation, it will be difficult for him to deny the crimes he has committed. Although Gingrich is the leader of the Republican Revolution, he may become more of an impediment to his own policies if action is taken against the long list of ethical violations in his political career. The question is whether Gingrich can continue to evade responsibility for his crimes by virtue of the power he holds as Speaker of the House.

Chapter 4

The Authoritarian Speaker: The Corruption of Congress

Gingrich's crimes have destroyed the integrity of the office of Speaker of the House, but his leadership in opposing political reform has corrupted the entire Congress as an institution. Where once lobbyists influenced Congress on legislation, in the wake of the Republican takeover they now sit in Congressional committee meetings, work in Gingrich's own office, and actually write some of the legislation. How did this change come about?

Gingrich remains so powerful and influential despite massive negative ratings in the polls because democratic rule means nothing in House chambers. His recent slump notwithstanding, Gingrich wields near-absolute control within the House, making him one of the most powerful Speakers in American history, even while he is one of the most despised. How did he do it?

In order for Gingrich to maintain power in the face of popular resistance, he had to seize control of the internal operations of the House and ensure that the Republicans would remain loyal to him even when there was a massive public outcry against Republican policies. To do this, he grabbed power within the House to a degree never before done by a Speaker. He required Republicans on the Appropriations Committee to write letters of commitment to the Contract with America. He forced committee chairs to impose a six-year limit on their positions. And he required all committee and subcommittee chairs to report to him when they scheduled hearings.[1]

Gingrich shifted control away from committees and caucuses (whose funding he ended, because he considered many of them too liberal) and placed it directly under his auspices. His first step in reorganizing the House was to eliminate the seniority system, which automatically made the longest-serving member of the majority party the chair of that committee. The seniority system did have its flaws; a more democratic practice, such as allowing committees to select their own chairs (as the Democratic representatives now do) would have been a real reform. But Gingrich moved in the opposite direction. Instead, he appointed each committee chair personally, mandating a maximum term of six years to prevent anyone from establishing a power network that might challenge the Speaker's control. As a Gingrich aide noted, "We reconfigured it to give Newt absolute power."[2]

Selling the Seats of Power

Gingrich announced his intentions long before he became speaker, writing notes to Republicans in the fall of 1993 (after House Republican leader Bob Michel declared that he would retire) to inform them that if he became speaker the seniority system would be eliminated. Instead, the key factor for earning a committee chair position would be money.

The end of the seniority system enabled Gingrich to sell committee chairs to the best fundraisers. In mid-July 1994, Gingrich wrote to Republican candidates, asking them to contribute $148,000 directly from their campaigns to Republicans challenging Democratic incumbents around the country. Bob Livingston became chair of the Appropriations Committee (ahead of several more senior Republicans) after giving the $148,000, and John Boehner and Susan Molinari also donated in hopes of getting leadership positions. Freshman Jon Christensen (R-Neb) got a seat on the powerful Ways and Means Committee after raising $80,000 for the House GOP Campaign Committee.[3]

Gingrich desperately wanted to seize control of the House in the 1994 elections, and he knew that Republican challengers needed financial support. Since many of the House Republicans in 1994 were excellent fundraisers and didn't expect to be seriously threatened, Gingrich essentially extorted campaign donations from the incumbents in the House. The number of Republican congressmen who contributed to the campaigns of Republicans challenging Democratic incumbents jumped from six in 1992 to 102 in 1994, since they knew that their power under Gingrich would depend on their fundraising for the Republican Party.[4]

Command Central

Gingrich also undercut the committee system by concealing most of his important legislation as riders to appropriations bills. It sped up the process and prevented opposition from building against the Republicans' proposals. It also centralized power in Gingrich's hands, instead of having proposals go through the committee process where they might be changed by Democratic opponents or less extreme Republicans. As Gingrich's whip, Tom DeLay put it: "We've known from the beginning that appropriations would have to carry much of the load of what has to be done."[5]

Gingrich also used appropriations riders to try to implement unpopular laws. When Republicans had difficulty getting their bills through the Senate, or faced a veto threat from President Clinton, they would add these riders to important appropriations bills. In addition, Gingrich cut the budget in areas such as environmental protection when he didn't have the votes to pass legislation undermining government regulation.

Although promising more openness than the previous Democratic speakers, Gingrich exerted greater control over the Republican majority than any other leader of Congress in history. When Henry Hyde, chair of the Judiciary Committee, opposed an NRA provision lifting the ban on Uzis and other assault weapons, Gingrich simply went around his committee to bring the bill to a vote. In the 104th Congress, Republican leaders brought an unprecedented 78% of all bills directly to the House floor, avoiding the committee process completely.[6] This enabled them to pass legislation much more quickly, and exert greater control over the process by changing bills and deleting or adding any provisions that they wanted.

One of Gingrich's strategies for centralizing power is to replace the House committees with a task force system. Gingrich considers the committee system "archaic" and declares that "eventually it would be better if committees could be replaced by task forces."[7] The task force process would establish temporary committees on specific issues to create particular bills and then dissolve. The Speaker would exert much more control over the legislative process, determining which task forces would exist and who would be on them. This would enable much stricter party discipline, since any representative who failed to follow the Gingrich line could be excluded from important task forces in the future, whereas under the current system it is nearly impossible to remove someone from a committee.

Journalist Weston Kosova wrote in the *New Republic* about "the authoritarian discipline of Gingrich's emerging leadership in Congress." As Kosova put it, "Gingrich is running the House with a hierarchy of yes-men."[8] Gingrich maintains his power by requiring obedience to his ideas. Only those who support Gingrich are allowed to hold positions of power and influence. As Columbia University historian Alan Brinkley observed, "In many ways Gingrich is an old-fashioned political boss within Congress."[9]

In the first 139 votes, Gingrich received unanimous support from Republicans 73 times, and the number of times he lost more than 10 Republican votes out of 230 was kept to a dozen times.[10] Gingrich accomplished all this by sheer force of will and threats of retaliation. For the first time in Congress's history, to gain a subcommittee chair on the plum Appropriations committee, Republicans were forced to sign a formal contract with the Speaker, promising to follow his lead and agreeing to be removed if they violated it.[11]

This was the true meaning of the "Contract with America": a contract with Newt Gingrich agreeing to follow his orders. When freshman Congressman Mark Neumann (R-Wis) voted against a $3.2 billion increase for the Pentagon, Gingrich hauled him into his office and threatened to force him to resign from the Appropriations Committee if he didn't change his tune.[12] In September 1995, he advised Agriculture Committee chair Pat Roberts about how to punish three Republicans on the committee with loss of assignments and chairmanships if they voted against Gingrich's farm bill. Eventually, Gingrich decided to avoid a confrontation by simply moving the bill to the more friendly Budget Committee under John Kasich.[13]

Rep. Pat Schroeder (D-Col.) notes that Gingrich "is a man who has figured out how to exercise power." She reports, "you have the committee chairmen saying, 'I hate this bill; I don't believe in this but I'm voting for it.'" This is happening because "Newt has taken all that power for himself and they let him do it."[14]

Gingrich got away with the power grab because no Republican in the House had ever before been in these positions of power under Democratic control. Gingrich, with a loyal band of freshmen, could crush all possible resistance. There wasn't much; even Republicans who hated Gingrich realized that he had given them what no one else could: the majority. Unity was the order of the day, and that meant following Gingrich's marching orders. Gingrich was also skilled at placating disgruntled Republicans, with his willingness to listen and his foresight in putting off part of the far right's agenda so that he would not alienate the party's moderates.

Gingrich's work as Speaker within the House was not a complete success: he was constantly running up against extreme conservatives who demanded more action, and moderates in the party occasionally broke party lines in votes on the Strategic Defense Initiative and environmental programs. But more than any other Speaker, Gingrich had imposed his agenda on the House and coerced members of his party to vote for it, often against their better judgment.

Defending Corruption: the Attacks on Campaign Finance Reform

With his hands on more power than any previous Speaker, Gingrich has systematically thwarted any efforts aimed at stemming Congressional corruption. One popular idea conspicuously absent from the Contract with America is campaign finance reform. Gingrich's pivotal opposition to campaign reform laws—laws which might crack down on the kind of abuses that were key to his rise to power—is not surprising. He has a personal vendetta against the Federal Election Commission, which he has called "dangerous." He's right; the commission is dangerous to corrupt politicians like him.It fined him $3,800 in 1994 for failing to report $30,000 in contributions of $1,000 or more in the last days of his 1992 campaign, and filed a lawsuit against GOPAC. Gingrich called the lawsuit "an outrageous power grab," and has enough political clout to stop any reform.[15] Part of the $17 billion rescissions package passed by House Republicans in 1995 was a 10% cut in the Federal Election Commission budget, an effort to punish the agency for its investigation of Gingrich.[16]

When asked about his priorities in May 1995, Gingrich declared: "In a country where children are dying of drug addiction, where children are illiterate, and we have huge problems with Medicaid and Medicare, I think the priorities are to restructure the underlying system. Eventually, we are going to get around to rethinking the campaign system. But I don't know when."[17] Although Gingrich promised in a June 1995 New Hampshire meeting with President Clinton to pursue campaign finance reform, he kept putting off the issue.

Clinton marveled at how Gingrich broke his pledge to create a bipartisan commission on campaign financing and lobbying: "When you shake hands with somebody in broad daylight and say you're going to do something, you ought to at least act like you're going to do it."[18] In response, Gingrich accused Clinton of playing "narrow, cheap political games."[19] To Gingrich, campaign reform is just another political game, not a serious issue.

Linda Smith, one of the new Republicans in the House who won't back down in the face of Gingrich's hypocrisy on finance reform, noted: "This polluted system has to be cleaned up completely."[20] Smith's reform ideas have been rejected by Gingrich and the other Republican leaders: "I asked nice, I followed the rules and they don't want to address it. All we're saying is: Just keep your commitment."[21]

Gingrich claims that he and Congress are engaging in reform by "putting every bill, every report, every conference report on the Internet so that every citizen has the same instantaneous access as the highest-paid lobbyist in Washington, D.C."[22] But posting bills in cyberspace is not reform of any kind. The idea that online availability of bills and reports puts citizens on a level playing field with top lobbyists is ludicrous. Access to information is only a sliver of the lobbyist's power compared to the power they exert through campaign contributions.

Reform is the last thing Gingrich and the Republicans want now that they are pocketing millions from wealthy donors anxious to influence the new Congress. The main effect of the 1994 elections was an enormous increase in money given to Republicans. Between October 1 and November 28 of 1994, the Republican Party took in $16.2 million, nearly four times as much as the Democrats. In the first four months of 1995, the Republicans raised $9 million in soft money from corporations and wealthy individuals, compared to $790,000 in the first quarter of 1993.[23] The battle to raise the most may swing to the Democrat's favor in the 1996 election or in subsequent elections. But whoever is in power, there are extraordinary forces of self-interest that will compel the ruling party to prevent real reform.

The Republicans used their newfound power as the majority party to raise record amounts of money. In 1993, Democratic candidates in the Senate had raised $41.2 million compared to only $34.5 million for the Republicans, but in the next non-election year, 1995, the Democrats' fundraising dropped to $32.3 million while Republicans' jumped to $35.5 million. The disparity in the House was even greater: gifts to Democrats fell from $53.8 million in 1993 to $46.8 million in 1995, while Republican money nearly doubled, from $40.9 million to $70.5 million. Gingrich became the leading fundraiser in the history of Congress, raising $1.9 million for his own campaign and over $50 million for the Republicans, including $6 million directly for other House Republicans.[24]

The Best at What He Does

In 1995, Gingrich became the leading fundraiser in the history of the House of Representatives. By the end of 1995, Gingrich had more than one million dollars in cash on hand. "Nobody in the House can or is raising more money than Newt," reported his old friend Eddie Mahe.[25] Gingrich's great skill has always been fundraising; he seized leadership of the Republican Party not because he had any original ideas, but because he learned how to dig deep into the pockets of his supporters.

Realizing the tremendous opportunity to consolidate their power with corporate money, Republicans immediately attempted to eliminate the $3 income tax checkoff that has supported the public funding of Presidential elections for two decades, leaving the money of special interests to decide the Presidential campaign.[26] Sen. Mitch McConnell (R-Ky) sponsored a bill to end public financing of presidential campaigns. His justification is that "most Republicans don't believe that is a good idea—and we won the election."[27] The last thing that Gingrich wants is to change the campaign finance system now that money is pouring into Republican campaign funds. As Fred Wertheimer, head of Common Cause, observes: "Newt Gingrich complained about the corrupt system when he was in the minority. Now he's running that corrupt system, and it's politics as usual."[28]

Gingrich started planning for this fundraising even before the 1994 elections. In October 1994, Gingrich told special-interest lobbyists that they should give money to Republican candidates as an investment in "future corporate savings."[29] If that wasn't explicit enough, he warned them that for anyone who didn't start giving large contributions to Republicans, "It's going to be the two coldest years in Washington."[30] Gingrich was explicitly promising to give special favors to groups that wrote the biggest checks, while freezing out anyone who supported the Democrats.

Former Gingrich aides and friends, like Tony Roda (legislative strategist until 1992), Steve Stockmeyer (informal advisor for 20 years), and Vin Weber (former congressperson and close friend), are now cashing in as lobbyists.[31] The path between Congress and lobbying also runs in the opposite direction. Rep. Bill Archer (R-Tex) fired the veteran chief of staff of the Joint Committee on

Taxation and replaced him with powerful tax lobbyist Ken Kies.[32] When the Consumer Products Safety Commission raised questions about a provision in a Senate bill requiring cost/benefit studies of new regulation, a law firm lobbyist working for an unnamed client was assigned by Republican leaders to negotiate a compromise with them.[33] Chip Kahn, a lobbyist for the Health Insurance Association of America, was appointed staff director for the health subcommittee on the House Ways and Means committee.[34]

Gingrich has even been lobbied by felons. Former Reagan official Michael Deaver, who was convicted of perjury for his influence-peddling activities, reported that after the 1994 elections, he "met with various people around Newt on a number of occasions." Gingrich spokesperson Tony Blankley declared, "Mike Deaver is a fine man who understands the way the media work in Washington."[35]

Gingrich's chief whip, Tom DeLay, keeps a book of the top 400 PACs and their donations to Democrats and Republicans, so that pro-Democratic lobbyists can be marked as "unfriendly." Not surprisingly, in the first half of 1995 Republicans got two-thirds of the PAC donations, compared to only one-third the year before.[36] The Republicans rented their majority to the highest bidder, hoping to use the money raised to establish themselves in power permanently.

Is There a Lobbyist in the House? The Don Jones Connection

Gingrich's pandering to big donors included opening up his office for their influence. Donald Jones owns millions of dollars of investments in Cyberstar, a company with cable interests in Wisconsin and the Virgin Islands. He invested $1.8 million in US Cyber, a new business selling Internet access and became unofficial "Telecommunications director for Speaker of the House Newt Gingrich," working as a volunteer in Gingrich's office with an official Congressional ID from December 1994 through July 1995. Jones spent two or three days a week in Gingrich's office, hanging around for two or three hours each day with Gingrich. The *Wall Street Journal* reported that "his volunteer job, by all appearances, made him almost a de-facto member of the speaker's staff."[37]

Gingrich's spokesperson claimed that Gingrich "did not turn to Don Jones for advice or recommendations on telecommunications legislation." But Jones wrote something quite different in a memo: "the content of the House bill is the subject of daily negotiations involving the Speaker, Committee Chairmen and a constant parade of TelCo CEOs. I participate as an observer and interpret and analyze the subtleties of the meeting for the Speaker, who is a remarkably good listener."[38] Gingrich listens for a good reason: Jones has given $125,000 to the Republican Party, and $25,000 to GOPAC. Jones also, according to a 1990 memo at a GOPAC meeting, "helped with Family Channel for

ACTV (30,000)"—the cable TV project for the Abraham Lincoln Opportunity Foundation, GOPAC's first tax-exempt subsidiary. Jones says, "In the eighties, I was one of the top donors in the country to the Republican Party."[39]

Jones influenced Gingrich's pro-industry views on the telecommunications bill, where Jones has a direct interest. Jones also used his inside information to help his partners in US Cyber, who were told by Jones about Gingrich's privately-expressed opposition to the Communications Decency Act, a matter of great concern to the company because it runs a computer pornography service which claims to have "gigabytes of the best adult files on-line."[40] "With a high level of certainty, I feel the Speaker would vehemently resist any ill-advised government control of Internet content," Jones wrote in a May 17, 1995 memo.

Gingrich first declared about Jones that "his primary contribution was to get in touch with New Zealand," which had privatized its telecommunications industry. Jones met several times with New Zealand Prime Minister Jim Bolgar in 1995. At the same time, Jones and his company Cyberstar were interested in New Zealand for their own reasons, since they were negotiating a $13 million deal in New Zealand to install a fiber optic network there. Jones noted, "The Cyberstar team, of which I am the Leader of Change, is excited about investing in the New Zealand telecommunications industry and the opportunities it presents."[41]

Gingrich sent his staffer Scott Klug to New Zealand for a $50,000 "fact-finding" mission in April to look at telecommunications privatization. Jones initially offered to finance the trip—until the ethics complaints against Gingrich made the issue too controversial for him. The *Madison Capital Times* noted in an editorial, "Klug did not go to New Zealand to learn whether privatization would work or not. He went to learn how best to advance the interests of people like Donald Jones."[42]

Despite his earlier claims that Jones provided a connection to New Zealand leaders who had privatized telecommunications, Gingrich later changed his story, saying that Jones spent "95 percent" of his time working on the Earning by Learning Program, a Gingrich nonprofit organization designed to avert criticism of his cuts in education and social programs by paying children to read books.[43] Even this explanation doesn't get Gingrich off the hook, since House rules declare that "official resources may not be used to assist the work of an outside organization."[44] Why would Jones spend all his time (supposedly sitting on a couch outside Gingrich's office) at Gingrich's Congressional office working on a nonprofit, nonpartisan program, and mention virtually nothing about it in his memos?

Gingrich's claim that Jones had no influence on the telecommunications bill is almost certainly a lie. According to the Ethics Committee, the Speaker's "office took caution to ensure that Mr. Jones performed no official duties." But Jones says otherwise. Jones wrote in a June 30, 1995 personal memo about his relationship to Gingrich, "I am a trusted listener and companion." Even Jones was shocked by the kind of influence he had in Gingrich's office: "To my surprise and sobering responsibility, on occasion am asked for an opinion or advice on what to do or how to handle a situation. I am told by staff and other friends of the Speaker he trusts and respects my judgment. There have been four times my ideas or opinions have resulted in decisions and actions on national strategic directives on huge matters."[45]

Standing Up for Internet Free Speech for the Wrong Reasons

One major part of the telecommunication bill was the proposal to regulate the Internet. Jones writes in a memo that he spoke to Gingrich "about concerns that entrepreneurs have making investments facing the possibility of government controls." He mentioned Campbell Lanier, a major Gingrich contributor, as one of those concerned about the regulation of the Internet, and reports that Gingrich replied, "I know Cam." Gingrich certainly did: Since 1991, Lanier and his family have given at least $56,000 to GOPAC and Gingrich's campaign. Lanier's uncle, Smith Lanier, has been a charter member of GOPAC for five years. One of Cam Lanier's companies, Interserv, was paid at least $10,000 to work on Gingrich's "Renewing American Civilization" course—and one member of Interserv's Board of Directors was Timothy Mescon, the Kennesaw State College administrator who arranged to have Gingrich teach the class. Lanier also has investments in National Vision Associates, whose founders, Ed and Rayna Weiner, gave $100,000 to GOPAC and Gingrich's course, and whose stock had been purchased by Marianne Gingrich.[46]

Lanier e-mailed Jones about a provision in the anti-terrorism bill that might regulate giving instructions over the Internet for how to construct a bomb. Jones in turn informed Gingrich about it, reporting in a memo that Gingrich hadn't been aware of it. Gingrich reportedly told him he opposed "central government control of anything. This is amazing and absurd—keep me informed." In the end, the Internet regulation provision was dropped from the bill at the insistence of House members.[47] As Jones reported, "I do not feel threatened by the possibility of such a public policy (as long as the Speaker is in leadership)." Although Gingrich was unwilling politically to stop the Communications Decency Act, Jones obviously had influence on the telecommunications bill and leaked information about Gingrich's views to people who were directly affected by the legislation. Whether one agrees or disagrees with Gingrich's views about Internet regulation, one thing is clear: they spring from an underlying motivation for money, and not from any principled view of Constitutional rights.

Gingrich was well aware that Jones's "volunteer" duty violated House rules, which prohibit the use of unpaid volunteers except for "educational programs that are primarily of educational benefit to the individual (volunteer), as opposed to primarily benefiting the Member or office, and which do not give undue advantage to special interest groups."[48] Jones, needless to say, wasn't a college student, but he certainly did represent a special interest group: himself.

The reason for this rule is obvious: without it, lobbyists could be installed in Congressional offices to "help" members of Congress who would be unlikely to refuse the assistance of a major donor. From this inside position, people like Jones would be able to manipulate legislation to benefit themselves—exactly as Jones apparently did with the telecommunications law, which Gingrich unilaterally altered before it reached the House floor, bypassing the committee system.

Getting Tough on Congressional Crime

Although the House Ethics Committee determined that Gingrich had violated the rules, it imposed no punishment. In fact, the Ethics Committee did more to cover up the incident than to expose it. Reporters for *Roll Call* found that "the committee ignored evidence provided to it that may have furthered the investigation."[49] Two former business partners of Jones, Tim Brown and Jeff Coleman, had their attorney write to Nancy Johnson, chair of the Ethics Committee, declaring that they "have information that will help to ensure that their actions are not cast in a false light and that the Members of your Committee are not misled in their investigation of the case involving Donald G. Jones. They are willing to cooperate in appropriate ways to ensure that the truth is revealed." Johnson never contacted these witnesses, and did not respond to the information sent to her.[50]

Both *Roll Call* and the *New York Times* condemned the incompetent investigation by the Ethics Committee and its weak response to Gingrich's violations. The "investigation" consisted solely of asking Gingrich, Jones, and Gingrich's staffers what Jones did in the Speaker's office, ignoring the contrary evidence that showed how Gingrich was covering up Jones's real role in the telecommunications legislation. It's not surprising that Gingrich's spokesperson Tony Blankey said he was "gratified" that the Ethics Committee took no serious action.[51] The Ethics Committee, apparently taking Gingrich's word as absolute truth, only gave him a minor reprimand for failing to "comply with applicable guidelines issued by this Committee governing interns or volunteers."

An April 24, 1996 *New York Times* editorial criticized "the committee's sagging credibility."[52] Rep. George Miller (D-Calif) declared that the Ethics

Committee "is either incapable or unwilling to properly investigate complaints against the Speaker of the House," and asked the Ethics Committee to have the independent counsel look into the Jones case.[53]

This was the second time in less than a year that Gingrich had broken House Rule 45, prohibiting outsiders from working in a Congressional office. The Ethics Committee determined in December 1995 that Gingrich violated the rule the first time by letting Joe Gaylord, a top political advisor and perhaps his closest friend, work out of his Congressional office.

Gingrich wanted Gaylord to work for him, but he didn't have enough money in his Congressional office account to afford the kind of salary Gaylord demanded. Instead, Gingrich used the various Republican Party groups he controlled (like GOPAC) to pay the salary of important advisors like Gaylord, who earned $326,000 in 1994 from GOPAC, Gingrich's campaign, and other sources (nearly three times as much as Gingrich's highest-paid employee). But despite the fact that he was only an unpaid volunteer, Gaylord ran the show in Gingrich's office. Elizabeth Drew reported that a close associate of Gingrich said, "Joe is really the chief of staff." According to one associate, "Newt delegates to Joe, and Joe calls other members of Newt's staff and gives instructions."[54]

The House Ethics Committee wrote Gingrich that "your use of Mr. Joseph Gaylord was in violation of House Rule 45," but in all of these cases, the committee did not vote to punish Gingrich in any way. Gingrich was repeatedly guilty of unethical conduct, and it should have been easy for the Ethics Committee to see through his lies. But Gingrich is too powerful for any member of the House to enforce the laws against him.

Chapter 5

Manipulating the Media

"We are engaged in reshaping a whole nation through the news media," Gingrich once said, and when it came to avoiding criticism about the Contract with America and his ethical lapses, Gingrich was an expert at manipulating the press.[1] Because of the media's reluctance to challenge his lies and the destructiveness of his plans, little of the truth about Gingrich or the Contract with America ever reached the public.

Whenever Gingrich runs into problems of his own making, he follows a standard cop-out: blame the media. According to Gingrich, "there is an elite, a remarkably isolated group of people who are mostly left wing."[2] Gingrich blames his high negative ratings on "unrelentingly negative press."[3] When the media reported a complaint by David Bonior about Gingrich's unethical conduct, Gingrich accused them of helping to "fan a piece of nonsense into a serious story."

He even tried to rewrite reality and blame his mistakes on a press conspiracy against him. After at least four different newspapers quoted Gingrich referring to the Clintons as "counter-culture McGoverniks," Gingrich claimed he was misquoted: "I used the term McGovernite, not McGovernik—it was one of those things that the *Times* picked up and therefore it's now history." In fact, tapes showed that he said McGovernik, not McGovernite. Gingrich also blamed the media for reporting the comment, claiming that "I didn't say that to attack the president, I was asked an analytic question."[4] Gingrich stopped having daily press briefings because the questions were too "nitpicking" and "adversarial." He's telling the truth here—reporters were asking him about his ethics problems and challenging his ideas.[5] Journalists in Washington quickly learned that if they wanted to have exclusive interviews and influential sources, they had to go easy on the man.

Gingrich also sought to influence the press by appealing to the corporate interests controlling most large media companies. He told *Broadcasting and Cable* magazine, "The business side of the broadcast industry ought to educate the editorial writing side of the broadcast industry." He reports that he was appalled at how "dumb" and "irresponsible" it was when "I went into a major cable company that owns a daily newspaper, and the newspaper's editorial page is attacking the very position of the cable company."[6] In Gingrich's mind, it is not only acceptable for owners to exert ideological control over the media, but it is irrational for them to allow freedom of the press. And if they fail to impose conservative ideas, advertisers should pick up the puppet strings. Gingrich contends that "most editors and editorial writers are 'socialist' purveyors of poisonous cynicism" and urges businesses to boycott liberal papers: "I think it's perfectly legitimate in a free society for people to decide where they'll put their money and their impact."[7] By spewing such nonsense about the press, Gingrich hoped to discourage any examination of his past, and condemned the media for being vindictive if they tried to criticize his agenda.

Gingrich gave enthusiastic support for the new telecommunications law—not because he thinks there is no reason to fear the loss of diverse voices from mergers and monopolies, but precisely because he hopes that a smaller range of opinion will be available to the public. If every media outlet is owned by a diversified conglomerate with interests in cable, broadcasting, communications, and other commercial endeavors, then editorial content and reporting will shift even further toward big business interests and its conservative advocates. If fewer and fewer corporations control the media (a trend throughout the 1980s and 1990s that will accelerate in broadcast media thanks to Republican deregulation), the monopoly over the thoughts and ideas that the public is allowed to hear will increase. When a handful of major companies are the only competitors in the realm of journalism, the kind of thought policing that Gingrich advocates will become almost inevitable.

Because business has not completely taken up Gingrich's call to be the Big Brother to the press, he must rely on his own tactics of media manipulation. Spokesman Tony Blankley observes that "he wouldn't be where he is today if he didn't know how to use the media."[8] A favorite tactic is to boycott the media when they question him. In 1994, the *Atlanta Journal and Constitution* published an editorial cartoon by Mike Luckovich which showed Gingrich with his arms around two bimbos ("D.C. highrollers") saying to a woman in a hospital bed ("Georgia Constituents"): "I want a divorce"—a clear reference to Gingrich's visit to his wife while she was in the hospital recovering from cancer. Gingrich responded by refusing to talk with any reporter from the paper for weeks; he would say "no comment" if a journalist from the newspaper asked a question at a public news conference.[9]

Gingrich regularly attacks the "elite" media, accusing them of a liberal bias. He told the Association of Opinion Page Editors, "I don't pay attention to letters to the editor because I assume they're just based on misinformation." According to Gingrich's paranoid theory, editorial page editors around the country conspire to give preference to liberals and refuse to print conservative letters. Yet he offers no proof for his absurd assertion that "the elite media is the offensive wing of the other team," in the service of the Democrats.[10]

Bashing the media is one of Gingrich's favorite games. He presents himself as a victim to gain sympathy, and his cries of being attacked make the press back off. Instead of scrutinizing the Republican agenda and Gingrich's authoritarian control over Congress, the media present Gingrich's views uncritically. Although a few stories exposed disturbing details of Gingrich's past, there was little follow-up or direct confrontation of Gingrich.

Reporters regularly downplayed the allegations against Gingrich for illegal conduct. John Cochran of ABC News declared on *Nightline* about the ethics charges, "so far these charges are not as serious as those leveled against Bob Packwood, or the 'Keating Five,' or Dan Rostenkowski, or even Jim Wright."[11] In fact, the ethics charges against Gingrich are far more serious and sweeping than those against any of these corrupt politicians. But because they are not being taken seriously by the press, and because Gingrich is not in danger of being forced out of Congress, the mainstream media do not consider it a serious story.

By trying to present the press as partisan, Gingrich ensures that journalists will do everything in their power to be lenient toward him. He uses the accusations of bias to manipulate the media, knowing that precisely because they are untrue, the media will try to avoid attacking him lest they appear partisan. Not surprisingly, Gingrich's ideal newspaper doesn't have any serious investigative journalism. He says, "I think *USA Today* is an extraordinary publication. It has more interesting pieces of information than you can find in eight or 10 or 12 pages of any other paper. It's almost the opposite of the *New York Times*."[12] Gingrich is the *USA Today* of politicians: high-tech, superficial, unable to concentrate on anything for more than a moment at a time, and fundamentally opposed to real journalism.

Yet the media have rarely attacked Gingrich, and often portray him as the revolutionary he imagines himself to be. A January 21, 1995 cover story in the *New York Times* declared, "While he has seemed consumed with breaking down the old order on Capitol Hill, he has also been applying himself to the future of the planet, of the human race, of the country and of his party."[13] This image of Gingrich as a revolutionary destroying the "old order" in Congress and a futurist devoted to saving America is exactly the kind of propaganda Gingrich has been successful at promoting.

Although the media have reported stories critical of Gingrich, they have almost always cast his systematic actions as "blunders." A substantial challenge to Gingrich's ideas, and an in-depth examination of Gingrich's corruption, have been largely missing from most of the media report. The major newspapers did publish serious critiques of Gingrich, but only *after* his ascent to power. When the *New York Times* finally detailed many of the ethical questions concerning Gingrich's college course, they published it on one of the days people are least likely to read the paper—Thanksgiving, 1994. The *Washington Post* ran a lengthy multi-part profile of Gingrich that same month. Yet, for

Gingrich, this bad publicity (which, given his past, was inevitably going to be revealed) came at the best possible time—following the election, when it was too late to change their votes.

The flurry of exposés didn't last long. Believing that they had said everything about Gingrich, the media quickly ended their critical stance and began swallowing Gingrich's rhetoric about the Republican Revolution. A *Washington Post* profile depicted Newt as a fighter against "entrenched authority" and "insider power." But the truth is that Gingrich has only fought the Democrats' power in order to establish himself as the new insider busy consolidating his own power.[14]

The media never took the Republican Revolution seriously until near election day 1994, when they concluded that a conservative shift among the American people had actually occurred—in essence believing that since the Republicans won, arguments about the widespread popularity of the Contract must have been right. A poll found that a mere 3% of the media considered the Contract with America a "serious reform proposal," while 59% dismissed it as an "election-year ploy." Conservatives pointed to this fact as evidence of a liberal bias, and Gingrich declared, "I unequivocally believe, as a Republican activist, that the core of the news media is biased, that the bias is amazing."[15] But the media's dismissal of the Contract was a sign of their cynicism, not their liberalism, and Republicans actually gained votes because the press paid little attention to the Contract with America.

The Contract was more than an election-year ploy. It was the framework for much of what was to come. But the media never scrutinized the conservative agenda until it was too late—after the elections, when it became clear that the Contract would form the foundation for the Republican Revolution. The Contract with America was perfect proof of how the media are not liberal at all; if it were, the press certainly would have struck out against Gingrich during the elections and discredited the Contract, or at the very least disproven the Republicans' claim that it represented popular demands. Instead, the Washington media act as a professional class, reporting on the latest political brawls but doing little truth-seeking. The media is not a liberal weapon used to attack the Right, but a tool manipulated by whatever side can feed the hungry press a story.

During the 1994 elections, Gingrich manipulated the media better than anyone else, staging the Contract's patriotic signing ceremony and then evading any critique of its specifics. The media, too caught up in the story of who would win the elections and whether the Republicans might take back control, missed what the elections were all about. Reporting on the possible consequences of a Republican takeover was practically nonexistent when voters were making their choices—hardly the goal of a "liberal" media. After Gingrich became Speaker of the House, the rare attacks on him in the media were much milder than the widespread hatred felt toward him by the general public.

After an embarrassing appearance on *Meet the Press* in December 1994, Gingrich immediately attacked the media for "trying to start fights" and promised to boycott Sunday morning talk shows for a month because of their "nit-picking argument." Gingrich was sending a direct message to one of the most politically influential kind of media: if they asked critical questions, he would refuse to appear on their shows. Because of severe competition for prestige, the Sunday morning shows are reluctant to confront guests like Gingrich with serious questions.

Gingrich told the media, "I would suggest to all of you that to make it work you've got to be positive." He condemned the press for its questioning: "It's a little bit like having a large household in which one person wakes up every morning, trying to start fights—spends the whole day trying to get people to fight each other." It may seem ironic for Newt Gingrich, the master of smearing his opponents, to complain about confrontation. But he always applied different rules to himself. Unfortunately, the press has let him get away with his double standard.[16]

When he took over as Speaker of the House in 1995, virtually all of the media coverage depicted his victory as a celebration. While Gingrich pushed the Contract with America through the House, the media ignored the ethics issues and devoted most of their time to publicizing Gingrich's accomplishments. The coverage of the Contract with America in particular showed the weaknesses of the press. Most of the stories focused on the horse race: whether Gingrich would get the bills passed, rather than what would happen to the country if the Republican agenda were enacted. Because the Republican Revolution's goals were so massive and complex, the media simply failed to give the public an adequate understanding of the Contract with America's consequences. Gingrich's radical restructuring of the House to weaken committees and centralize power directly under himself passed virtually without a word of coverage, let alone critique, in the mainstream media. The same was true of Gingrich's illicit behavior being revealed in ever-increasing detail by various ethics complaints.

Gingrich and the Republicans not only set the agenda in Congress; they also set the agenda in the media, determining that only the Republican spin on issues would be the focus. Gingrich continued the old tactic of the Conservative Opportunity Society to create an "issue of the day," faxed to all Republican members of Congress, which would often dictate what made the news.

Whitewater and Newtgate

While ignoring all the scandals surrounding Gingrich, the media devoted an extraordinary amount of attention to the Whitewater scandal. The American people didn't agree with Gingrich's self-perceived media victimization. A mid-1995 poll found that 32% thought the media had been biased against Bill Clinton, but only 24% felt there was bias in the press coverage against Gingrich and the Republicans.[17] A mid-1995 study by *Mother Jones* found that stories about Whitewater in the *New York Times* and the *Wall Street Journal* outnumbered stories about GOPAC by more than ten to one, even before the Whitewater hearings began.[18] When it came to one of the most influential kinds of media coverage—late night talk show monologues—Gingrich and fellow Republicans were ridiculed far less than Bill Clinton. The Center for Media and Public Affairs found that in 1995, Clinton was the top target of jokes by Jay Leno, David Letterman, and Conan O'Brien. The 338 jokes about Clinton more than doubled the total told about Bob Dole (56) and Newt Gingrich (103) combined, who were mocked less often than Kato Kaelin.[19]

The "liberal" *New York Times* broke the Whitewater story and has run dozens of front-page stories about the scandal, but ethics complaints against Gingrich usually generated only small stories on its inside pages. Although its editorials have criticized Gingrich's efforts to stop the ethics investigations, the *New York Times* has never condemned Gingrich's illegal conduct—or labeled it as such. Nor has the *New York Times*—or any other major newspaper—reported on more than a small number of Gingrich's crimes and unethical pandering to corporations.

By virtually any standard that can be applied, the Gingrich scandals are far more serious than the Clintons' involvement in Whitewater. The payoff to Gingrich was far more direct than anything Bill and Hillary Clinton ever received. Hillary Clinton's infamous $1,000 investment that turned into $100,000 was an aboveboard investment in which the Clintons risked far more than $1,000 because they were liable for any losses. The only advantage they had was a skilled trader using inside information; many others made much more money than they did.

The Clintons were given the opportunity to take another risk by investing in Whitewater; the fact that the Whitewater investment was not a payoff is proven by the Clintons' financial losses on the deal. Although the Clintons obviously had a special connection, there is no evidence that it was an outright bribe. And the Clintons never regarded this as anything other than a good business deal they were lucky to find, and certainly not as a favor they owed to anyone.

The Clintons' friends and business associates were involved in illegal activities, and the Whitewater case certainly merited an investigation into whether the Clintons did anything illegal. The problem was that the press never gave similar attention to far more substantial evidence of crimes committed by Gingrich.

Gingrich knew exactly what was happening when business "investors" for his books gave him money. He knew that he owed these friends a favor, and in some cases he returned it. Gingrich regularly and openly used his political influence on behalf of contributors to GOPAC and his college course, and explicitly tied his help to big donations—as did his donors. It's one thing for a friend of the Clintons to invite them to join a risky but potentially highly profitable investment that many others were involved in; it's quite another for business leaders to give money directly to Gingrich for two "investments" in his books, deals so irregular that they have never been imitated in the history of publishing.

In the area of tax evasion, the Clintons were guilty of taking deductions for their investment losses that should not have been allowed. These were mistakenly approved by the IRS or eventually paid back by the Clintons. Gingrich was guilty of violating numerous IRS and federal election laws that prohibit the use of nonprofit organizations for political purposes. To date, Gingrich has never sought to rectify his blatantly illegal actions.

While there may have been a cover-up by the Clintons and their people on the Whitewater case, it pales in comparison to the cover-up by Gingrich and his staffers. GOPAC and the Progress and Freedom Foundation kept their donors and their misconduct secret from the IRS and the media. Gingrich himself repeatedly lied to the Ethics Committee and the American people in order to silence inquiry into the extent of his crimes.

Most important of all, there has been no evidence that Whitewater had any connection with electoral politics. No money involved in the project was funneled to Clinton's campaigns or the Democratic Party, while Gingrich's scandalous activities were aimed directly at taking over the political system. The Clintons' illegal actions (if there were any) amounted to an attempt to increase their bank accounts. Gingrich's illegal activity, which has already been proven beyond any reasonable doubt, led to a political revolution, perhaps one of the most important events in 20th-century American politics.

Gingrich's corruption was directly tied to the empire he created in order to take over the House and become Speaker. If he had not illegally used GOPAC to help elect Republicans to Congress, it is doubtful that he would have generated the support he needed to narrowly win the vote for Minority Whip in 1990, which made him heir apparent to the position of Speaker. If he had not illegally used GOPAC's "Newt Support" to help himself win re-election in 1990 and 1992, he probably would not be a member of Congress today, let alone Speaker. If Gingrich had not illegally used nonprofit groups like the Progress and Freedom Foundation to give taxpayer-subsidized pep talks to party activists and donors, it is doubtful that he would have had the fundraising and organizing infrastructure he needed to win in 1994.

One of the things that made the Watergate scandal so shocking was its attempt to illegally manipulate electoral politics by spying on Democrats. The worst of the Whitewater accusations paint a far less serious picture, an old story of a powerful governor in a small state whose friends tried to help him make some money (and failed). In contrast, the scandals surrounding Newt Gingrich are far closer to Watergate proportions: a member of Congress violating the rules of the House and the laws of the United States in order to give himself an unfair advantage within the political system.

Why, then, are the media obsessed with Whitewater but indifferent to Newtgate?

One main barrier to press coverage of Newtgate was that Gingrich's crimes were almost purely political—and therefore dull by Washington standards. Although a small portion of the money was used for Gingrich's personal benefit (notably the 1977 and 1984 book partnerships), most of it went to promote his political ambitions. There were no close friends committing suicide in suspicious circumstances, no diaries bragging about his sexual exploits and revealing the inner workings of Congress, no relatives being given patronage ghost jobs. Gingrich had broken the law, but he hadn't done it in an interesting way.

Scandal has become so common in Washington, D.C., that mere corruption isn't considered newsworthy. The press wants lurid sex stories like Bob Packwood's (and it has told a few about Gingrich, but they are unrelated to his most serious crimes). Yet there is a clear double standard when it comes to Clinton and Gingrich. The entire country is aware of the sexual allegations of Gennifer Flowers and Paula Jones, helped in part by right-wing legal groups who filed a lawsuit against Clinton. Virtually no one has heard of Anne Manning—a far more credible source who reported having had an affair with Newt Gingrich, a claim he has never refuted. A NEXIS search of "Clinton AND Paula Jones OR Gennifer Flowers" came up with 7,668 references in the past two years in major newspapers and magazines; a search of "Gingrich AND Anne Manning" resulted in only 87 references. Why is old news about Clinton's illicit sex life (which was dealt with during the 1992 campaign) considered nearly a hundred times more important to the press than Gingrich's hypocrisy concerning adultery and morality?

Journalists certainly know about Gingrich's corruption. The Capitol Hill newspaper *Roll Call* has done an extraordinary job of revealing many of the scandals, and numerous ethics complaints against Gingrich have detailed these charges—but virtually no one reading the mainstream press knows much about these facts. As media reporter William Glaberson noted in the *New York Times*, "Mr. Gingrich makes such 'good copy' that the news are showering attention on him. And even if much of the attention is negative, the sheer volume of coverage has helped establish him as 'King of the Hill.'" Glaberson observed that Gingrich was "handled with kid gloves" on the ethical issues. *Wall Street Journal* Washington bureau chief Alan Murray admitted, "How many times can you hit a story?"[20] Because Gingrich's ethical violations are so numerous and complex, journalists looking for a simple story got bored with all the details of his crimes.

The disproportionate coverage of Whitewater to the exclusion of Newt's crimes is due to the Republican control of Congress and the dearth of true investigative reporters in Washington. The mainstream media are stuck in a responsive mode, reporting the latest confrontation or official action in Washington, while ignoring the real news. The media are reporting on every detail of Whitewater because the Republicans control Congress and can set up endless investigative committees to look into every deal. Sen. D'Amato's Whitewater hearings have reached epic mini-series proportions, with the press printing stories about each daily development. Meanwhile, the Republican-controlled Ethics Committee operates entirely in secret and constantly delays any serious inquiry into Gingrich's crimes.

The right's dominance over the media is also a dramatic factor in the biased coverage. It makes a difference when Accuracy in Media promotes the Whitewater conspiracy theories in advertisements on the *New York Times* op-ed page. It makes a difference when the *Wall Street Journal* editorial page and the *Washington Times* attack Clinton but always stand in defense of Gingrich. It makes a difference when Rush Limbaugh promotes rumors about Vince Foster's "murder" to millions of people on his radio show and defends the Republican agenda daily. It makes a difference when right-wing talk show hosts are constantly talking about Whitewater, while entirely ignoring Gingrich's illegal activity.

The timidity of the press toward Gingrich's crimes is unusual. The mainstream media were largely responsible for the downfall of Jim Wright, with newspapers like the *Washington Post* uncovering damning evidence of Wright's corrupt book deal and other unethical conduct that Gingrich's aides were not competent enough to find. In contrast, not one major newspaper has seriously investigated Gingrich. Virtually every revelation about his illegal conduct has come from independent agencies (notably the Federal Election Commission) and his political opponents filing ethics charges against him. As a result, reporters were never very interested in the Gingrich case: it was old news that had been reported before. Newspaper and newsmagazine editors and reporters want to highlight the stories *they* break, not someone else's investigative work.

Corporate Spin Control

Gingrich uses his power as Speaker to push for more than just money from lobbyists. When the people seeking his influence run media conglomerates, Gingrich asks them to control the reporters who work for them. On January 19, 1995, Gingrich met with the CEOs of top communications companies behind closed doors. After Gingrich sharply attacked the media for critical reporting about him, Time-Warner Chief Executive Gerald Levin asked what he and other media CEOs could do to make coverage more "fair." Gingrich told them they were responsible for keeping their journalists in line. According to a staffer at the event, "It was like, 'Get your children to behave.'"[21] In an earlier age, the media and the public would have been appalled to learn that the most powerful politician in Congress wanted positive media coverage in exchange for doing favors on behalf of their corporate leaders. Today, no one in the media considers it newsworthy, perhaps because the corporate conglomerates which own virtually all of the major media would be upset if there were any coverage of Gingrich's demands for editorial control. It was precisely this kind of "spin control" that allowed Gingrich to avoid negative coverage of his crimes.

Part II

The "Contract with America"

Chapter 6

The "Contract with America" and the Attack on Democracy

The anti-government ideology of the Contract with America masks its service to the wealthy donors who support Gingrich and the Republican Party. According to the Contract with America, we face a debate "between smaller government with lower taxes and fewer services or bigger government with higher taxes and more services."[1] But this is a particularly senseless way of presenting the issue. The issue is not small government versus big government. After all, even the Republicans favor more government spending when it comes to the defense budget and prisons. The idea that bigger government is always bad takes a ridiculously simplified approach; a far better way to deal with wasteful spending is to make government programs more effective, reducing or eliminating them when they are unnecessary, and creating them when they serve an important social good.

Nor is it clear that the American people really want the smaller overall government advocated by the Republicans. Although the public opposes higher taxes, it also opposes cuts in services (and, at the same time, opposes large budget deficits). To call this a mandate for conservatism is absurd. Rather, it is the desire to have everything, much like Gingrich (and Reagan before him) want to have tax cuts, military increases, and a balanced budget.

Rhetoric to Shock Even Orwell

The Contract declares, "Big Brother is alive and well through myriad government programs usurping personal responsibility from families and individuals."[2] Borrowing their ideas from the militias, the far right Republicans made our own government the greatest villain of the world now that the Cold War is over. They claim that America's government is a totalitarian state that imprisons people within the welfare state, trapping free enterprise under the yoke of rules and regulations. With hate speech against government workers from top politicians like Gingrich, it is not surprising to find extremists ready to blow up government buildings. It is one thing to argue that certain welfare programs and environmental regulations are ill-conceived or poorly administered; it is something quite different when the leaders of the Republican Party compare our government to a police state in their platform.

The Republicans' invocation of "Big Brother" is particularly hypocritical given their support for a "gag rule" against doctors discussing abortion, a Constitutional amendment to ban flag burning, a law to repeal the Exclusionary Rule's protections against illegal searches and seizures, and the Communications Decency Act's violation of the First Amendment. Gingrich isn't an advocate of individual empowerment, nor is he opposed to the ideal of "Big Brother." Instead, he wants to take power away from individuals and the government they elect, and put the power in the hands of big corporations so that they become our Big Brothers.

Nothing exemplifies Gingrich's anti-government views more than his attacks on the AmeriCorps program which pays slightly above minimum wage to young people, enabling them to work full-time at volunteer projects in local communities. AmeriCorps members help build houses, immunize infants, and clean up dirty rivers and inner city vacant lots.

Unlike the wealthy businessmen Gingrich helps with his influence and his tax cuts, the participants in AmeriCorps don't get rich from their government sponsorship: the program pays only $600 a month, plus health benefits and a voucher for education worth $4,725 after a full year of service.

Gingrich condemns the AmeriCorps program: "I am totally, unequivocally opposed to national service. It is coerced voluntarism."[3] Of course, nothing about AmeriCorps is coerced. It's the only way for people who aren't as wealthy as Gingrich and his friends to serve their community. While unpaid volunteerism is important, it's impossible for most young people to spend more than a few hours a week volunteering in their community. They often work full time, and must raise money to pay off college debts or save money to pay for college—a feat made that much harder by Republican efforts to cut education funding and keep the minimum wage as low as possible. AmeriCorps is a beautiful solution for the problem: with only a minimal amount of money, unskilled workers who want to help their community can be paid to do good work instead of flipping burgers.

Gingrich thinks that government-supported community service is "gimmickry." His true fear is not that AmeriCorps might be a failure or a waste of money, but that it might succeed. If AmeriCorps works—and it does—then everything Gingrich believes about the evils of government is utterly wrong. If the free market doesn't help people, and a government program can, then the irrational Republican goal of killing social programs will be exposed as a morally corrupt idea. If AmeriCorps helps people, encourages lifelong volunteerism, and performs social services at a small expense, then it might become the model for a much larger jobs program to invest in America and provide employment opportunities to welfare recipients and the unemployed. Gingrich, of course, is firmly opposed to this idea because his corporate donors depend upon high unemployment (and a large supply of poor people looking for work) to keep wages down. If the government offered subsistence-level wages to work in the community, private employers might be forced to pay a living wage in order to attract workers away from these jobs.

AmeriCorps survived the first year of the Gingrich Congress with "only" a 15% cut. But Republicans plan to completely eliminate the program, depriving tens of thousands of members each year of the opportunity to serve their community. According to Gingrich, a much greater social good is produced if the money is used to give tax breaks to millionaires, who can hire these workers to clean their mansions and maintain their lawns.

Gingrich doesn't want less government; he wants a government that does less to ensure social justice. He wants a government that serves the corporate CEOs who financed the Republican Revolution, rather than a government that tries to help the disadvantaged. It is only by demonizing the government that Gingrich and the Republicans can justify their enormous transfer of wealth, reverse Robin Hood-style, from the poor to the rich.

GOPAC Writes the Contract

Gingrich originally conceived the idea behind the Contract with America back in 1980, when he convinced reluctant Reagan officials to stage an event with Ronald Reagan and the Republican congressional candidates on the Capitol steps, where they promised to pass tax cuts. Gingrich's goal was to nationalize Congressional elections, so that a Reagan victory would also draw in a Republican majority in Congress.[4] Gingrich's plan was a failure: Reagan won a decisive victory, but Republicans were not swept by his coattails into the House of Representatives. However, he successfully revived the idea a decade later.

The current Contract was born in GOPAC meetings held in 1989 and 1990 to plot the Republican takeover of Congress. GOPAC functioned as the main planning organization for Gingrich and the Republicans to take over the House, especially after the National Republican Congressional Committee ran into financial and organizational problems in the early 1990s.

In 1989, GOPAC advisors outlined an "Agenda for America for the '90s" in order to nationalize local campaigns: "Platform gives candidates legitimacy, keeps President from walking away. Leads to ability to run national campaign." Another 1989 planning meeting proposed a "100 day agenda" for when the Republicans took over the House. GOPAC head Bo Callaway wrote in an August 13, 1990 memo to Gingrich: "We would give it a name (for now '100 day agenda') and would ask all candidates running in 1992 to sign off for supporting all or essentially all of the program." Callaway reported that GOPAC would help "make a real run at recruiting quality candidates" and sign up candidates for Congress to support their agenda.[5] Long before GOPAC registered as a federal political action committee, it was secretly organizing the Republican Revolution.

Of course, the text of the Contract with America omits GOPAC's role in its creation, telling a pleasant myth about the Contract's origins. At a February 1994 House Republican conference in Salisbury, Maryland, Republicans supposedly expressed disappointment that Bill Clinton "did not intend to govern on the agenda which people elected him to lead the country." Shocked at this revelation, the Republicans decided to make a Contract as "an agreement and a covenant between our now elected representatives and the American people with whom we sought a common bond."[6]

But this contract signed on behalf of the American people wasn't really a contract with America at all; it was a contract with Newt Gingrich, an agreement by Republican candidates to follow his "blueprint for action" once they were elected—regardless of what the American people wanted.[7] The Contract had little impact on the 1994 elections, but it had a dramatic effect on Gingrich's ability to centralize power and set an agenda for Congress. His friend Vin Weber noted, "The closer we got to the election, the more Newt saw the Contract as a device for managing the first six months."[8]

Buried beneath the seeming transparency of the Contract was a secret contract with Newt Gingrich. Few people, even among the Republican candidates, knew much about what the Contract with America contained. The Contract was the combination of a campaign ploy and a political blank check made out to Newt Gingrich. The specific provisions of the Contract (most of which were not mentioned until after the election) revealed the real goal of the Republican Revolution: to help wealthy corporations by cutting taxes on the rich, curtailing enforcement of health and safety regulations, and expanding corporate welfare programs.

Block Grant Magic

Perhaps Gingrich's most brilliant innovation was the "block grant" scam. By assigning social programs to the states, Gingrich wants to escape the political repercussions of severe budget cuts. The original Contract with America mentioned little about block grants; but once in power, Republicans in Congress realized that block grants offered a perfect way to cut welfare programs without having to make the difficult (and unpopular) decisions themselves. As recently as 1994, Gingrich had attacked block grants in the Clinton crime bill; he feared that block grants to local governments with "destructive bureaucracies" would "let the local politicians build a bigger machine with more patronage."[9] Less than a year later, Gingrich had flip-flopped completely, and was heralding block grants to state and local governments as the model of efficiency and innovation.

Gingrich knows that state and local bureaucracies are not magically more efficient than the federal government. He also knows that the block grant program violates every principle of good government: there is no mechanism for oversight, no reward or punishment for success or failure, only a federal check that can be used for anything. Currently, the Congressional committees and Washington media can monitor the federal bureaucracy when corruption and abuse occur; it is difficult to imagine any similar scrutiny of 50 state governments and thousands of local bureaucracies. The "block grant" plan was exactly what Gingrich has always criticized about government programs: it throws money at a problem without any supervision or incentive for success. But Gingrich would much rather see a failed government program than a successful one. If "block grants" lead to wasteful spending and a failure to solve social problems, then this will provide Gingrich with a perfect excuse to cut them back even more. Preventing government from working is the primary goal of a man whose political career is based on the presumption that government always fails.

Gingrich likes to point out a few successful state programs as evidence of the superior ability of states to deal with social problems, but he often does so inaccurately. For example, Gingrich praised a Massachusetts initiative that cut a $200 million welfare program for the disabled in half simply by requiring doctors to confirm the disability. Was this a sign of the superior ability of states to innovate? In fact, Governor William Weld admitted, "We modeled our program on the one used by the feds; it works."[10]

Several Republican governors have enthusiastically endorsed the idea of getting federal money without any strings attached. However, even if a few states manage to do a better job than the federal government, many more states are likely to have enormous waste and corruption. A *Wall Street Journal* report found that an $8.3 million block grant for child care had been wasted on personal furniture and designer salt and pepper shakers for state bureaucrats.[11] If the Republicans were really committed to reform, they would improve federal welfare and anti-crime programs, rather than throwing the problems at the states.

Because states under the Republican plan are no longer obliged to continue contributing to welfare programs, many of them will simply cut back their own welfare benefits. The Center on Budget and Policy Priorities estimated that states would lose $7.8 billion over four years due to the Republican block grant proposal.[12] The idea that efficiency will make up for all these cutbacks isn't credible. The real goal, as Gingrich knows, is to cut welfare programs.

During a recession, the poor will be especially hard hit because the amount given in block grants would not necessarily increase, as current programs do to meet rising needs. Republican Ohio Governor George Voinovich observed that block grants would put states "in an extremely vulnerable position should the welfare-eligible population increase significantly."[13] In the case of an economic downturn, states would face a severe strain on their budgets and the poor would suffer large cuts. Nor would the block grants always be adjusted for population changes. If a state cut back welfare benefits dramatically, pushing welfare recipients out of the state, it could still get the same block grant and effectively eliminate its own welfare spending, saving millions of dollars, and leaving the problem for someone else to solve. The buck would never have to stop anywhere.

Nor were Republicans consistent in their advocacy of state authority. Even while they argued for block grants to give state governments more flexibility for welfare programs, they added rules for virtually-impossible-to-meet work requirements, lifetime limits on welfare, and restrictions on money to teenage single mothers and anyone having additional children. As Republican Rep. Christopher Shays admitted, "we want block granting and freedom for local and state government when it fits into our agenda and we want restrictions when that fits our agenda. We make contradictory arguments."[14] Although his rhetoric was contradictory, Gingrich's goal was always consistent: to destroy all government programs to help the poor.

Concealing Corruption: The Congressional Accountability Act

One of the most loudly trumpeted Republican proposals was to "require all laws that apply to the rest of the country also apply equally to the Congress." But the truth is that Gingrich has spent his career evading the laws applied to other Americans, and to other members of Congress. The Republicans are interested in political manipulation, not Congressional reform. In 1994, the Senate Republicans stopped a Democratic effort to pass a House bill which would have removed exemptions for members of Congress from laws that regulate the private sector. After its defeat, the House Democrats passed a House rule that had the same effect as the proposed law. Gingrich and the Republicans wanted to get exclusive credit for reforming Congress by promising to pass a useless and purely symbolic "accountability" law that the Democrats had already enacted. If the Republicans had allowed the Democratic law to pass, then they might have faced pressure to implement real Congressional accountability, including campaign finance reform and stricter anti-corruption laws.

In the Contract with America, Gingrich promised to "cut the number of House committees, and cut committee staff by one-third."[15] While one might think this would be part of a Republican effort to cut spending in the House, it wasn't. Instead, staff reductions gave Republicans an excuse for getting rid of staffers they considered liberal holdovers from the era of Democratic control. Gingrich wanted to weaken committees so that he could have direct control over legislation.

While Gingrich was cutting committee budgets and staff dramatically, he increased the budget for the Speaker's office by 30% (and used "volunteer" workers like Joe Gaylord and Don Jones to supplement his office staff). Gingrich also expanded the Speaker's security forces. While the last three Democratic Speakers had only one police officer to guard them, Gingrich has had groups of three, four, or even five police officers following him to his district.[16] House Republicans even created a new post for Director of Protocol.[17] These expenditures reveal the intention behind the rhetoric: Gingrich's budget cuts were not designed to save money, but to undermine the opposition by cutting off funding to House caucuses in order to remove a potential source of competition. Gingrich's "accountability" rhetoric was used only to expand his own power as Speaker of the House.

Lying About Deficits: A Devious Balancing Act

One of the most widely publicized but insignificant proposals of the Contract with America was the Balanced Budget Amendment, which passed the House but failed in the Senate by only one vote. Although Gingrich presented the Balanced Budget Amendment as the Republican response to Democratic overspending, the truth is that most of the national debt has been built up under Republican presidents pursuing "conservative" fiscal policies. During the Reagan Administration, it was the president who proposed large deficits and the Democrats who reduced them.

The Balanced Budget Amendment was a ploy of political posturing and symbolism, since no amendment to the Constitution can make hundred-billion-dollar deficits disappear. It takes political agreement, not messing around with the Constitution, to balance the budget. Republicans seized upon the idea of the "balanced budget" as an excuse for their larger agenda: to cut taxes on corporations and the wealthy, and destroy the social safety net for the rest of America.

What few people realize is that the federal government is not bloated beyond what it can afford; there is no "spending madness" as the Contract with America claimed.[18] In fact, the current Federal government operating budget, taken alone, is already balanced: in fiscal year 1995, the deficit was only $164 billion, but interest on the debt alone was $235 billion. If it were not for the excessive spending on the military, the $150 billion S & L bailout, and tax cuts for the rich during the Reagan and Bush Administrations, when more than $3 trillion of the debt was created, we would have a balanced budget right now. The only reason why a deficit exists is the hundreds of billions of dollars which the federal government must spend each year for interest on the national debt. The problem is not too much government today, but the excesses of the 1980s—which helped fuel economic prosperity for the wealthy.

Unfortunately, today's taxpayers must pay the interest for the fiscal irresponsibility of the Reagan years—there is a deficit that we cannot ignore—but it should be clear that the problem is not a "welfare state" which has grown too large. Instead, the problem is a "military state," fueled by the Cold War paranoia of Gingrich and other hawks, that grew too large in the 1980s (and remains far greater than current military needs), and a "corporate welfare state" that subsidizes the wealthy with direct payments and tax loopholes. If AFDC, food stamps, and other social programs were eliminated completely, it would only have a small impact on the overall budget, but a devastating effect on the poorest Americans..

Rule By the Few

The Balanced Budget Amendment was also part of a concerted effort by the Republicans to enhance their power. The Republicans realize that their control over Congress is likely to be a temporary phenomenon, which is why they are moving quickly to alter the political system to strengthen their future position in the minority. Because the Contract was written while they were in the minority, it includes their plans for measures—including Constitutional amendments and the line-item veto—that would enhance the power of the minority party in Congress.

Since everyone knows that there will be deficits for years, and probably decades, to come, the balanced budget amendment is purely symbolic in every respect but one: it includes a provision that allows Congress to vote by a three-fifths supermajority to overrule the Constitution and run a deficit. The main effect is to ensure that the minority party in Congress has a great deal more sway than normal; if the majority party cannot pass a budget on its own, then a Republican minority will have more leverage to impose its demands.

The concept of the minority veto directly contradicts the Founding Fathers' vision of the government. As Yale law professor Bruce Ackerman points out, James Madison explicitly rejected the idea of a supermajority for normal legislative business, arguing in *Federalist* No. 58 that "the fundamental principle of free government would be reversed. It would be no longer the majority that would rule; the power would be transferred to the minority."[19]

The requirement of a balanced budget would offer Republicans the kind of budgetary veto power that they have never before had in the minority, even when they controlled the White House, because Republican presidents might be reluctant to veto appropriations bills and shut down the government.

One provision of the Contract that got passed and signed into law was the line-item veto. Knowing that Republicans have been more likely than Democrats to be elected president in the past half-century, and that even a Democratic president is more likely to cut welfare programs for the poor than for corporate welfare, the Republicans sought the line-item veto. Moreover, since much of the corporate welfare comes in the form of special tax breaks or tariffs rather than direct appropriations, it could not be affected by a line-item veto. The line item veto would do almost nothing to reduce the deficit; its main effect would be to shift more power to the president in negotiations with Congress, since a promise not to exercise the line item veto will be part of future budget negotiations. President Clinton, hoping to be able to use the veto, signed the Republican bill into law even though it is likely to increase Republican power over the long term.

The most ridiculous part of the Republicans' plan to protect their power in the minority is the Contract's proposal to require a three-fifths majority for any tax increase. This is blatantly unconstitutional, since no Congress is allowed to impose a supermajority requirement based on the content of legislation. Moreover, it was a stupid law that would create a tangle of lawsuits, since a three-fifths vote might be required even for a bill that generally lowered taxes (such as majority leader Dick Armey's flat tax) if it increased *anyone's* income tax rates. But it was a sign of the Republican's unease about their future as the majority party. They want to impose their reforms as quickly as possible and change the rules to prevent the Democrats from repealing any of them.

The Republicans used the Balanced Budget Amendment for political purposes, but they have no serious commitment to balance the budget. If they really wanted to balance the budget, Republicans would reject their tax cut and cut defense spending. But again, budget-cutting is just a knife to slash unwanted programs. Milton Friedman, the Nobel Prize-winning conservative economist, has often expressed the economic theory that Republicans generally follow: their key concern is the size of government, not the size of the deficit. The goal, according to Friedman, should be to retain a moderately large deficit in order to create pressure for budget cuts, and never to raise taxes to meet the gap. On the contrary, taxes should be lowered under the Friedman scheme in order to increase the deficit and spark further reductions in the size of government. What the Republicans want is not fiscal responsibility, but the decimation of government.

When the goal of political leaders is to destroy government, not improve it, the result is even greater inefficiency and bureaucracy. Although Gingrich will rarely come out and admit it, the last thing he wants is a government that works. The best way to downsize the government, Gingrich has discovered, is to make it as ineffective as possible, thereby making government programs less popular. This is one reason why Gingrich was so anxious to shut down the government during the budget crisis of 1995-96. By disrupting government operations and making people angry with the current state of government, he hopes to convince them that it is futile to expect anything useful from government.

No Exit

This helps explain one of Gingrich's most serious mistakes in dealing with the budget. In November 1995, after flying with Clinton to Israel to attend Rabin's funeral, Gingrich complained about being forced to leave Air Force One by the back exit, and whined that he "didn't talk to the president at all on the plane." Gingrich announced to the president that his "snub" was "part of why you ended up with us sending down a tougher continuing resolution." Gingrich declared, "It's petty, but I think it's human." Americans who were mildly irritated that the government would be shut down over a speaker's inflated ego were not so forgiving.[20] Although Gingrich's goal was to pin the blame for the budget delay on Clinton, it was a PR disaster. Gingrich was openly ridiculed for his arrogance and pettiness.

But media coverage missed the fact that Gingrich's misstep was caused because he couldn't admit the real reason for the government shutdown: his desire to get rid of the government if he didn't have his way. Gingrich could not say that he really wanted to force a shutdown, and instead blamed his refusal to compromise on a personal resentment against Bill Clinton.

Gingrich presented the balanced budget act as an ethical necessity:

> No truly moral civilization would burden its children with the economic excesses of the parents and grandparents....We're talking about hard economic consequences that will limit our children and grandchildren's standard of living. Yet that is what we are doing for the children trapped in poverty, for the children whose futures are trapped by a government debt they're going to have to pay.[21]

Yet Gingrich says nothing about the future of the children who will suffer from the budget cuts he proposes (supposedly to help pay off the debt).

In Gingrich's Orwellian rhetoric, helping children is hurting children. And hurting them, by cutting off welfare benefits, really helps them. The fact that this Gingrichian "tough love" happens to cut the budget and pay for tax cuts for the rich (who, unlike the poor, are better off having more money) is mere coincidence. Beneath this contempt for the poor lurks a bizarre form of self-delusion, Gingrich apparently believes it is better for children if their mothers are condemned to complete poverty. Since welfare is the primary reason why poor women have children, he reasons, then sacrificing a few children to the depths of poverty will be necessary to save the rest from the evils of welfare.

The Contract for the Rich

As if slashing poverty programs wasn't enough, the centerpiece of the Contract was an expensive bribe to the "family values" constituency: the $500-per-child tax credit. The child tax credit was designed to cover up the real goal of the Republican tax reform: to dramatically cut taxes on the rich. Gingrich's plans will benefit the richest 1% of Americans by raising the exemption on inheritance taxes from $600,000 to $750,000, a move which would cost the government $27 billion over the next ten years. He would open tax-deferred IRAs to people making up to $95,000 a year. But the primary goal of Republicans is to cut the capital gains tax sharply, at a cost of more than $50 billion. The Joint Congressional Committee on Taxation calculated that the Republican tax cuts would cost $196.3 billion in the first five years and $369.9 billion within seven years.[22] Most of the cuts would go to the wealthiest Americans.

While Gingrich and his allies loudly promote the free market and oppose government interference in it, they suddenly change their tune when it comes to special tax breaks for the rich. Cutting capital gains taxes is considered essential, even though a huge government subsidy for investment (usually by the wealthy) goes completely against the notion of the unregulated free market.

Of course, investment is important for America. But rather than have government invest in the infrastructure of this country and the education of its citizens, Gingrich only wants to encourage corporate and private investment, no matter how wasteful it may be.

His plans make no effort to cut back on corporate tax breaks which, according to Citizens for Tax Justice, include excessive depreciation write-offs ($164 billion over five years), tax breaks for mergers and takeovers ($9 billion), taxes evaded by multinational corporations ($46 billion), and subsidies for "business" meals and entertainment ($29 billion). The Center on Budget and Policy Priorities estimates that tax breaks to corporations and the rich will amount to $400 billion in lost revenue this year alone.[23]

When Democrats planned to slightly tighten a loophole in tax laws that allowed wealthy Americans to renounce their citizenship for tax purposes, Republicans resisted. In 1995, the Senate passed a bill to close the "expatriate tax" loophole, which allows Americans to avoid estate and capital gains taxes by renouncing their citizenship. But in a conference meeting with the Senate, House Republicans insisted on dropping the bill, which would bring in $2.4 million over five years.[24] Sen. Phil Gramm (R-TX) compared it to "Nazi Germany" and Gingrich personally cut down the proposal.[25]

According to the Republicans, the fact that their tax cut favored rich Americans hardly mattered since everyone in America is potentially wealthy; it's only a matter of entrepreneurial skill and effort—not economic opportunities—that separates the rich from the poor. Their lesson is clear: choose to be rich.

Republican Majority Leader Richard Armey's book, *The Freedom Revolution*, argues that "a person in the poorest income group in 1979 was more likely to end the decade in the richest quintile than to remain at the bottom."[26] This, to Armey, is proof of upward mobility. But in fact, it's only proof that people get older. The median age of those rapid risers who went from the poorest income group to the richest was 22 in 1979. Obviously, the child from a wealthy family who's attending Harvard Law School in 1979 (and technically has no income) is quite likely to join the richest quintile in a decade; but this isn't exactly what most people mean by equal opportunity or upward mobility. As economist Paul Krugman commented, the study Armey cited was one done by Bush Administration officials which "experts immediately ridiculed."[27]

The U.S. has the widest gap between rich and poor in the industrial world[28] and a report by the Center on Budget and Policy Priorities discovered that the working poor are 50% more likely to fall below the poverty line today than in the late 1970s.[29] A recent study of 18 Western industrialized nations found that the United States had by far the largest gap between rich and poor families. Although the United States had the wealthiest affluent families of four (who earned $65,536 after taxes at the 90th percentile), America ranked 16th among the countries for poor households, who (at the 10th percentile) had $10,923 in salary and government welfare. This means that 10% of American families of four have to live on less than $11,000 a year, far below the poverty line. So much for the myth that people are getting rich on welfare. Poor children in Europe are better off than poor children in America, even though our wealth is far greater than most European nations. The only two countries in the survey whose poor households were more impoverished than those of the United States—Israel and Ireland—had affluent households that earned just half as much as American ones.[30] The Republican response to studies like these is denial and destruction: deny that it means anything, and cut back the budgets of the National Science Foundation and similar agencies which financed the study.

The Contract with America was only the first step in the plan for government giveaways to the rich. The Republican leaders in Congress appointed a special commission led by Jack Kemp which proposed the idea of a flat tax. Dick Armey writes in his book that "a flat tax seems almost a certainty—with only the timing and exact rate in doubt."[31] Even Gingrich—who had never expressed any interest in the flat tax until it became politically trendy—endorsed the concept, and condemned the progressive tax system as an artifact of the Cold War.[32] Economist Robert Eisner calculated that under the Armey flat tax, Americans earning less than $100,000 would pay more income tax, while the tax rates for those earning over $200,000 would be cut nearly in half.[33]

Destructive as the Contract with America's promises would be to American democracy, the most dangerous part by far of Gingrich's agenda never appeared in print. In order to quiet the opposition, the Republicans were silent about the programs they would eliminate in order to finance the large tax cuts for the wealthy and the increases in defense spending. The Gingrich budget turned out to be a massive assault on the poor in America, with destructive cuts not only in welfare, but in school lunches, food stamps, education, and a long list of programs which are strongly supported by the American people. While cutting funds for poor children, *Newsday* noted, Republicans in the House Appropriations Committee "left virtually untouched nearly $3 billion in their own pork barrel projects."[34]

When Rep. Richard Durbin (D-IL) tried to eliminate the government's $42 million in subsidies for tobacco (including $23.2 million for crop insurance, $2 million for marketing, and $16.5 million for tobacco price supports), the Republicans quickly crushed the proposal.[35] The tobacco industry has taken steps to make sure Republicans do not end tobacco subsidies or allow FDA regulation of cigarettes; big tobacco companies donated $1.5 million to Republicans in the first half of 1995, ten times what they gave in 1993. Tobacco donations, which five years ago were split evenly between Democrats and Republicans, now favor Gingrich and his colleagues by a five-to-one margin.[36] After the FDA suggested that tobacco should be regulated as a drug, Gingrich declared that the agency had "lost its mind."[37]

Members of Congress have always made secret deals with corporations, exchanging money for influence, but today, the Republicans who rule Congress are openly demonstrating their obedience to corporate dollars. Gingrich's majority whip, John Boehner (R-OH), recently walked around the House floor handing out checks from tobacco lobbyists to his Republican colleagues. Boehner stopped this outright bribery only when colleagues pointed out to him that it might create an "appearance" problem.[38]

Instead of going after corporate profits, the Republican Congress defended the subsidies to big business. Although Gingrich promised to cut corporate welfare and defense spending along with poverty assistance, his House bills only contained cuts in programs to help the poor.

Terminal Limits: The Citizen Legislature Act

The Contract with America's crusade for term limits in the name of creating a "citizen" legislature was ironic, considering that career politicians like Newt Gingrich were the ones in charge of the party. In fact, Gingrich and the Republicans want term limits only because they believe it will increase their institutional power.

In 1992, columnist George Will declared that Gingrich had become "a case study of the primacy of careerism in the life of the modern congressman." Will observed that Gingrich "was beginning to be perceived as one of those unsavory creatures he had long been excoriating for fun and profit." To defend his political career against a challenge in the primary, Gingrich gave up his government Lincoln Town Car and $60,540-a-year driver/bodyguard which were perks for whips (David Bonior, the Democratic Whip, had refused to accept his).

Gingrich argued that his wealthy suburban district should reelect him to preserve the massive federal funding that it received. Cobb County, Georgia receives $1.80 in federal funding for every dollar they send to Washington. In contrast, New York City, the center of bureaucracy and welfare programs, only gets 82 cents back for every dollar they sent to the federal government. Accustomed to telling wealthy GOPAC donors about the influence they could buy with contributions, Gingrich had no problem making what Will called a "pledge of servility" to the voters: "If you had the choice between the No. 2 ranking Republican in the House or you can have a freshman who doesn't have any idea who the Cabinet members are, has never met any of them and has never worked with the president, which one do you think can do more for Cobb County?"

As Will commented, "Gingrich may have saved his career as a professional legislator, but he ended his career as the scourge of the 'corruption' of the welfare state in the hands of career legislators. And he unwittingly made himself a textbook example of why term limits are now necessary."[39] But Will never realized that Gingrich was always a professional politician who attacked "career legislators" as a political ploy, not as part of any philosophy of government.

To reduce the pressure on members of Congress for term limits, Gingrich allowed four versions of the term limits amendment to be voted on, so that representatives could vote for one to protect themselves politically while making sure that none of the bills would get the necessary two-thirds vote.[40] This tactic also appeased the conservatives who wanted to vote on more radical proposals. Gingrich never wanted term limits because he feared it might undermine the Republican majority that he had finally established, especially since he believes that dismantling the welfare state would require a long-term effort. Gingrich considered term limits an unnecessary distraction from the real work of implementing Republican policies; but it did have the benefit of putting many Democrats in the unpopular position of opposing term limits, a stance which the Republicans hope to exploit in the 1996 elections and beyond.

The idea of term limits is not anathema to an experienced politician like

Gingrich. He knows that even if there were term limits, he could influence Congress from the outside, and continue his political career by running for the Senate or for president. From Gingrich's perspective, term limits only increase the important power of outside lobbyists and political donors who can trump the popularity of an individual politician and use their money to influence elections. Gingrich has learned from personal experience that popular opinion, not a law against term limits, is the most powerful way to stop corrupt politicians, because he was nearly a victim of it himself in the 1990 election.

Gingrich knows that term limits have their advantages and disadvantages, and sees them primarily as a way to manipulate popular resentment against Congress and make Democrats appear to be the establishment fighting off outsiders. However, term limits would help the Republicans resist a Democratic movement to take back Congress. It took Gingrich more than a decade of careful organizing to bring about a revolution in the House, and term limits would effectively prevent any Democrat from imitating his long-term planning. Although the Republican members would have to leave their jobs after 12 years, their superior farm system and access to money would give conservatives a substantial advantage in future elections.

Gingrich supported term limits in one area by creating a six-year maximum term for chairs of congressional committees. Again the reasons are self-serving, not principled—Gingrich wanted to prevent the powerful committee chairs that dominated the Democratic majority because he desired to centralize power under himself as Speaker. The term limits ensure that committee chairs need to toe the Gingrich line in order to secure another plum position. And all the other representatives would know that many opportunities existed to rise quickly among the House Republicans—if they followed Newt's orders.

To impose this term limit, Gingrich agreed to an eight-year limit on himself as Speaker. It wasn't too much of a sacrifice. Gingrich is too restless to stay in the same position for decades, and he is obviously planning to run for president in 2000 or 2004, depending on political circumstances of the time. Gingrich spent several weeks in 1995 laying the groundwork for a presidential run in New Hampshire, and seemed to even consider making an early attempt at it before realizing that his massive unpopularity made success unlikely.

Chapter 7

Let Them Eat Orphanages: The War on Welfare

No politician in recent decades has advocated policies as cruel to the poor as Newt Gingrich has. Where America once declared a war on poverty, Gingrich today declares a war on the poor. Gingrich writes in his book, *To Renew America*, that we should follow Captain John Smith's statement in 1607 in Jamestown, Virginia: "If you don't work, you won't eat."[1] This starvation principle is what Gingrich promotes as "traditionally American." Gingrich sees nothing wrong with letting children starve and watching people go without food. This, he thinks, is the meaning of the American "work ethic." Gingrich urges the most draconian of measures to be taken against the poor, without ever offering them employment and educational opportunities. What Gingrich advocates is not a shift away from the welfare state to an "opportunity" state; instead, his policies will cause deepening poverty and foster social indifference to the harm created.

But beneath all the attacks on the poor is a deeper agenda: to benefit the corporations and the wealthy business leaders who bankrolled Gingrich's rise to power. The "Personal Responsibility Act" is the Contract with America's euphemism for taking money away from the poor and diverting it to defense contractors and wealthy investors. Throwing people off welfare not only saves the government money, but it increases the number of untrained people who are desperate for employment and who are willing to work at a sub-poverty wage.[2] The Republicans declared that they would "end welfare as we know it," and make it a "helping hand rather than a handout." In reality, nothing like this will happen. Welfare will continue exactly as we know it, but the poor will be made even poorer as welfare cuts get used to subsidize a tax cut for the wealthy. It is precisely because Gingrich's troops oppose anti-poverty programs that welfare is doomed to continue for a long time in its present state. By perpetuating a system in which large numbers of children grow up in poverty—without hope, without opportunity—the Republican Revolution's "helping hand" is really just a shove into deeper poverty.

The poorest Americans bore the brunt of the Republican attack on government. On March 24, 1995, the House passed the welfare reform bill, repealing the Food Stamp Act, the Child Nutrition Act, the National School Lunch

Act, the Emergency Food Assistance Act, and other federal programs. Block grants—with a $69 billion cut over five years—would replace the programs which affect millions of children and women. As conservative Senator Rick Santorum (R-PA.) observed, "you're going to have millions of women and children with absolutely no support out there."[3]

Preventing the Crime of Poverty: Filling Up Orphanages

Gingrich's Contract represents the most radical plan to strip social programs for the poor in American history. The Contract specifically prohibited or cut aid to children if their mothers were unmarried and under age 18; were legal immigrants; did not know the identity of the father; or had been on welfare for 60 months in their lifetimes. Although Gingrich later dropped the ban on welfare for legal immigrants because he considered it too extreme, the rest of the plan was dramatic enough. The Department of Health and Human Services estimated that as many as five million children could be denied benefits under the Gingrich plan.

Gingrich is clearly aware that his plan will cause devastating poverty for those who are cut off from government support. He came up with an answer for the massive number of children whose poor mothers cannot find jobs: orphanages. Like many of Gingrich's ideas, the orphanage solution was conceived while watching a movie: *Boy's Town*, a glamorized portrayal of an all-white world where children learn American values from a caring (private) charity. When the cable network TNT showed *Boy's Town*, Gingrich introduced the movie by declaring, "I can't imagine a better antidote to the modern welfare state than the sense of love, caring, and spirituality conveyed in this movie."[4]

Ironically, Gingrich's defense of orphanages brought welfare reform full circle. The orphanage idea was abandoned earlier in this century because it was a failure—it proved too expensive and disruptive to families. AFDC originated from an Illinois mothers' pension program started in 1911, which enabled single mothers to keep their children at home instead of in high-cost state institutions like orphanages.[5] In 1935, Franklin Delano Roosevelt created the Aid to Dependent Children program as part of the Social Security Act, which gave a small monthly payment to single mothers. The percentage of children in institutions fell from 57.8% in 1933 to 31% in 1962 and 17.1% in 1989.[6]

Today, Gingrich wants us to return to the age when children were taken from their impoverished parents for the "crime" of being poor. These "poverty orphans" have parents whose only flaw is their failure to find a job. Republican welfare guru Charles Murray advocates converting all AFDC money into funding for orphanages; with the shift toward block grants that allow states to use federal money in any way they want, orphanages are one way to solve the welfare "problem." However, Gingrich was guilty of believing his own rhetoric about the cost of welfare when he suggested orphanages. Considering that Gingrich is too cheap to support the current meager level of welfare benefits, it is impossible to imagine where he would find the $47,000 per year (not including capital expenses) it costs for each child at Boy's Town.[7]

Realizing that orphanages were too unpopular and expensive to be a realistic alternative to welfare, the Republicans came up with another solution to deal with the problem of poor children: adoption. There are a large number of Americans who cannot have children and want to adopt, often spending tens of thousands of dollars to adopt children overseas. The Republicans proposed a highly popular tax credit that would encourage middle-class parents to take these expensive refugees from a childhood of poverty off the hands of the government. The law also banned attempts to match adoptions by race. Although it is wrong to enforce segregation in adoption, leaders of minority groups are understandably disturbed by the idea of children being taken away from impoverished black and Hispanic parents who are denied welfare assistance, while white middle-class families are paid with a large tax credit to adopt them. Republicans are entirely opposed to a much more effective solution to the adoption problem: creating a government program which would establish a national database of people seeking children, reducing the high cost of adoption.

But Gingrich has never explicitly identified either adoption or orphanages as the solution to the problem of impoverished children. The truth is that he has no solution, only a blind assumption that the problem will disappear once government gets out of the way. And the children who suffer under his policies will not be able to call Gingrich and ask for a favor, like the wealthy businessmen he courts endlessly. No, these children will suffer in silence from the debilitating effects of dire poverty, and when anyone points out the consequences of an inhuman social policy—drug abuse, crime, illiteracy, and an ever-increasing cycle of poverty—Gingrich and his allies will turn away and blame the tattered remains of the welfare state for all of our problems, refusing to stop until every last example of public compassion is destroyed and the social safety net is ripped to shreds.

Workfare Without Work

Perhaps the biggest scam of the Republican war on welfare was its promise to increase work by welfare recipients. The Contract originally promised day care programs and "support for work efforts" as part of welfare reform. In the end, the reforms were killed: funding for day care will actually be cut under the Republican plan, and the work program is one of the largest unfunded mandates ever imposed on the states. Although no money is provided for the work program, and the block grants for welfare programs are cut sharply, the

Republicans expect states to magically enable 50% of welfare recipients to work 35 hours a week by the year 2002. Welfare reformers have always found that truly changing welfare as we know it requires more—not less—money in order to provide work and education programs. Welfare reform on the cheap never works, but the Republicans are more concerned about saving money than saving people from poverty.

Workfare costs more than just mailing a check; it needs organization, supervision, and child care programs. According to the Congressional Budget Office, it will cost $15 billion a year to put 50% of welfare recipients to work. Although the Contract with America originally promised $10 billion to fund workfare, the money disappeared to fund the tax breaks planned by Republicans.[8] But states will only lose 5% of their funding for failing to meet the work participation goals; even if the federal government enforces this penalty, it will be far cheaper for states to simply ignore work programs than to try to meet this requirement with the Republican budget cuts.

Aid to Families with Dependent Children (AFDC) costs $14 billion a year, plus $11 billion in matching money from the states. It provides basic sustenance for 13 million poor Americans, two-thirds of whom are children. But Republicans spread the myth that welfare programs are giving recipients a life of lazy luxury. The average value of AFDC benefits in real dollars fell from $644 a month in 1970 to $380 in 1994—a drop of 41%. Welfare doesn't even come close to bringing anyone up to the poverty line. Nowhere in the country does welfare pay as much as a minimum wage job. Because of inflation, AFDC no longer provides an adequate amount to live on.[9]

There was no mandate from voters for Republicans to punish the poor. Most Americans believe that the poor don't get enough money from the government: a 1994 poll showed that 58% of U.S. citizens thought that welfare payments that bring families up to the federal poverty line (just under $15,000 at the time) were too low. Even when the value of welfare payments is taken into account, 21.5% of America's children live in poverty—more than 50% higher than any other industrialized nation in the West.[10] However, the American public doesn't get to pass welfare reform; the Republicans, desperate to find the budget cuts needed to finance corporate welfare and tax cuts, intended to destroy most of the programs designed to help the poor. The Center on Budget and Policy Priorities found that although "welfare" (broadly defined as discretionary spending for poor people) consisted of only $64 billion (12% of government discretionary spending), the Republicans planned $10.8 billion (63%) of its cuts to fall on welfare.[11]

The Root of All Evil

One of Gingrich's favorite myths is that welfare causes all of the crime and immorality in America. When he became Speaker, Gingrich declared that in the welfare debate he would wage "an entire 120-day offensive on language."[12] If he could make "welfare" the ultimate evil, then he might be able to avoid the politically uncomfortable fact that he was responsible for cutting programs to help the poor. What followed was an irrational and often incomprehensible attack on the "welfare state," which became the scapegoat for all the evils of the world.

In 1994, Gingrich claimed that Susan Smith's drowning of her two sons was a good reason to vote for Republicans—even though the most likely cause of her disturbed mind was the sexual abuse she suffered from her stepfather, who was a prominent figure in the local Christian Coalition.

Gingrich blamed the welfare state (along with daytime talk shows and tenured teachers) for the bizarre murder of a pregnant woman (and her two children) in Chicago and the abduction of her near-term baby, which was ripped out of her corpse: "What's gone wrong is a welfare system which subsidized people for doing nothing, a criminal system which tolerated drug dealers, and then we end up with the final culmination of a drug-addicted underclass with no sense of humanity, no sense of civilization, and no sense of the rules of life in which human beings respect each other."[13] In fact, the woman murdered was the welfare recipient. Gingrich admitted the remark was "dumb" but blamed the "elite media" for making it impossible to explain what he meant.[14]

Gingrich explained to the U.S. Chamber of Commerce that child abuse was caused by welfare programs because children would be beaten by their parents if they failed to fake a disability in order to get Supplemental Security Income: "They're being punished for not getting what they call crazy money, or stupid money. We are literally having children suffering child abuse so they can get a check for their parents." Naturally, Gingrich's solution to this imaginary problem was to cut welfare spending, not to stop child abuse.[15]

Most of Gingrich's attacks on welfare were so irrational that a logic teacher would give him a failing grade. In September 1995, Gingrich blamed the murder of a three-year-old child in Los Angeles on Lyndon Johnson's "Great Society" programs, which he called "a 30-year experiment in destroying America.[16]

Gingrich also declared, "If you are comfortable with 4-year-olds being killed and you are comfortable with 11-year-olds being buried with their teddy bears, and you think your money is being spent intelligently, you don't need us. But if you are sick of the carnage and sick of the debt and sick of the waste, we would like to work with you to change it."[17] Gingrich never bothered to explain how a government safety net led to the murder of four-year-old children, but he continued to spread misinformation. He stated that "800 babies a year" were left in dumpsters in Washington, D.C. alone (the actual number was four, which were highly publicized cases), and blamed welfare policy, which he claimed was telling "a 13-year-old drug addict who's pregnant, 'Put your baby in the dumpster; that's O.K.'"[18] Gingrich imagines that welfare encourages teenage girls to have children so that they can get free money and housing. But if welfare created these incentives, why would teenage mothers leave their highly profitable babies in dumpsters?

These stories are the '90s version of Reagan fairy tales about welfare mothers driving Cadillacs: then, as now, the parables are designed to portray welfare as the cause of social ills. But whatever sweet finesse Reagan's lies had, Gingrich's barely coherent ramblings sound as though Darth Vader accidentally got on the bus in *The Electric Kool Aid Acid Test*.

Welfare mothers are not having children to get government checks. States provide between $40 and $65 per month for each additional child, which is far less than the cost of raising a kid. The average tax deduction for each child is more than that amount (and will be greater with a $500 tax credit), but neither tax breaks nor welfare cause people to breed like rabbits to make more money. Women, whether poor or rich, usually have children for non-monetary reasons—they want children or they get pregnant accidentally—and the idea that a eugenics program can be created via the tax code and welfare limits is ridiculous. The results of the Republican plans will be tax breaks which the rich can make the most of and welfare cuts forcing more children into deeper poverty. Over the course of a generation, this will inevitably lead to more poverty, illiteracy, teen pregnancy, crime, and, ironically enough, more welfare recipients.

Lying with Statistics: The Myth that Welfare Causes Illegitimacy

In his April 7, 1995 address to the nation at the culmination of his first 100 days in office, Gingrich declared that "welfare spending now exceeds $300 billion a year" (a completely false figure) and complained that "despite all the trillions that have been spent since 1970, the number of children in poverty has increased 40 percent." Gingrich then pulled out a chart which showed that "welfare spending goes up and so does children born outside marriage. Year by year they track each other."

Yet there is no evidence whatsoever for Gingrich's illogical assertion that welfare spending causes poverty or illegitimacy. In fact, contrary to what Gingrich thinks, welfare spending has gone down while poverty and the number of children born outside of marriage have skyrocketed. Spending for AFDC fell from 1.4% of the federal budget in 1974 to 1.1% in 1994. When adjusted for inflation, the real value of family assistance (AFDC, food stamps, housing subsidies) fell dramatically in the past two decades.[19]

All the empirical evidence shows that cutting welfare, not increasing welfare, leads to higher teen pregnancy and poverty rates. If welfare benefits cause teen pregnancy, then how does one account for the fact that the nation's highest teenage pregnancy rate is in Mississippi, the state which also provides the lowest welfare payments (only $120 a month for a family of three)? Among the states with the highest welfare benefits, 14 out of 16 have below-average teen pregnancy rates. Between 1985 and 1991, teenage pregnancy rates rose in 24 of the 25 states with the lowest benefits.[20] If welfare causes teen pregnancy, why is the rate of teen births in the U.S. (97 per 1,000) much higher than in countries like Canada (40), Sweden (35), Denmark (25), and the Netherlands (10), where welfare benefits are dramatically higher?[21]

Gingrich draws a line connecting welfare benefits and single mothers as if there were an absolute cause-and-effect relationship, when the evidence is exactly the opposite. Even an anti-welfare zealot like Charles Murray admits, "It seems likely that welfare will be found to cause some portion of illegitimacy, but not a lot."[22] In fact, Murray was also wrong. High welfare spending has not been found to cause any portion of illegitimacy. But low welfare spending has been connected to increased illegitimacy. Sociologist Mike Males found that in the five states with the most generous welfare payments, the teen birth rate was 5.5 per 100, while the five least generous states averaged more than twice as many teenagers giving birth: 11.5 per 100. According to Males, 15 to 20% of the teen births were, statistically speaking, linked to low welfare payments.[23]

Why is Gingrich so wrong about the connection between welfare and teen pregnancy? Conservatives think women have children because they're greedy people trying to live off the government. Gingrich's complete misunderstanding of why people have children makes it impossible for him to create a rational social policy. The truth is that a life spent in poverty, not the allure of sub-poverty welfare payments, creates the conditions that lead to teenage women having children. And when the Republicans, ignorant of all the sociological evidence, cut back even more on welfare and thereby increase poverty in America, they are actually exacerbating the social problems they pretend to solve.

We could, of course, pursue Gingrich's politics of cruelty and conduct an experiment on our youngest citizens by ending welfare spending to see if they starve. But it seems much more logical to realize that we know what's wrong with welfare. All welfare experts know that there are flaws in the welfare system that need to be dealt with, but they also know that cutting the budget is the greatest barrier to true welfare reform. Instead of encouraging innovation, budget cuts mean that the poor will get poorer, and will be further deprived of the few opportunities they have.

Yet Gingrich promotes the delusion that welfare spending is the cause of poverty rather than one of the few counterweights to it: "The more tax money we spend on welfare, the more children who are born without benefit of family and without strong bonds of love and nurturing."[24] Of course, this kind of Orwellian lie—compassion is cruel, and cruelty is compassionate—is necessary because Gingrich cannot admit the truth to himself or the country: he is cutting welfare to save money, it will cause pain and suffering, and he doesn't really care as long as his corporate donors keep him in power.

The irony is that much of what Gingrich says is true: the welfare system has largely failed, and we need to replace it with a system to increase opportunity. But there is an enormous gap between the message and the messenger. Gingrich's welfare reform sounds good on the surface; his actual program is a fraud, promising results he knows it will never deliver, and banishing the poor to deeper poverty and fewer opportunities.

By disguising his budget cuts as humanitarian measures, by blaming welfare payments for all the evils in America, Gingrich is trying to evade moral responsibility for his actions. If welfare were truly the source of all evil, it would be easy enough to eliminate it and save both money and America's future. But the truth is that America's social problems are not caused by the welfare state, and cutting welfare will only make problems caused by poverty even worse.

Destroying the Safety Net: Undermining Social Programs

Cutting social programs is one of the dumbest ways to try to balance the budget, because the poverty that results from eliminating the social safety net ends up costing all of us much more than the price of a few small programs to help the poor. The Republicans proposed turning the Supplemental Nutrition Program for Women, Infants, and Children (WIC) and the food stamp program into block grants. They wanted to cut the $24.5 billion food stamps program by 15%, inevitably reducing the amount of assistance to the poor. Since food stamps are directly allocated to individuals, it is difficult to imagine how any money could be saved by greater efficiency, and putting states in charge of food stamp programs might actually increase fraud by enabling people to receive food stamps from several states at once.

Many of the cuts in social programs will end up costing the American people much more money in the long run. A House panel eliminated $186 million from a program to provide housing with social services for people with AIDS, but as a result many people with the disease will end up in much more expensive hospital beds.[25] Other cuts in investments for education and nutrition will have a similar long-term cost in reduced productivity and higher health-care costs.

Congress intends to finance the Republican tax cuts by undermining the infrastructure of America, both human and physical. The Senate and the House voted to reduce operating assistance for public transit by 44%, cutting it from $710 million in 1995 to $400 million in 1996. Although the Republicans claim that they want to move people from welfare to work, they are destroying the public transportation system which is essential for low-income workers to get to jobs. Even though buses and trains serve a public good (and save money) by reducing traffic, pollution, and wear and tear on highways, Gingrich and the Republicans want to eliminate public subsidies.[26] While Republicans seek to cut back on "public transportation"—buses and trains—they have no plans to reduce the subsidies that disproportionately benefit businesses and the wealthy: the subsidized airline user fees (which amount to $11 billion a year) and massive road construction projects.

The Gingrich welfare "plan" is really a plan for funding tax cuts, not a strategy for helping the poor. The Republicans want to "help" teenage mothers by punishing them for having children. The basic concept is simple: if you punish someone harshly enough, it will make them stop. Still, executing thieves in the old days didn't stop theft for a very obvious reason: it didn't address the underlying poverty that prompted people to steal. Punishing young unmarried women and their children for the crime of being poor is hardly the way to create the conditions for people to lift themselves out of poverty.

One of the cruelest provisions in the Contract with America cuts welfare to any teenage mother below the age of 18 who does not live with her family. According to the Republicans, welfare is subsidizing women who resent their parents and want an apartment of their own. Even though a 1990 study found that only 4% of mothers under 18 live entirely on their own without any other adults, Gingrich treats teen mothers on welfare as an epidemic that must be stopped by punishing women for sexual misdeeds. Not a word is said in the Contract with America about the epidemic of sexual abuse and rape that is affecting young women. Only 6% of fourteen-year-olds report having had sexual intercourse; two-thirds of them were victims of sexual assault.[27] Nor does the Contract with America mention the fact that a large number of teen mothers are abused by adult male family members. A 1994 study determined that 70% of pregnant teenagers receiving social service aid had been sexually abused at home. A 1992 study in Washington found that two-thirds of teenage mothers had been sexually abused and 70% had been physically abused.[28] Yet Gingrich wants to promote "family values" by forcing poor young women on welfare to stay in homes were they are beaten and sexually assaulted.

Making lives more miserable as punishment for having children will do little to change behavior because it's clear to anyone who thinks about it (except Newt Gingrich) that poor women don't have additional children in order to line their pockets with ill-gotten government money. If welfare mothers really wanted to get rich on government largesse, they'd pick a much more profitable source of federal spending—defense contracts, for example.

The Republicans believe that there is a "welfare trap" which makes "welfare more attractive than work to many families."[29] However, welfare does not snare people; poverty and joblessness are the trap. The problem with welfare is not the lack of a work ethic, but the lack of jobs. Until the Republicans—or Democrats, for that matter—create real programs to address the lack of educational opportunities, the lack of child care for young parents, and the lack of available jobs, all of their promises to transform welfare are transparent lies.

It is certain that Gingrich's welfare plan will make the lives of poor children and their parents much worse. Plans to cut off welfare after five years (in a lifetime) bring up a serious question: what will happen to the parents (and their children) who are cut off from welfare? Will they starve? Will all of them get jobs? It is possible that private charities will give enough to prevent death by starvation, but if the problem is too much charity, how will private gifts be an improvement over government programs? Of course, it is unlikely that millions of children will face starvation and homelessness because of the Republican plans. But certainly some will, and many more will suffer the damaging effects of malnutrition and deprivation, while private charities will be devastated by the cuts in government programs that support them, and unable to meet the increased need from the poor people whom the government refuses to help.

Although Gingrich hopes that private charity will replace the lost federal dollars, this is highly unlikely. The wealthiest Americans give only 3.3% of their income to charity, and that figure includes "donations" like the money given to Gingrich's Progress and Freedom Foundation.[30] Gingrich contends that "decentralized charities that have a sense of spirit and passion are vital," while "bureaucracies that are anonymous are devastating."[31] Ironically, the private charities that Gingrich glorifies are likely to be among the worst victims of the Contract because most of them rely on government grants to subsidize their charitable operations. A large portion of federal welfare spending is already "privatized" in the hands of local charities.

It would be one thing if Gingrich were planning to punish able-bodied adults who refused to work despite employment opportunities, but the majority of the people he plans to throw into deeper poverty are children. Of 13 million AFDC recipients, nine million are children and most of the adults are mothers with young children. Gingrich has no plan to create jobs for these women. He has no plan to make sure they have inexpensive, quality child care available so that they can afford to take a job. His free market safety net has a large hole at the bottom.

Vignettes from a Man in Bed with the Christian Coalition—Females in a Ditch

As if Gingrich's poverty policy of women and children first wasn't bad enough, the Speaker also spews out admonitions about the need for "family values." Yet his personal history is checkered with former lovers now disgusted by him, former friends who feel betrayed by his move into the Washington establishment, and a former wife he abandoned for the sake of political opportunism.

In morality, as in politics, the standards he stridently demands of others just aren't meant to be applied to himself. Gingrich was much more of a participant in America's moral problems than someone on the moral high ground qualified to preach about their solutions. He secretly started dating his geometry teacher during his senior year in high school.[32] As a freshman at Emory University, he continued to pursue her and married her after he finished his first year of college. But when his political career was advancing, he decided she was "too frumpy" for a Washington politician.

In his 1974 campaign, Gingrich's slogan was "Newt's family is like your family." But Kip Carter, Gingrich's former campaign treasurer, was once walking Gingrich's daughters back from a football game and saw a car with "Newt in the passenger seat and one of the guys' wives with her head in his lap going up and down. Newt kind of turned and gave me this little-boy smile." During the 1974 campaign, Carter notes, Gingrich had an affair with a volunteer: "We'd have won in 1974 if we could have kept him out of the office, screwing her on the desk." Former Gingrich staffer Dorothy Crews reports that "he had girlfriends—some serious, some trivial."[33]

Anne Manning had an affair with Gingrich during the 1976 campaign when she was married to one of Gingrich's colleagues at West Georgia College. She now calls him "morally dishonest." Manning reports, "we had oral sex. He prefers that modus operandi because then he can say, 'I never slept with her.'" He also told her, "If you ever tell anybody about this, I'll say you're lying."[34] Another married former friend says that Gingrich repeatedly made advances to her, and once tried to seduce her while visiting to comfort her after the death of a relative.[35] Gingrich has never denied any of the stories about his adultery.

At the same time that Gingrich was routinely cheating on his wife, he used the rhetoric of family values to win an election to Congress. During the 1978 campaign, his office put out a pamphlet that declared, "Let Our Family Represent Your Family." His campaign advertising showed a photo of Gingrich, comparing him with his opponent, Virginia Shapard. "Newt will take his family to Washington and keep them together," read the ad. "Virginia will go to Washington and leave her husband and children in the care of a nanny."[36]

By 1980, he was having another affair, with Marianne, the woman he would marry after divorcing his first wife. By that time, Gingrich had decided to end his marriage. Carter notes that when Gingrich told him that he planned to divorce his first wife, Gingrich had said, "The bottom line is, Jackie isn't young enough or pretty enough to be the wife of the president of the United States." And, "she's got cancer."[37] Gingrich denies he ever said it. But it's perfectly in line with his history of political calculation and brutal honesty. His wife did not have the image he needed to rise further in politics; she was a burden to him now that he was finally in Congress and could use his position to get re-elected. Newt's mother reports that he said, "I'm either going to get a divorce or I'm going to have a nervous breakdown. I can't take it." But his mother added, "I've often wondered if she had taken that weight off maybe they would still be together."[38] When Gingrich's own mother suspects that Newt dumped his sick wife because she weighed too much, it shows how low his character is—and how much political calculation affected every decision in his life.

The decision was particularly cruel because of everything Newt had done to invoke the importance of his family. Newt had pursued Jackie when she was his high school geometry teacher, and the two had a secret affair together. While Newt was in his first year of college, he went to Atlanta to tell Jackie he wanted to marry her, and eventually did so at the end of his freshman year. But Newt quickly grew bored with his old conquests. For a decade, Jackie's salary as a teacher had kept the family afloat while Newt finished graduate school and pursued his political career. Jackie had campaigned constantly on Newt's behalf, devoting her life to his political career and making handwritten pleas for donations to support "a good husband, a good father, and a good Christian."[39] When he demanded a divorce, she pleaded with him to work out their problems, but Newt refused.

Newt informed Jackie that he wanted a divorce in April 1980, when Jackie was suffering from uterine cancer. In September 1980, a day after Jackie had surgery for the third time and was in the hospital recovering, Newt came to her hospital room and started discussing the terms of their divorce. According to former friend Lee Howell, "Newt came up there with his yellow legal pad, and he had a list of things on how the divorce was going to be handled."[40] Jackie threw him out of the hospital room. Newt had good reason to worry about the divorce. Despite a substantial Congressional salary, by 1980 Newt had a $34,000 debt, and became one of the "deadbeat dads" he would later rail against and pass legislation to stop. Jackie eventually had to take Newt to court before he would give her adequate support. He was paying her only $400 a month (plus $40 for allowances for his daughters), the same amount he listed spending on himself for food and dry cleaning. Members of Gingrich's church took up a collection to help Jackie with food and utilities bills.

Gingrich preaches, "Our culture should be sending over and over the message that young people should abstain from sexual intercourse until marriage, that work is a part of life, and that any male who does not take care of his children is a bum and deserves no respect."[41] That's a remarkable statement from a man who repeatedly cheated on his first wife, divorced her, and then failed to pay the alimony and child support he owed her. Jackie took Newt to court again in 1993 because he "failed to pay alimony on a timely basis" and hadn't kept up his life insurance policy as required. Even apparent offers of generosity only concealed his selfishness. In March 1994, he negotiated to raise the monthly alimony he paid her by $350, in exchange for Jackie renouncing her right to any of his future added income; by the end of the year, he had signed a $4.5 million book contract.[42]

Gingrich is infamous for his difficulties in dealing with strong women, as exemplified by what he told his mother about Hillary Rodham Clinton: "She's a bitch." In graduate school, he reportedly "got very upset when a woman graduate student joined one of his seminars."[43] One male former campaign supporter, Glyn Thomas, reports that when he turned down a job in Gingrich's office because of the low salary, Gingrich replied, "Well, I'm sorry you can't...but I could probably hire two women for that anyway."[44]

In 1989, during a troubled period of his marriage to Marianne, he read *Men Who Hate Women and the Women Who Love Them* and cried because he saw himself: "I really spent a period of time where, I suspect, I cried three or four times a week. I found frightening pieces that related to...my own life." He admitted to the *Washington Post* that he and Marianne had separated from time to time, and he calmly calculated the odds of their marriage surviving at 53-47.[45] Newt complained about Marianne because "she doesn't gear up every morning to be a Viking!" They argued about trivial things like what to have for dinner because, Newt admitted, "It's just the habit of dominance, the habit of being the center of my staff and the center of the news media."[46]

Newt's ideas about male dominance cause him to reach strange conclusions about women. A few days after becoming Speaker of the House, he told his "Renewing American Civilization" class: "If combat means living in a ditch, females have biological problems staying in a ditch for 30 days because they get infections and they don't have upper body strength. I mean some do, but they're relatively rare. On the other hand, men are basically little piglets, you drop them in the ditch, they roll around in it, it doesn't matter, you know. These things are very real."[47] Gingrich was actually trying to pose as an open-minded feminist when he said this, explaining why women should be able to participate more in a modern, high-tech army than men (a man "gets very, very frustrated sitting in a chair all the time because males are biologically driven to go out and hunt giraffes"). Gingrich is too smart a politician to reveal his neolithic views about women, knowing that it is politically necessary to attract female voters in this emancipated age. But sexism pervades much of Gingrich's decision-making—from blaming single mothers for all the problems in the world to his opposition to family leave and child care proposals.

While unceremoniously dumping the "family" he used to get elected, and throughout all of his sexual improprieties and marital problems, Newt remained a leading advocate of family values. Gingrich defends the practice of allowing members of Congress (unlike all other government employees) to keep the frequent-flier miles they earn on public business for their own personal use as a "pro-family benefit" because, he claims, that for young, impoverished congressmen, it "allows their family to come to Washington." Gingrich protected the frequent-flier miles perk from being eliminated in the Congressional Accountability Act, although perhaps his decision was motivated by the fact that he himself had accumulated 1.2 million frequent-flyer miles on taxpayer-funded airplane rides.[48]

In 1992, Gingrich tried to paint the Democratic Party as anti-family, pointing to Woody Allen's relationship with Mia Farrow's adopted daughter. "I call this the Woody Allen plank," said Gingrich. "It's a weird situation, and it fits the Democratic Party platform perfectly. If a Democrat used the word 'family' to raise children in Madison Square Garden, half their party would have rebelled, and the other would not vote. Woody Allen had non-incest with his non-daughter because they were a non-family." As conservative commentator George Will observed about the comment, "That would cost Gingrich his reputation for seriousness if he had one."[49] For Gingrich, "family values" is just another political tool, one more piece of rhetoric used to bash the opposition in his climb to power.

Gingrich's "pro-family" rhetoric is pure hypocrisy. He complains about the immorality caused by the welfare state, but he is reticent in explaining his own philandering and his cruel treatment of his first wife. He preaches family values to underprivileged people who have far more integrity than he has ever displayed. And he defends an assortment of personal and corporate benefits under the guise of the "family," from protecting his own frequent-flier miles to concealing a tax cut for the rich as "pro-family" by including a $500 per child tax credit. Gingrich's own promiscuity and adultery would not be quite so fascinating were it not for the intensity of his lectures to the American people about the moral decline supposedly caused by the welfare state.

Chapter 8

Dirty Politics: Gingrich's Betrayal of Environmentalism

As a child, Newt Gingrich made the news as an animal-lover: at the age of 10, he approached the mayor of Harrisburg, Pennsylvania with a proposal to start a publicly-supported zoo. In his teens, he convinced a local TV station to give him a five-minute weekly spot for him to lecture the public about zoology.[1]

When Gingrich first ran for Congress in 1974, he was a committed environmentalist running as a liberal Republican against an old conservative Southern Democrat. Teaching at West Georgia College, Gingrich helped start the Environmental Studies program and even led students on a field trip to a "famous industrial-pollution site." Gingrich was endorsed by the League of Conservation Voters and the Sierra Club, and he criticized the pollution spread by a local copper wire manufacturer named Southwire.[2]

How times have changed. Two decades later, Gingrich is the leader of a Republican movement to destroy the Environmental Protection Agency, gut regulations that protect the environment, and allow corporate America unimpeded access (often subsidized by the federal government) to our natural resources. In 1994, Gingrich was one of only nine representatives who got a zero rating from the League of Conservation Voters on environmental issues.[3] And Southwire, the polluter that young Newt once condemned, became one of his leading contributors, and perhaps his most important constituent.

Gordon Johnson, who was the Executive Vice-President for Manufacturing at Southwire, remembers Gingrich as an early critic of polluters: "Newt was anti-business; he was going after Southwire, saying it was polluting, a big business in a small community. He was an environmentalist." Gingrich reconciled with Southwire after visiting its plant in the mid-1970s, and hearing Southwire's side of the pollution story. This was around the time that company president Roy Richards started giving him money (Richards gave to both parties in his district). After Gingrich's pro-Southwire conversion, Johnson also contributed money to his campaign, although he questioned whether political pragmatism motivated Gingrich's change of heart. The People's Bank of Carrollton, which Richards also ran, allowed the Gingrich campaign to roll over its debts without paying them back. Gingrich's office was in a bank-owned building, and he was not evicted despite though he fell far behind on the rent. Three bank officials personally loaned Gingrich's campaign $750 in 1976 and were never paid back. Richards also paid Gingrich thousands of dollars when he needed the money desperately, hiring him to give motivational speeches to bank employees.[4]

In 1980, Gingrich voted against the Superfund legislation because it required polluters to pay part of the clean-up cost for hazardous waste sites; that same year, Southwire made its first PAC donation to Gingrich. In the past decade, Southwire's leaders have given $18,000 to Gingrich's campaigns. Company president James Richards has donated $80,200 to GOPAC. Gary Crook, a top aide, reports that in the early 1990s, Southwire officials came to Gingrich's office and "helped reorganize the place to make our office staff more responsive."[5]

In 1992, Southwire and a South Carolina subsidiary were convicted of violating federal environmental laws. They pled guilty to knowingly failing to "report the distribution of hazardous waste." The company combined 3,400 tons of hazardous waste with fertilizer and illegally sent it to Bangladesh. Southwire and its subsidiary were ordered to take out full-page newspaper ads in apology and pay a $1 million fine, a record in South Carolina. Since then, Southwire has paid hundreds of thousands of dollars in fines for more than two dozen civil actions against them. But Gingrich refuses to criticize the company, calling them "good citizens" and blaming the crime on "the complexity of our environmental and OSHA regulations." Southwire has also been penalized by the Occupational Safety and Health Administration and the National Labor Relations Board for safety and labor violations. While he refused to criticize Southwire's actions, Gingrich claimed it would be "irresponsible to not have a concern for that particular corporation." Gingrich admitted to helping Southwire in a Customs dispute, writing the Department of Commerce and urging them "to pressure the Japanese to open their markets to aluminum conductor imports," one of Southwire's key products. Gingrich claimed, "I would be derelict in my duties if I did not do so."[6] As Gingrich noted in 1989: "Southwire automatically has my attention every morning."[7]

From Environmentalism to De-Regulation: The Political Odyssey of Newt Gingrich

Early on, Gingrich was a supporter of the environmental movement in Congress. In 1979, he voted for the Alaska Lands Act, which protected natural resources from oil drilling. In 1983, he was one of the first members of Congress to call for the resignation of Interior Secretary James Watt.[8] He co-sponsored the Clean Air Act and the Endangered Species Act, votes that he now renounces.[9] Nevertheless, he has maintained the pretense of defending the environment. In 1991 and 1992 he co-sponsored commemorations of Earth Day—of course, in those same years he also co-sponsored "National Convenience Store Appreciation Week," so it was hardly much of a commitment.

What, Me Worry?

Today, Speaker Gingrich keeps a $5,000 model of a Tyrannasaurus rex skull from the Smithsonian in his office—and he seems determined to add to the extinct species list. Last year, he put on his triceratops tie to talk about the environment. The triceratops is extinct, he said, but "life is like that." According to Gingrich, conservationists in the Paleozoic Age couldn't have stopped the forces of nature with a "Society for the Preservation of Troglodytes." And besides, he says, the Earth will tilt "at some point in the next 50,000 years" which will "change totally the ecosystems you're prepared currently to spend endless quantities to save." Gingrich says, "I'm very much in favor of the environment"—he only opposes the "static preservationists" who want to "regulate the human race out of existence."[10]

Here, Gingrich's New Age, futurist lingo serves him well: since the environment is constantly changing, anyone who objects to human modification of it—such as poisoning a lake—is simply stuck in the Second Wave static industrial age model of life. Gingrich seems unconcerned about the fact that natural changes in the environment over vast stretches of time are completely different from the massive destruction caused by human activity in the past century.

He claims to be a champion of the natural world, proudly displaying his activity at Zoo Atlanta. But the people Gingrich has put in charge of natural resources are not so coy about their hatred of the environment and those who would protect it. Rep. Don Young (R-AK), who Newt appointed as chair of the House Natural Resources Committee (and whose first act was to remove "Natural" from the committee's name), has condemned environmentalists as a "waffle-stomping, Harvard-graduating, intellectual bunch of idiots" and "the most despicable group I've ever heard of." Young proposes eliminating the National Forest Service, creating a National Parks Closure Commission, and turning the Arctic National Wildlife Refuge into an oil pumping project.[11] When Rep. Ralph Regula (R-OH) was being considered for the House Interior Committee's appropriations subcommittee, he had to assure his colleagues that he was thoroughly pro-business, telling the *Washington Post*, "My environmental record wasn't all that great."[12]

Newt's majority whip, Tom DeLay, is the point man on the environment. A former exterminator, DeLay doesn't believe that chlorofluorocarbons harm the ozone layer. He says it's a "media scare" and has introduced legislation to end US compliance with the Montreal Protocol, under which most of the world is committed to eliminating chemicals like CFCs that destroy the ozone layer.[13] DeLay complains about regulations on DDT and other "safe" pesticides: "They banned chemicals and drove up the cost of doing business." He also urges repeal of the Clean Air Act of 1990, and, along with Rep. Bud Shuster (R-PA.), refers to the EPA as "the environmental Gestapo."[14]

Rep. Jim Hansen (R-UT), chair of the National Parks, Forests, and Lands Subcommittee, is author of the "Utah Wilderness Act," a bill allowing the sale of most of Utah's public land. The bill would take 22 million acres of Bureau of Land Management wilderness and designate only 1.8 million acres as protected, permanently preventing the remaining land from ever being designated as a protected wilderness. Roads would be maintained and motor vehicles permitted anywhere in the wilderness, regardless of its environmental impact. Although conservationists in Utah have proposed keeping 5.7 million acres of the desert land as protected wilderness, the Republicans in the House are anxious to get rid of environmentally precious land—to raise money for their tax cuts.[15]

The ideology behind the Republican attack on the environment is not a belief that the free market will solve environmental problems, but that there are no problems to solve. After all, unless you think the destruction of the environment is a bad thing that should be minimized by regulation, you don't need the government (or anyone else) to stop it. According to this mindset, government regulations protecting the environment are, like all regulations, the tools of anti-capitalist villains that stifle economic growth. Republicans have abandoned the concept of a social good. In their view, the free market is the absolute god which we shall worship, no matter what damage it does to us collectively.

The Environmental Destruction Act

The Job Creation and Wage Enhancement Act, Gingrich's Orwellian title for the bill which would gut environmental laws and safety regulations, was a central feature of the Contract with America. The Republican agenda is a simple one: end protection of habitats for endangered species, freeze the current list to prevent new additions, cut EPA funding by one-third and enforcement by one-half, exempt oil refineries from clear-air regulations, reduce funding for national parks, open the Arctic National Wildlife Refuge to oil drillers, exempt polluters from paying part of the Superfund cleanup of toxic sites, end the ban on tuna caught in nets that also kill dolphins, allow mining companies to buy public land at nominal rates, and transfer national parks and forest to state governments friendly to commercial interests. As Rep. George Miller (D-CA) says, "This is the most systematic and comprehensive assault on the environment and the environmental laws of this nation in the history of the country."[16]

The House should follow the principle expressed by Gingrich on July 13, 1995, when he suddenly appeared on the House floor to plead for the preservation of an $800,000 appropriation to African and Asian nations to help them stop the poaching of the rhinoceros, tiger, and elephant. Gingrich declared, "We don't have to cut mindlessly just because we want to get to a balanced budget." The House voted 289-132 in favor of saving the Speaker's pet program, heeding his warning about the danger of cutting aid to the environment: "Don't allow them to disappear and join the dinosaur skull in my office."[17]

But saving endangered species was not the goal of the Republicans in Congress; one bill imposed a ban on adding new species to the endangered species list, even if they are seriously threatened. Congress also passed (and Clinton signed into law) a bill to prohibit unfunded mandates on state and local governments. Unless the federal government provides complete funding for any environmental regulation (or other law, such as the "motor voter" act), state and local governments are now free to ignore it. The unfunded mandate law is the ticking bomb in the Republican agenda. Although it will not affect laws already in force, if the Republicans are able to decimate environmental regulations, the unfunded mandates law will prevent them from being reinstated later, when the public becomes aware of the enormous harm caused by its policies. The unfunded mandates law is the main Republican scheme to prevent all future regulation of business.

Dead Meat: The Unsafe Contract

The Republican Contract with America's attempt to halt regulation will lead to serious harm by exposing Americans to dangerous products. According to the Department of Agriculture, contaminated meat and poultry cause 4,000 deaths and five million illnesses each year. However, the current meat inspection program relies solely upon sight, touch, and smell inspections which cannot detect deadly bacteria like E. coli and salmonella. A new meat inspection process using microbial testing could stop up to 90% of these sicknesses.[18]

Even though the proposed regulations are a vast improvement over the outdated system, the anti-regulatory climate in Washington means that they will be delayed for several years, costing thousands of lives. A Republican bill banning new regulations would not only keep meat dangerous, but it would also stop improved testing of seafood, repeal the ban on adding carcinogins to food, and stop the EPA from removing cancer-causing pesticides from the market. The ban has serious effects on the health of Americans. After there were 100,000 cases of iron poisoning in children from 1988 to 1993, the FDA planned to put warnings on iron supplements. The FDA rule will now be dropped or delayed by several years.[19]

Senate Republicans rejected a Democratic amendment to the moratorium on Federal regulations that would allow the Agriculture Department to pass new rules to stop E. coli bacteria in meat. The Senate passed an amendment allowing emergency actions to deal with the E. coli problem, but the proposed Agriculture rules on meat inspection would not be emergency measures.[20]

The E. coli scandal was so egregious that Gingrich and the allies of the meat industry felt obliged to back down, promising that they would make an exception for it. The Republican bill included a provision requiring the Agriculture Department to rewrite its rules and negotiate with industry groups. In order to avoid the spectacle of delaying changes in meat inspection rules, Republicans agreed to allow the regulations to be changed. But under pressure from the Republicans, Agriculture Secretary Dan Glickman agreed to hold several meetings with industry lobbyists to listen to their concerns.[21]

Takings for the Contract

The Private Property Rights Act passed by the House on March 3, 1995, required the federal government to compensate property owners whenever federal regulations lower the value of their property by more than 20%. A provision inserted by Western Republicans would also require the government to compensate farmers and miners if it stops subsidizing 90% of water costs from federal irrigation projects.[22]

The problem with this "takings" legislation is that it greatly expands the original idea of just compensation, which in the past always meant the physical seizure of land. If any regulation is a "taking," then almost all regulations, from zoning laws to pollution limits, could require restitution from the government. The assumption of Republicans is that the unregulated state, in which people are entitled to pollute the air and destroy the environment, is natural. Any limitation on the right to pollute is therefore a violation of property rights and must be compensated.

The consequences of this Republican plan would be disastrous to the environment. Almost any regulation could become too expensive for the government to enforce, particularly when the EPA budget is being severely cut back. And it would create a bizarre situation where property owners could repeatedly make money by having regulations imposed, lobbying to have them removed, and then having the regulations reinstated, with compensation provided each time.

Public opinion is wholeheartedly opposed to conservative efforts to leave the environment defenseless. In fact, most property owners want environmental regulations in order to maintain property values, which suffer when overdevelopment or destructive actions harm the surrounding area. Studies have found that 77% of real estate property owners possess nothing but their own house and lot, which makes up only 2% of all privately-owned land. It is the small minority of American families and corporations who have vast real estate holdings who are pressuring Congress to give them absolute power over the use of their land.[23]

But the views of the American public don't determine what laws are passed by Congress: money does. When it comes to the environment, the business of Republicans is business. Michael Kehs, an expert for Burson-Marsteller, a PR firm specializing in anti-environmental issues, was ebullient over Gingrich's victory and the help it would offer for the business community: "although the word 'environment' is never mentioned, many observers believe it's less a Contract with America than a contract on environmental busybodies."[24]

Lobbyists: Sleepless in Washington

The 1994 elections represented a takeover of Congress by business interests and the Congressmen who front for them. Where corporations once lobbied politicians to help them with legislation, after 1994, the lobbyists were writing the legislation themselves. The House Job Creation and Wage Enhancement Act included a provision requiring all agencies to cut through enormous amounts of red tape and cost/benefit analyses, with approval by "peer review" panels. The Republican law required that the panels "shall not exclude peer reviewers merely because they represent entities that may have a potential interest in the outcome"—in other words, lobbyists and business executives would get to decide the fate of regulations directly affecting them.[25]

Michael Bean of the Environmental Defense Fund noted, "The task of rewriting our nation's most important environmental laws is being done by the major corporate interests whose practices created much of the problem in the first place."[26] One of the most explicit examples came in 1995 when three lawyers from Hunton & Williams, a firm which contests environmental regulations for corporate clients including Philip Morris and electric utilities, led a briefing for Senate Judiciary Committee staff about the Republican bill on health and environmental laws. During the hearing, staff director Larry Block deferred to the lobbyist-lawyers sitting next to him for information on the sweeping environmental law reforms. David Vladek, director of the Public Citizen Litigation Group, noted that this was "a bill by big business, for big business, and of big business."[27] During a House Resources Subcommittee hearing, a lobbyist for irrigation companies sat with Republicans on the dias.[28]

Norman Mineta (D-CA) and Robert Borski (R-PA) reported that the process "has been limited almost exclusively to the regulated business community."[29] The House Transportation and Infrastructure Committee excluded Democrats but invited lobbyists from the Chemical Manufacturers Association and the Chlorine Chemistry Council into closed meetings where the clean water legislation was revised. The proposed House regulations would allow companies to dump liquid waste directly into sewers without removing poisonous chlorinated compounds and heavy metals.[30]

Corporations have formed innocuous-sounding lobbying groups to promote their agenda, and some of them are even funded by the EPA. In 1992, the EPA gave a $300,000 grant to the Water Environment Federation (WEF), a sewer operator lobbying group, to promote the use of sewer sludge as fertilizer (the money was used to hire a PR firm which offered advice on how to attack environmentalists and came up with a new word for sludge: biosolids). WEF supported the Republican Dirty Water Act because it would be "relaxing federal pre-treatment standards." Until recently, the sludge was classified as toxic waste, and much of the sludge currently being used on food crops contains pathogenic organisms and chemical contaminants. Toxic sludge was re-classified as fertilizer by more than doubling the allowable amounts of lead, arsenic, mercury, and chromium. Some sludge can be so contaminated that it would be banned from landfills by the EPA.[31] While environmentalists and the American public support much stronger efforts to pressure the EPA into enforcing environmental laws, the Republicans have shifted the agenda so that the fight is now simply to maintain the status quo.

A corporate propaganda group called Citizens for a Sound Economy (which includes General Motors, Amoco, Bell Atlantic, Citibank, and General Electric) sent C. Boyden Gray—former counsel to President Bush—to testify to a House subcommittee last year that FDA delay "kills American citizens". In reality, the FDA has sharply reduced the time to approve important new drugs. Gray accused delays in FDA approval of the drug Nitrazepam of causing nearly 4,000 deaths. Unfortunately, Gray didn't actually know what Nitrazepam was used to cure until Rep. Dick Durbin informed him: insomnia. Still, one can't blame Gray for being upset: death by sleeplessness must be a particularly painful demise.[32]

The attacks on regulation are rarely as comical as this. On the contrary, they raise a serious question about whether corporate profits can be put above public health. In the eyes of the Republicans, the best way to regulate potentially dangerous drugs is to sell them now, and let the lawsuits sort them out later. Not coincidentally, the Republicans in Congress have proposed new laws to sharply limit the damages that can be assessed when irresponsible companies sell dangerous products. The combination of deregulation and damage caps will be a nightmare for American consumers who are accustomed to safe products.

The consequences of deregulation can be severe. In 1983, the FDA under the Reagan Administration cut quality-control inspections of the blood industry by 50%.[33] The result was massive contamination of the blood supply with

AIDS, and the transmission of the HIV virus to thousands of people who received transfusions. The cost in medical expenses and lost wages—not to mention the value of human life—far exceeded the trivial amount of money saved by reducing regulations. A report by *Public Citizen* found that the FDA kept 47 drugs off the U.S. market that had been approved for sale in major European countries and then withdrawn because of safety problems.[34] One of the most famous public health crises—the 8000 deformed babies born because their mothers took the drug Thalidomide in the late 1950s—was almost completely avoided in America because regulations prevented an under-tested drug from reaching the market. Contrary to what C. Boyden Gray's employers and the Republicans in Congress believe, the threat to American lives comes from the free market, not the FDA bureaucracy.

Gingrich himself spun myths to denigrate government regulation. He condemned the EPA for imposing the "absurdly irrational" cost of ripping out asbestos, even though Gingrich has twice voted for such bills in the past and the EPA has opposed mandatory asbestos removal since 1990.[35] Gingrich claimed that the FDA was causing the deaths of heart attack victims by waiting to approve the Cardiopump, a device like a toilet plunger. On December 4, 1994, Gingrich appeared on *Meet the Press*, claiming that the Cardiopump "increases by 54 percent the number of people with CPR who get to the hospital and have a chance to recover." A gripping statistic. But turning to the facts, a study in the *Journal of the American Medical Association* a few months later found that the Cardiopump led to no significant improvement in survival over regular CPR. Moreover, the makers of the Cardiopump had not yet applied for FDA approval. By contrast, a device that had been proven effective at preventing heart attacks was approved in just six days.[36]

Grimm Fairytales of Regulation

Anti-environmentalist myths are regularly spread by right-wing pro-business think tanks and their allies in Congress. James DeLong of the Competitive Enterprise Institute wrote in the *New York Times* about the evils of environmental regulation, citing a forum held by Republican members of Congress at which it was claimed that the endangered Stephens' Kangaroo rat caused 30 homes to be destroyed in a California fire: Because one family was "not allowed to disturb the land in any way, the underbrush grew impenetrable and the kangaroo rats all left. This became evident after a fire, fueled by the uncut brush, destroyed the habitat, along with 29 nearby homes."[37] A General Accounting Office report found that "the loss of homes during the California fire was not related to the prohibition of disking in areas inhabited by the Stephens' Kangaroo rat." Disking—using heavy equipment to make fire breaks—threatens the rat by destroying vegetation in its habitat, but the GAO determined,

"We found no evidence to support the view that disking would have saved homes," since weed abatement had no connection to whether or not a home was destroyed.[38]

Rep. David McIntosh attacked the Occupational Safety and Health Administration (OSHA), claiming that it required dentists to confiscate baby teeth. But this is "absolutely not true," according to the agency. McIntosh refused to back down, saying "Don't believe OSHA. They'll lie to you." In fact, OSHA only requires that teeth—like anything that may be contaminated with blood—be handled properly. The Consumer Products Safety Commission was accused of recommending that all five-gallon buckets should be built to leak. The practical reason for this measure is that 500 babies have drowned in these buckets in the past 10 years. One possible solution for buckets used to carry solids in plastic liners was to put holes in the bottom to prevent reuse for liquids, but no regulations were ever issued. [39]

Regulate the Regulators

The House passed a bill in 1995 that would sharply reduce future regulations on business by requiring burdensome bureaucratic rules to be followed whenever a change in regulations is proposed. While the Republicans complained about too much government bureaucracy in other areas, when it comes to the environment or safety every regulation will require a rigorous assessment of risks and compliance costs certified by an independent peer review panel.

The irony is that the cost-benefits bill would actually impede efforts to overturn ineffective or harmful regulations. Regulators would be reluctant to overturn old regulations because of the difficulty in reinstating them.[40] But when the real aim is to obstruct needed regulations and drain money away from regulatory agencies, more bureaucracy is what the Republican Revolution wants.

Interior Secretary Bruce Babbitt noted that the Republicans had launched a "crude and misguided attack," by proposing to eliminate agencies like the U.S. Geological Survey, the National Biological Service, the U.S. Bureau of Mines, and the Office of Technology Assessment in order to silence scientific expertise. As Babbitt observed, these agencies "insulate science from the regulators and the politicians." But by eliminating the source of accurate scientific knowledge, the Republicans hope to allow their corporate donors to control the debate over environmental policy. Without reliable scientific information, lobbyists would be able to bombard members of Congress with distorted data.[41]

The Dirty Water Act

The Clean Water Act of 1972, one of the great triumphs of environmental regulation, was ripped to pieces by Republicans who sought to limit the definition of wetlands in order to allow millions of acres of land to be used by developers and oil companies. The Republicans ignored a definitive 268-page study of how wetlands should be defined that was published by the National Academy of Sciences. The report, which had been requested by Congress in 1993 to resolve the issue, concluded that "the Federal regulatory system for protection of wetlands is scientifically sound and effective in most respects" and that the new Republican definition of a wetland (designed to open up more than half of America's wetlands to commercial development) had no scientific basis.[42]

This attack on the environment comes at a time when more regulation, not less, is needed to preserve natural resources. More than half of America's wetlands have already been lost. Each year, 35 square miles of coastal wetlands along the Gulf of Mexico are destroyed. The Association of State Wetland Managers estimates that 60-80% of our wetlands, including parts of the Everglades, would no longer exist under the law and could be filled.

The Republicans would like to take us back to the 1970s, when free enterprise reigned supreme and the environment was always a secondary consideration—but also a time when we had 30% more smog (despite many fewer cars), when half as many rivers and lakes were safe for swimming, a time of large chlorofluorocarbon emissions destroying the ozone layer, and rapid destruction of endangered species with virtually no effort to stop environmental losses.[43]

In May 1995, the House enacted this "Dirty Water Act" to amend the Clean Water Act. Although 34 moderate Republicans voted against the bill, one of the highest defections yet from the Contract with America, 45 conservative Democrats supported it. Fortunately, the "environmental destruction act" was not passed in the Senate. But if the Republicans ever consolidate their power in the Senate and elect a president who is not committed to defending the environment, all of these proposals—and worse ones to come—will become the law of the land.

Even without a budget agreement or a successful Republican environmental bill, the behind-the-scenes attacks have already begun through the use of riders to appropriation bills. In a July 17, 1995 letter, 38 Republicans and Democrats objected to efforts to use riders instead of independent legislation, declaring that "the House should not be debating fundamental questions of environmental policy as part of appropriations bills" and adding that Congress "should not be prohibiting agencies from enforcing Federal law."[44]

That same July, a budget rider surreptiously overturning legislation that regulates logging became law. The new law doubled the amount of logging in national forests under the guise of salvaging trees "imminently susceptible to fire or insect attack," and prohibited environmentalists from blocking any logging with lawsuits.[45] The *Seattle Times*, which originally supported Sen. Slade Gorton's "salvage logging" plan, realized it was a lie a year after implementation: "Gorton's plan has generated little or no salvage logging. Instead loggers are attempting to clear-cut an ancient stand of Douglas firs in the Olympics, where fire is not an issue. Gorton's backers, including this newspaper, feel lured into a bait-and-switch game."[46] A House Appropriations Committee report found that "salvage timber" was a common way to conceal as much as $100 million in timber thefts, with the help of corrupt Forest Service workers.[47]

While the Republicans destroy environmental regulations, they say nothing about the government subsidies for major corporations, such as the $300 million lost each year thanks to below-cost timber sales, the ranchers who pay one-fifth of the market rate for grazing on public lands, or the laws which allowed the Barrick mining company to pay $9,000 for public land which contained $34 billion worth of gold.[48]

The American people are strongly opposed to the Republican anti-environment proposals. Republican pollster Linda DiVall found that popular opinion is only 35% in favor of but 46% against the conservative plans to cut the EPA. Among Republicans, 55% do not trust their own party to protect the environment. Thirty Republican moderates wrote to Gingrich in January 1996, criticizing the "missteps in environmental policy" and warning that "If the party is to resuscitate its reputation in this important area, we cannot be seen as using the budget crisis as an excuse to emasculate environmental protection."[49]

A study by the Natural Resources Defense Council found that very small airborne pollution particles (which are currently unregulated) cause at least 56,000 deaths annually that could be prevented.[50] However, the Republican plans to halt all additional regulations and hamper EPA enforcement would slow down the kind of regulation necessary to save lives. The Republicans do not want to make our environment cleaner; they want to redefine dirty air and dirty water and call it clean.[51]

Killing the Environment Softly

Republicans face a difficult dilemma: their opposition to government regulation and their desire to serve the interests of big business drive them to attack environmental laws, but the overwhelming popularity of environmental regulation prevents them from attacking it openly. Even with heavy public relations and spin control, Gingrich has been unable to convince the House to eliminate all laws protecting the environment.

But if they cannot openly overturn environmental laws, the Republicans will win by a process of gradually undermining existing laws and fiercely resisting any new laws or efforts to enforce current regulations. A National Biological Service review of 261 major ecosystems in the United States found that 126—nearly half—are endangered or threatened.[52] Strong action is needed to stop the threats posed to the environment, but the Gingrich Revolution makes environmental groups struggle just to maintain the status quo.

The Republicans have already successfully punished the EPA and the FDA by sharply cutting funds for enforcement during the 1995/96 budget crisis, hoping that they can eviscerate by disuse the laws that are too popular to overturn. The EPA was forced to suspend clean-ups of Superfund toxic waste sites when Congress cut its operating budget during the crisis.[53]

Unlike the war against the welfare state, the Republican attack on environmental laws and regulations is something done in secret, behind closed doors, led by politicians like Gingrich who try, on the surface, to proclaim their commitment to the environment. But the anti-environmental movement represents what is happening to nearly every major policy in Washington: a Republican crusade, financially supported by big business, to overturn laws that the American people want and to prevent the enforcement of laws needed to protect the environment.

Chapter 9

Senseless Legal Reform: Defending Corporate Criminals

If the Republican Revolution succeeds, the American legal system, which has always favored the wealthy over the poor and the corporation over the consumer, will be tilted even more dramatically in favor of a monied elite. The victimized consumer who tries to sue a business for the damage it has caused will find a brand new set of barriers protecting corporate irresponsibility. Limits on punitive damages will prevent adequate punishment of corporations who recklessly threaten public health. "Loser pays" rules for legal expenses will discourage the poor from going after corporations who have deep pockets and a large stable of lawyers. Cuts in legal services programs will prevent the poor from getting adequate legal representation. The end result will be a vast increase in the widening gap between justice for the rich and justice for the poor.

The Contract with America's Common Sense Legal Reform Act only makes "common sense" if you're a major corporation. It seeks to free businesses from product liability laws by nationalizing standards and sharply limiting punitive damages. Stockholders would find it much more difficult to sue companies that deceived them. And the plan would revolutionize the American legal system by creating a "loser pays" system to favor the wealthiest companies.

Supporters called it "the Girl Scout Bill," and Rep. Jon Christenson (R-NE) declared that the Girl Scouts organization "has been beset by predatory lawyers looking for anybody with pockets to pick." Ads supporting the bill described the number of boxes of cookies each girl scout must sell to pay for liability premiums. However, the Girl Scouts don't face a litigation nightmare. Bonnie McEwan, Director of Communications for the Girl Scouts, declared: "It is not true at all that we have been barraged with frivolous lawsuits. That is absolutely not the case."[1]

The attempts to limit punitive damages will increase the incentives for companies to reduce safety. Knowing that there is a maximum amount of punitive damages ($250,000 or three times the amount for damages and harm, which ever is greater), companies will be able to calculate when it is more profitable to keep an unsafe product on the market than to correct it. Punitive damages give juries and judges the flexibility to determine the social harm created by corporate misconduct and pressure them to change.

Punitive damages are one of the few ways that the poor, elderly, and disadvantaged can have an equal impact. Currently, in assessing damages, the law proclaims the rich to be more valuable human beings than anyone else. Damages are generally assessed based on what an individual would have made working. As a result, people who face discrimination in the workplace, such as women and minorities, also face discrimination in the courtroom. Homemakers, the aged, and the unemployed are considered virtually worthless. Punitive damages often help to equalize this unfair system, since they punish a company for its behavior, not for the economic value of the individual who is harmed.

Of course, punitive damages can be excessive and can be awarded where they are not deserved, but the answer is to create a system where punitive damages are reviewed for their fairness, not to impose an arbitrary limit. The Republicans claim to be the representatives of small business; but large penalties are rarely imposed on small businesses, for whom a $250,000 payment would still be devastating. The limit on punitive damages, however, helps the multi-billion dollar corporations for whom a $250,000 ruling would be small change.

Another part of the Republican plan, the Securities Litigation Reform Act, is a license for corporations to lie when seeking to lure investors. It would ban all class action lawsuits and dramatically raise the standard of proof to require clear evidence that company executives "knowingly" or "recklessly" tried to deceive. By anyone's standards, there is no litigation explosion requiring this reform. In 1994, only 300 out of 235,000 federal lawsuits were securities class actions.[2] While a handful of debatably frivolous lawsuits may be prevented, the overall effect of the law will be to dramatically increase fraud. Arthur Levitt, chair of the Securities and Exchange Commission, feared that the bill would restrict private monitoring of financial companies, placing oversight responsibility entirely on the SEC.[3] However, for the Republican supporters who want to avoid lawsuits holding them accountable for their actions, this was an important piece of legislation.

Loser Pays, Big Business Wins

Perhaps the most important part of the "Common Sense Legal Reform" is the plan to force the losing side in a lawsuit to pay the legal costs of both parties. Although ostensibly advocated to stop frivolous lawsuits, the real result will be to stop legitimate lawsuits against major corporations.

"Loser pays" does not fundamentally reform the legal system and stop frivolous lawsuits. On the contrary, it mainly serves to give advantages to the wealthiest individuals and corporations by imposing a heavy burden on anyone who initiates a lawsuit. Because big companies have much deeper pockets than litigants and their lawyers, they can afford to risk taking a case to trial. The average individual cannot afford to bring a lawsuit and face liability for hundreds of thousands of dollars in legal fees generated by the other side.

The Republicans argue that the "loser pays" rule would only apply if a settlement is offered by the other side but rejected, and it turns out to be larger than the eventual court award. But as Philip Howard, author of *The Death of Common Sense* and one of the thinkers most often cited by Republican reformers, points out, "this would allow corporate defendants to make low-ball offers to legitimate victims, still leaving them the ruinous prospect of paying the corporation's fees."[4] It will become standard procedure for any company being sued to immediately make a token $1 settlement offer—creating the same consequences as a straightforward "loser pays" system.

In fact, the Republican plan suggests an even more radical "winner pays" system: if you win a lawsuit, but the court award is less than the settlement offer, you must pay the legal fees of the company that was found at fault. Ironically, this provision will discourage settlements, the exact opposite of how it has been promoted. Because companies have a great deal to gain from having a court award fall below the settlement offer, they will pursue all avenues of appeal. Litigants who receive an award below the settlement (who might otherwise be happy to take the money) will appeal to avoid the other side's legal fees.

Howard urges a sounder policy: "let the judge decide at the end of a case if a claim or defense lacked substantial merit....It puts litigants at risk for making unfounded claims, but not for the fact of losing."[5] However, Gingrich and the Republicans do not propose this because their goal has never been to stop frivolous lawsuits. Instead, the Republicans want to free businesses from the threat of legitimate lawsuits.

However, Gingrich's support for legal reform only applies when the defendants are rich corporations. When the average person faces frivolous lawsuits, Gingrich proposes nothing to help them. One growing trend in the past decade is the use of SLAPPs—Strategic Lawsuits Against Public Participation. Companies file SLAPPs against individuals and neighborhood groups who publicly speak out against real estate development or other corporate activities. They use defamation or business interference as the excuse for intimidating citizens, imposing high legal costs on anyone who resists their corporate goals. Since the Republican plan for "loser pays" applies only to product liability cases, it doesn't apply to defamation suits used by companies to silence dissent. Ten states have passed laws to oppose SLAPPs, giving judges the discretion not only to dismiss a case but also to impose damages and legal costs on companies if they act with malice for the purpose of intimidating people. But Gingrich and the Republicans have never proposed protecting individuals from corporate censorship.[6]

Killing Legal Help for the Poor

Another Gingrich target is the Legal Services Corporation (LSC), which Republicans plan to destroy because it defends the poor in civil cases (such as tenant's rights issues and divorces involving battered women). Republicans hope to turn the LSC into a block grant and eliminate funding altogether after two years, leaving 50 underfunded state bureaucracies to provide legal representation for those who cannot afford an attorney.

The Republican plan will also impose highly restrictive new regulations on federally-funded legal service groups. The legislation would ban legal service groups from receiving legal fees awarded by courts, depriving them of $15 million a year in funding. The goal is to undermine legal representation for the poor by removing any federal funding for their lawyers. The Republican bill would also ban any legal services group receiving federal funding from representing illegal immigrants, lobbying state legislatures or helping to write government regulations (including those meant to protect battered women from abuse), or dealing with abortion rights cases. Legal service groups are already banned from using federal funding for these purposes, but now the Republicans want to prohibit any group from doing this, even with their own money. They will also be banned from "solicitation"— educating people about their legal rights, and outreach for those whose rights are being violated. These provisions, along with the elimination of the migrant-worker legal-aid program, were written into the bill at the request of the American Farm Bureau to prevent migrant workers from exercising their legal rights.[7]

For lawyers and their clients, this is the equivalent of the gag rule that prevented doctors in federally-funded clinics from mentioning abortions to their patients. This would prevent effective legal representation for people who cannot afford lawyers. While the leaders of the Republican Revolution complain about excessive regulations and bureaucratic rules, they impose extraordinarily intrusive and ideologically motivated restrictions on the Legal Service Corporation and its agencies.

A provision of the Republican appropriations bill attacking the Legal Services Corporation even prohibits it from receiving lawyer's fees for winning a case. Although permitting these fees would save the government money, it would also give Legal Services an independent source of revenue safe from Republican intimidation. The bill also includes a gag rule preventing anyone working for an organization that receives even $1 in Federal funds from Legal Services from testifying in Congressional hearings.[8]

The underpaid lawyers (salaries start at $25,000 a year) employed by Legal Services offer legal help to the poorest Americans. Less than a fourth of the people requesting help can be assisted.[9] The real effect of destroying the

Legal Services Corporation will be to increase the disparity between rich and poor in our justice system.

For now, the Republicans are only proposing to cut the LSC's $415 million budget by 35%. However, because it occasionally assists the poor by suing government agencies that fail to meet their legal obligations, LSC is at the top of the list of Republican targets. Rep. Robert Dornan (R-CA) says it "functions like a queen bee who sends out little liberal worker bees everywhere to drive the left-wing agenda in this country."[10]

The attempt to bring the Republican Revolution to the legal system will not reduce lawsuits or stop the cascade of litigation in America. On the contrary, businesses are more likely to flood the courts with cases because they know that the legal system has dramatically shifted in their favor. "Common Sense" legal reform will not stop frivolous lawsuits, but it will stop many consumers from securing justice in the courts.

Chapter 10

Criminals in Politics: The NRA's Crime Bill

Republicans guard their reputation as the party that fights crime, hiding Gingrich's efforts to weaken law enforcement and cut anti-crime social programs. His plan wastes money on the most expensive and least efficient kind of crime prevention—building more prisons—while it sharply cuts effective crime prevention programs and efforts to enforce the law against white-collar criminals.

Instead of addressing the underlying problems caused by poverty, lack of hope, and the absence of educational and job opportunities, the Republicans (and many Democrats, including President Clinton) promise only to turn Generation X into Generation Ex-Convict. Building penitentiaries instead of schools, paying for prison guards instead of better teachers, investing in handcuffs rather than library books, they offer a costly vision of fear and hopelessness for the future.

Good Cop, Bad Cop

Gingrich's tough anti-crime rhetoric does have an exception. He loudly denounces one arm of the law (but not the criminals) when it comes to one kind of crime: tax fraud. In his speech commemorating the first 100 days of his reign as Speaker, Gingrich attacked "an arrogant, unpredictable and unfair Internal Revenue Service."[1] Gingrich told Charlie Rose, "people are sick of the Internal Revenue Service being able to audit them."[2] Gingrich wants to let criminals go free and prevent the police from enforcing the law—if the crimes are committed by wealthy corporations and individuals who cheat on their taxes, harm the environment, and endanger the lives of workers. These corporate criminals should, according to Gingrich, be trusted to follow the law without any punishment or supervision.

Although Gingrich wants to make it tougher for the poor to win lawsuits against corporations, he is encouraging frivolous lawsuits against the federal government. In April 1996, the House passed a "taxpayer bill of rights" allowing taxpayers to sue the IRS for up to $1 million—ten times the current limit—for supposedly "reckless" attempts at collection of overdue bills. The "bill of rights" also makes it easier for taxpayers to get legal fees back after suing the IRS, raising the cap on reimbursement from $75 an hour to $110 an hour.[3] The Contract's "tough" stand against crime is notably lenient when it comes to corporate crime.

Hatred of the IRS is a perennial American sport. But while everybody despises the IRS, most people are strongly opposed to letting tax cheats violate the law at will. The ones who want the IRS enforcement powers eviscerated are the corporations and wealthy individuals who regularly cheat on their taxes by taking false deductions and concealing income. Not surprisingly, this is also the core of the Republican Party's financial supporters who put Gingrich in power.

There is an amazing hypocrisy in Gingrich's approach to crime. When the criminals are drug dealers and the poor (usually from minority groups), he wants to build more prisons, increase the length of sentences, conduct mass executions, deprive them of adequate legal counsel, and enlarge the budgets for law enforcement. But when the criminals are wealthy, white-collar, and usually white, Gingrich wants to eviscerate the laws, cut the budgets for law enforcement, and let the crooks go free.

The Taking Back Our Streets Act: "We Will Kill You."

After President Clinton pushed through a $30 billion anti-crime bill in 1994 despite Republican attacks against it as "pork" and "welfare programs," Gingrich decided to overturn the measure. Clinton's bill had established $8.8 billion to help put up to 100,000 new police officers on the streets and $4 billion for crime prevention programs, while designating most of the money for more prisons. The Republicans decided to cut crime prevention by combining these two programs in a $10 billion block grant to local governments, allowing them to decide how to use the money. Although the Contract claims that "this grant money is intended to supplement, not supplant, state funds," there is no way to enforce this, and local governments are likely to cut back their own law enforcement funding in order to deal with all the cutbacks proposed by the Republicans in other areas. However bad the Clinton crime bill was, the $2.8 billion Republican cut in crime programs will hurt nascent efforts at crime prevention.[4]

This irrational policy—which increases crime and causes higher costs for taxpayers—exists because Gingrich believes that government is incapable of doing good. His anti-government attitude leads him to think that the state should only punish offenders, not help prevent crime or rehabilitate criminals.

The Contract denigrates Clinton's moderate crime prevention efforts as another "welfare program." In fact, it is far cheaper to stop crime by preventing it in the first place than by building more and more prisons where incarceration costs more than an Ivy League education. By investing in education, establishing more drug addiction programs, and exploring alternatives to imprisonment such as heavy fines and community service, we can deal with crime cheaply at its source. Further, fighting poverty is critical to fighting crime. Gingrich's overall agenda increases poverty; so too will it increase crime, regardless of how much he pretends to be "tough on crime."

The Contract's proposal for more prisons will never increase prison-building enough to allow the massive increase in sentences it promotes, and most of the money will probably do no more than replace what states would have spent on new prisons anyway. The Republicans want to spend $10.5 billion over six years, with incentives for states to increase time in prison and meet sentencing guidelines. The "truth-in-sentencing" law is a well-known political scam. Obviously, you can't increase prison sentences if there's not enough room in prisons. The result will be shorter sentences or special maneuvers around the law if "truth-in-sentencing" is imposed.

Although the Contract has "stop violent criminals" as one of its chapter headings, it mentions nothing about the fact that excessive sentencing for minor drug dealers and drug possession is the primary reason why prisons are filled to capacity and violent criminals must be released. The Contract proposes that anyone who is found in possession of illegal drugs and a gun will face a 10-year mandatory minimum prison sentence for a first offense—no matter how small the amount of drugs, and even if the gun is never drawn or used. This and other illogical and inflexible mandatory sentencing is exactly what prevents increases in the prison terms of serious criminals. At a time when most rapists are never brought to court, and most convicted rapists serve a year or less in prison, it is ridiculous to say that drug users with guns should spend 10 years in prison.

Gingrich's other answer to the drug problem is mass execution: "The first time we execute 27 or 30 or 35 people at one time, the price of carrying drugs will have gone up dramatically."[5] He says that the message to international drug traffickers should be, "we will kill you." This is unlikely to discourage major drug traffickers (who often kill each other), and the most likely result is that drug smugglers will murder Drug Enforcement Agents rather than surrendering.

Even his fellow Republicans admit that Gingrich deceives the public with his demagogic inaccuracy about the crime issue. When Gingrich claimed that a discretionary sentencing program "would release over 10,000 drug dealers who are currently in prison," Rep. Henry Hyde (R-IL) had to point out that Gingrich was wrong: the law applied to future sentencing, not to drug dealers currently in prison, and only non-violent drug dealers who did not have a weapon and who cooperated with police would get the discretionary sentencing.

Gingrich's posturing about the drug issue is often contradictory. He condemned President Clinton because former Surgeon General Joycelyn Elders suggested studying the issue of drug legalization without endorsing it; yet Gingrich himself has declared that the choice about drugs is "either legalize it or get rid of it," and conservatives like William F. Buckley and Milton Friedman have supported legalizing drugs.[6] Gingrich also spread false rumors about Democratic drug use, claiming that he "had a senior law enforcement official tell me that in his judgment, up to a quarter of the White House staff, when they first came in, had used drugs in the last four or five years."[7] Gingrich's harsh anti-drug rhetoric stands in sharp contrast to his admission that he smoked marijuana in graduate school, only a few years before he ran for Congress.

The Good Faith Effort to Destroy the Bill of Rights

While Gingrich vehemently supports a "bill of rights" for taxpayers, he is busy trying to weaken the real Bill of Rights. One aspect of Gingrich's plan to be tough on crime was to overturn the Fourth Amendment and allow illegally seized evidence to be used in federal trials. Even though the Republican plan would have almost no impact on stopping crime (it only applies to a few federal cases, which are only 3% of all criminal trials), it is the beginning of the erosion of our rights.

Protections against searches without warrants have been in place for generations. In 1914, in order to stop massive police abuses of civil rights, the Supreme Court banned federal courts from hearing evidence that was seized without a valid warrant, and in the 1961 case *Mapp v. Ohio*, state and local police were prohibited from making searches without a warrant. As a result, police today must follow the Exclusionary Rule, which excludes from a trial any evidence gathered illegally. In 1984, the Supreme Court made an exception to the Exclusionary Rule for evidence found in a "good faith" police search with a warrant later declared illegitimate.[8] However, the Republican bill goes far beyond the existing "good faith" rule, applying it to cases where there was never a warrant issued. As long as a search was made with a vague and subjective definition of "good faith," any evidence seized could be used.

The Contract declared that the judicial system was being undermined by cases dismissed due to the Exclusionary Rule. However, evidence indicates that the 4th Amendment has a tiny impact on criminal cases. A 1978 study of 2,804 U.S. cases found that only 0.4% of cases were rejected by prosecutors because of 4th Amendment problems; evidence was excluded from trial in only 1.3% of the cases (and in more than half of these cases, the defendants were convicted even though some evidence was suppressed). A 1982 study by the National

Institute of Justice found that 0.79% of felony complaints in California were dismissed because of the Exclusionary Rule. And a 1983 study of nine Midwest counties found that if the Exclusionary Rule were eliminated, conviction rates would increase by less than 0.5%.[9] The Exclusionary Rule helps prevent police abuse, but its impact is mainly at the state and local levels, where most law enforcement is done. Since only 3% of criminal cases are in federal court, only about one in six thousand criminals on trial would be affected by Newt's proposal—hardly a war on crime.

Even though it has minimal effect on punishing criminals, Gingrich's proposal represents a dangerous erosion to the Bill of Rights. It's quite plausible that without the Fourth Amendment's protections against search and seizure, conviction rates could decline because police actions and evidence would seem less credible in the eyes of jurors, who might be more likely to believe conspiracy stories (such as those presented in the O.J. Simpson case) if they knew that the legal system offered no barriers to illegally seized evidence. FBI director Louis Freeh opposed the Gingrich plan to eviscerate the 4th Amendment, noting that "the Exclusionary Rule has not been an obstacle to the FBI with respect to performing our mission."[10]

On February 7, 1995, the House Republicans voted 303-121 to kill an amendment introduced by the Black Caucus to the bill about the Exclusionary Rule. It turned out to consist of the exact same words as the Fourth Amendment in the Bill of Rights.[11] It was an embarrassing moment for Gingrich and the Republicans, to vote against the Constitution they revered so much in theory—but none of this stopped the anti-crime crusade against the Fourth Amendment.

The Fourth Amendment was not the only victim of the Contract with America's conservative assault on the Bill of Rights. The First Amendment was ripped up in the name of symbolic politics, with the Republicans promising to amend the Constitution to ban flag burning. The Communications Decency Act was passed as part of the telecommunications reform, and signed into law by President Clinton in 1996. In the name of protecting children and fighting pornography, Congress imposed extraordinary new censorship of free speech in cyberspace. The rules imposed on everyone involved with the Internet are even harsher and more restrictive than the current FCC rules regulating dirty words and pictures on radio and television. Gingrich initially opposed the law, but he refused to use his power as speaker to stop or reform the bill. Even though a federal court recently ruled that the law was unconstitutional, the passage of this new "decency" law shows how willing the new Republican majority (joined by many Democrats) is to abridge the First Amendment.

Killing the Poor

Another phony Republican "anti-crime" proposal was to limit appeals for criminals and kill programs which provide legal representation for the poor. The right way to reduce death row appeals is not to ban death-row appeals, but instead to make sure that defendants have fair and adequate legal representation in the first place. This is the only constitutionally and morally sound death penalty; the alternative is to allow unfair trials to stand and to possibly execute innocent people.

One part of the Republican legal "reform" plan was conducted in secret: the attempt to destroy legal aid programs in order to deny legal representation for the poor. The House Republicans plan to eliminate a $19.8 million program which pays for groups to represent inmates facing the death penalty. Death penalty appeals are a highly complex specialty that most lawyers are unable to take on pro bono, and most public defenders are already too burdened to handle the cases. Ironically, cutting the death penalty resource centers will actually end up costing taxpayers more money and delaying the death penalty process. Because the law requires counsel in death-penalty cases, the government will have to pay private attorneys' fees which will be more costly than maintaining the resource centers. And because private attorneys may be inexperienced with death-penalty cases, the process of appeals is likely to be lengthened. If the accused who are poor cannot be represented by lawyers, the result will not be more convictions, but more appeals and overturned verdicts because the constitutional right to have adequate counsel will have been violated. It is far better for the government to ensure a fair and just system at the start by funding legal aid than to face all the appeals that will result when legal representation is not available.

But the death-penalty resource centers were too successful. In one case, Walter McMillian was sentenced to death in 1987 for killing a white woman in Alabama. Although one appeal was rejected, a $27,000-a-year lawyer from one of these centers found that prosecutors concealed crucial evidence. The main witness against him recanted, saying that he was pressured by a week of police interrogation. An appeals court overturned the conviction, and prosecutors decided there wasn't enough evidence to try McMillian again. Cases like these show that innocent people will be executed if the Republicans are able to limit prisoners to one appeal and eliminate effective representation. But in the name of appearing to fight crime, House Republicans are willing to slow down the judicial system, allow innocent people to be executed, and make criminal justice more expensive for taxpayers.[12]

Guns Don't Kill People, Welfare Does

Although the Republicans pretend to be tough on crime, they oppose the most important anti-crime measure: gun control. Despite 100 deaths a day from guns, the National Rifle Association wants more guns in America, more assault weapons, more cop killer bullets, and more laws to allow people to carry concealed weapons.[13] As with every other issue he purports to be principled about, Gingrich recognizes the political power on the far right of the NRA, and is a leading "gun rights" advocate.

On January 25, 1995, Gingrich and three other top congressmen met secretly with NRA representatives to submit to their demands for the repeal of gun control legislation.[14] Gingrich quickly moved to appease the NRA, writing a letter two days later to NRA official Tanya Metaksa in which he promised, "As long as I am Speaker of this House, no gun control legislation is going to move in committee or on the floor of this House and there will be no further erosion of their rights." This declaration was an extraordinary ban on any kind of gun control bill, no matter how popular or necessary.

According to Gingrich, "What we are going to have is a partnership of strengthening laws against the criminal misuse of firearms, which everyone agrees is the real problem issue, and eliminating harassment of law abiding gun owners who are not the problem." But throughout his congressional career, Gingrich has opposed efforts to keep guns out of the hands of criminals. He voted repeatedly against the Brady Bill waiting period that allows a background check for a criminal record or mental illness. As early as 1986, Gingrich voted to weaken the 1968 Gun Control Act. Although Gingrich and the NRA claim to be tough on crime, in 1995 Republicans restored funding to a federal administrative review program that allows convicted criminals to have their gun rights restored.[15]

Gingrich proclaimed to the NRA, "Our purpose is to remove ill-conceived and unnecessary government interference in those rights." He thinks these rights include the right to own assault weapons, which he has twice refused to ban, and the right to use cop-killer bullets. Gingrich concluded his letter to the NRA by writing, "I look forward to working with you." The NRA has donated generously in order to ensure his unqualified support.[16]

Although Gingrich was careful to avoid pressing a controversial issue like overturning gun control in his first term as Speaker, he is strongly devoted to ending the ban on assault weapons and removing virtually all limits on the ownership and use of guns. Gingrich created a Task Force on Firearms, which was packed with NRA supporters.

In March 1996, Gingrich pushed a bill through the House which would eliminate the assault weapons ban. As he put it, "I challenge the news media to go add up the number of people killed by those 19 guns this year and come back with a list. And then compare the bombing in Oklahoma City." In fact, the Bureau of Alcohol, Tobacco and Firearms tracked 229 homicides from assault weapons, and this is probably only 10-15% of the assault weapon crimes each year.[17] But Gingrich would never suggest that we should legalize homemade bombs like the one used at Oklahoma City—at least not until the militias start donating more money to Republican causes.

The NRA has unprecedented power in the new Congress under Gingrich. In one case, an NRA consultant interviewing a witness claimed to be "with the Waco hearings team that's putting together the Waco hearings."[18] The NRA lobbyist was working closely with the staff of the Government Reform and Oversight Committee.[19] The House Republicans invited NRA consultants to examine the guns in the Waco hearings, and claimed that witness Robert Sanders was an agent for the Bureau of Alcohol, Tobacco and Firearms, even though Sanders turned out to be an NRA-connected critic of the ATF.[20] The NRA is also lobbying the House to eliminate a Center for Disease Control and Prevention research program which studies the medical effects of firearms on public health. Gingrich and other NRA allies in Congress will be promoting similar attempts to silence the truth.[21]

Gingrich blames welfare programs for the epidemic of homicide with guns, even though European countries maintain much larger welfare states with far lower homicide rates, perhaps because very few murders are committed with welfare checks. He urges long prison sentences for criminals, but he avoids the cheapest and most effective way to address the crime problem: keeping guns out of the hands of criminals. Gingrich's pro-NRA philosophy can be summarized in a simple phrase: Guns don't kill people, the welfare state kills people.

For Gingrich, it doesn't matter that the Republican crime bill is expensive, wasteful, or undermines the right to a fair trial. As long as he can manipulate the debate, and make this symbolic stand for a "war on crime" more important than actually reducing criminal activity, he will win the only war he is truly concerned about: the political one.

Chapter 11

Welfare for Bombmakers: Gingrich's Military-Industrial Complex

While hacking apart programs to help the poor, Gingrich proved to be the defender of a far more wasteful welfare program: the corporate welfare budget, especially in the Department of Defense. Gingrich plans to add billions of dollars every year beyond what the Department of Defense has requested. Even though the Cold War is long over, Gingrich—who has always been one of the most extreme pro-military hawks in the House—wants to sustain (and increase) a huge military-industrial establishment that bears little relation to any current security needs.

Discussing the budget soon after he became Speaker, Gingrich claimed that there was "a lot on the table—corporate welfare, subsidies of every special interest. Defense is on the table. I'm a hawk, but a cheap hawk."[1] But when Gingrich's final proposal appeared, it turned out that the rich got most of the tax cuts, and the poor got most of the spending cuts. Corporate welfare was barely affected. Defense spending was increased by billions, far beyond any rational estimate of what our defense needs would require.

This certainly isn't because the Pentagon spends our money efficiently. In 1994, the Congressional Budget Office found 37 defense programs and weapons systems that could be cut, saving $200 billion over a five-year span. Other areas of the military could easily be trimmed without significantly affecting our preparedness for war. We spend more than $4 billion a year to keep the Air National Guard ready, even though such preparedness serves little military purpose. We have $36 billion in needless inventories for national defense and pay to keep factories ready for a world war that seems less likely than ever.[2] We give $1 billion a year to commercial ship owners in exchange for permission to use their ships during war, even though the government could simply take the ships and pay the fair market price in the event of a war. This subsidy to large ship owners persists because of massive lobbying—not by the Pentagon, which wants to get rid of the program, but by the maritime industry.[3]

In 1995, the House approved a plan to spend $267.3 billion on the military in 1996, nearly $10 billion more than the military actually requested. The

House allocated $553 million just for parts to make two extra B-2 bombers, which will cost about $1 billion each when they are finally constructed.[4] A General Accounting Office report found that "the Air Force has yet to demonstrate that the B-2 design will meet some of its most important mission requirements." Among its problems was the fact that "the B-2 radar cannot distinguish rain from other obstacles."[5] Waste on this scale far exceeds any inefficiencies in social welfare programs, but Gingrich is noticeably silent about it.

The defense budget's size is also concealed by the fact that other departments, like the Department of Energy, are primarily devoted to defense programs. Of the $17 billion energy budget, $4 billion is spent each year on controlling nuclear weapons and $6.5 billion is budgeted for cleaning up the waste generated by producing nuclear weapons.[6]

Yet the American public is resoundingly opposed to increasing defense spending; in a 1993 poll, only 17% felt we spend too little on defense, while 42% said we are spending too much.[7] It is now clear to everyone that even when the Soviet Union existed and posed a serious military threat, the U.S. was spending tens of billions of dollars each year beyond its true military needs. The paranoia about the Soviet Union, fueled by the institutional needs of the military-industrial complex and false CIA estimates of the Soviets' economic and military capabilities, drove the massive spending in the 1980s which (in combination with the Reagan tax cuts) created most of America's national debt. Yet despite the fact that unneeded and unproductive military spending caused so many of our current financial troubles, the Republicans under Gingrich insisted on increasing military spending beyond what the Defense Department itself requests—a request that goes far beyond military needs.

The justification is that the United States must be capable of fighting two large regional wars simultaneously—something that has never happened in our history. As the Persian Gulf War indicated, the U.S. military can overwhelmingly defeat one of the world's largest regional powers in the span of six weeks despite using only 20% of our troops. The American armed forces are never forced into a military situation until we feel ready, since no one is plotting an invasion of the United States. Even a substantially reduced military would be able to fight two wars simultaneously.

If we were really experiencing the serious economic problems that Gingrich claims to be solving, it would be insane to spend so much on military readiness when the National Guard can provide sufficient defenses. The current level of military readiness is designed to fight an enemy like the former Soviet Union. To have the military in a state of permanent readiness is irrational in a world where few countries are crazy enough to challenge the United States and none have the military resources to launch a blitzkrieg offense or threaten an invasion.

It is irrational to spend $270 billion each year on the military when the U.S. is the only superpower and has no substantial enemies. The Defense Department could have its budget cut below $200 billion immediately without losing any military superiority; in the long term, the budget could go below $150 billion, and we would still have by far the biggest, most advanced, and most expensive armed forces in the world.

We spend $50 billion a year for soldiers to defend South Korea (which spends $12 billion on its own defense) against North Korea (which spends only $2 billion). While a token U.S. force in South Korea may be important to prevent attacks, there is absolutely no reason for a state of total military readiness.[8]

Perhaps the biggest boondoggle proposed by Gingrich and the Republicans is the resurrection of the Strategic Defense Initiative, better known as the "Star Wars" fantasy of shooting enemy missiles out of space. Billions of dollars annually have been wasted on this frivolous science fiction project that has become entirely useless now that the Soviet Union has disappeared. But Cold War nostalgists like Gingrich continue to demand funding for "Star Wars," and want to pass legislation to require the Department of Defense to implement a missile defense system by the year 2002, regardless of whether or not it would work or would enhance our defenses.

All reports indicate that various "terrorist states" like Iran, Iraq, Syria, Libya, etc., are at least a decade away from possessing a missile capable of attacking the United States, and even these estimates assume that nothing would be done to stop the production of these nuclear weapons—although concealing an ICBM facility from spy satellites is virtually impossible today. Nor is it rational to imagine that any of these states would launch an expensive and incredibly complex missile, easily traced to the country that launched it, when it could simply smuggle a nuclear weapon into the United States and expect a much higher degree of success.

To spend hundreds of billions of dollars implementing a Strategic Defense system that probably won't work, all to protect us from a nonexistent threat, is insane. It is far better to protect our nation for the long run by cutting wasteful military spending and investing in the skills of our citizens, than to continue a useless program like SDI. But Gingrich's fascination with gee-whiz technology and science fiction stories makes missile defense a part of the Republican program to increase spending for a military that already outspends the rest of world. The real utility of military spending is political. By bringing home military pork, members of Congress satisfy defense industries and workers who need jobs. Gingrich's obsession with an ever-increasing military budget is not surprising when one considers the dependence of his home district, Cobb County, on military spending.

Baby Blue Helmets and CIA Plots: From Gun Nut to Foreign Policy Nut

In 1984, when Ronald Reagan was president and Democrats controlled the House, Gingrich stood on the floor and declared, "we should have nothing to do with implementing foreign policy in the House."[9] But now that he is in control, he wants to run U.S. foreign policy from the House. When it comes to foreign policy, Gingrich is one of the most dangerous politicians in the country, mixing a hardline Cold War approach with genuine diplomatic incompetence. But as always, Gingrich has apologists in the media. A front-page *New York Times* story which was headlined, "Newt Gingrich, Foreign Policy Novice," treated him as an newcomer to foreign policy, making the inevitable mistakes of inexperience. Gingrich himself admitted, "I don't do foreign policy."[10] In fact, Gingrich is not a novice when it comes to foreign policy; he's a loose cannon with a foreign policy philosophy shaped by his history as one of the most right-wing Cold War hawks in Congress. His famous confrontation with Tip O'Neill in 1984 was provoked by Gingrich's attacks on Democratic views about foreign policy.

One of the most shocking examples of his foreign policy incompetence (and his power to run the country) came in the fall of 1995, when Gingrich decided that he wanted to overthrow the government of Iran. It was an idea that neither the Clinton Administration nor the Central Intelligence Agency considered possible or wise. Yet Gingrich pushed through an $18 million appropriation for a "covert" action by the CIA against Iran, and continued pressing for the legislation even though the plan had been publicly revealed.

A covert action against Iran is an idea virtually doomed to failure; a covert action that has already been publicly exposed is so certain to fail that it would be remarkably stupid even to suggest it. But Gingrich's dumb ideas have serious consequences. In addition to wasting $18 million, Gingrich's foreign policy forays have already killed people. In response to Gingrich, Iran announced it will "ruthlessly quell any moves by the enemies of the revolution within the country," including a $20 million operation "to counter the Great Satan" and plans for the execution of several "spies." Iran also promised that Gingrich's plot "will not go unanswered" and that Islamic nations will "make America regret its spiteful acts," which led CIA director John Deutch to predict an increase in terrorism.[11] Gingrich blamed the media, declaring that "it's very hard for a free society to be effective doing anything in secret if it's on page one of the *New York Times*." In fact, the news had appeared three months earlier in *Congressional Monitor*, the *Wall Street Journal*, and international news wire stories. Yet Gingrich continued with the "covert" operation that Iran already knew about and the CIA said wasn't feasible.[12]

When Gingrich caused an international incident by urging the United States to recognize Taiwan, he quickly backtracked after being criticized by

Henry Kissinger and declared, "I don't think we should recognize Taiwan." Gingrich explained, "I was trying to rattle their cage, to get their attention," and said he was just toying around with his power. He got the idea from Allen Drury's novel, *Advise and Consent*, where the president shocks the Russians with his plans: "They said, 'You can't do this.' And he said, 'Watch me.'"[13]

Gingrich's foreign policy notions are still frozen in the Cold War era. When Rep. Robert Torricelli (D-NJ) revealed that a Guatemalan military officer in the pay of the CIA had been responsible for the murder of an American innkeeper and a guerrilla leader married to American lawyer Jennifer Harbury, Gingrich responded not by expressing his horror at CIA involvement in political murders, but by urging the House ethics committee to punish Torricelli for "totally unacceptable" behavior. In Gingrich's moral universe, the CIA-sponsored murder of Americans is a secret that no member of Congress should ever reveal, even if they discover the information from non-classified outside sources. Gingrich claimed that Torricelli should have concealed the truth about the CIA's illegal interference in Guatemalan politics because it caused "a public embarrassment to the United States."[14] The Republicans tried to punish Torricelli for violating a House oath not to "disclose any classified information received in the course of my service with the House of Representatives." The House Ethics Committee determined that Torricelli had not violated any rules, but it still suggested that members of Congress check in advance with intelligence agencies to "make a good faith effort to determine if information they mean to make public is classified."[15]

Gingrich strongly opposed the Clinton Administration plan to stop the genocide in Bosnia, declaring that Republicans "disagree deeply with the way they would risk American lives around the planet."[16] Gingrich said that the idea of having peacekeepers in Bosnia "is utter, total insanity" and mocked the United Nations soldiers for having wimpy "baby blue helmets." "Any system which would put soldiers out in such an unmilitary manner as to allow them to be taken hostage is a disgrace to civilization."[17] No one knows what manly helmet color Gingrich proposed as an alternative, but his plan for Bosnia was silly no matter what color the headgear: withdraw peacekeepers, bomb the Serbs in "every target in every part of the country simultaneously," airlift the Bosnian Muslims to a foreign country for military training and supply them with weapons (even though Gingrich said, "if they were winning, they'd be about as brutal as the Serbs"), and let the blood flow.[18] Failing this, Gingrich suggested free market entrepreneurs as the solution to the Bosnia problem by "creating a Balkan-wide development zone."[19] As ridiculous (and dangerous) as Gingrich's ideas are, he has gotten a free ride from the major media, which overlook his destructive influence on foreign policy and, like the *New York Times*, apologize for his idiocy on the grounds that this politician, whose career spans more than 20 years, is a "novice."

Gingrich is one of the leading Republicans who want to demolish the United Nations and return to the good old days when America ruled the world. Gingrich attacked President Clinton for believing in a "multinational fantasy" and wanting "to subordinate the United States to the United Nations," a complete impossibility given our enormous power in the organization. He pushed the National Security Revitalization Act through the House; the Act would prohibit the President from putting U.S. troops under "foreign" control and cut U.S. support for UN peacekeeping by over $1 billion (even though we already owe billions in unpaid dues to the UN). Arthur Schlesinger Jr. noted that the bill would "eviscerate the American role in collective security."[20] Gingrich's neo-isolationism is particularly dangerous because few people pay attention to foreign policy, so the protests against his attacks on social programs have not been matched by protests against his attacks on the United Nations.

Gingrich's attacks on the UN are designed to produce international chaos, and he forces the Pentagon to waste more and more money preparing for wars that we will never fight with adversaries who have, quite literally, disappeared from the map. Under pressure from Republican threats to cut the funding for operations in Bosnia, Clinton agreed to spend an additional $25 billion on defense over six years. Republicans claimed that we maintain a "hollow military," using the same rhetoric of underpreparedness that had been repeatedly proven wrong throughout the Cold War. The Republican House voted to cut $9 billion from the Departments of Labor, Education, and Health, while increasing defense spending by $7 billion beyond what the Defense Department wanted. Gingrich will take $1 billion from the poorest schools in America, and 50,000 kids will be thrown out of Head Start—all so the Navy can have a $1.4 billion boat it doesn't need, built in the home state of Senate Majority Leader Trent Lott.

We spend hundreds of billions of dollars every year on a welfare program for defense contractors. The rest of the industrialized world invests in citizenry rather than weaponry, but Gingrich is prepared to undermine education and social programs in order to increase a wasteful defense establishment. His priorities will not change as long as the manufacture and sale of weapons remains an excessively lucrative business.

Part III

Fine Print:

The Hidden Contract With the Far Right

Chapter 12

Praying for Power: The Deal with the Christian Coalition

Although the Contract with America featured economic issues, Gingrich's triumph brought another contract to Washington that was never mentioned in the 1994 elections. At a May 18, 1995 press conference, Gingrich stood with Ralph Reed, executive director of the Christian Coalition, to announce the next stage of the Republican Revolution: a 10-point social agenda called the "Contract With the American Family." This contract includes mandating school prayer, abolishing the Department of Education, creating school vouchers to help fund religious schools, tax breaks for children and homemakers, restricting abortion and banning federal funds for Planned Parenthood, abolishing the National Endowment for the Arts, the Public Broadcasting System, and the Legal Services Corporation, increasing parental rights, supporting private charities, requiring criminals to pay their victims, and restricting pornography.

While even Bob Dole did not endorse the full "Contract with the American Family" or appear at the press conference, Gingrich enthusiastically supported every measure, declaring that the Contract embodied "key values that matter overwhelmingly to most Americans." Gingrich readily acknowledged the deal he had made with the religious right for their support: "We are committed to keep our faith with the people who helped with the Contract With America." Although not a die-hard cultural conservative, Gingrich recognized the political power of the Religious Right and promised to pursue their agenda after he successfully guided the Contract With America through the House.[1]

Many of the Christian Coalition's ideas, like the ideas of the original Contract, are unpopular. A Gallup Poll after the election found that there was enormous opposition to Republican plans to limit abortion. Only 44% of Americans favored "making it more difficult to get an abortion," while 53% opposed the idea. A "gag rule" for health care workers at federally-funded clinics, prohibiting any mention of abortion, was opposed by 59% and supported by a mere 38%. The Gallup Poll analysts noted, "outright opposition to abortion now matches its lowest levels (13 percent) in Gallup's twenty years of tracking the issue."[2]

Yet the Labor/Health and Human Services bill planned by the Republicans would allow states to ban Medicaid money for victims of rape or incest who seek an abortion. It would also eliminate the Title X program because anti-abortion groups oppose providing money for family planning to organizations like Planned Parenthood, even though the money cannot be used for abortions.[3]

Praying for Power

Gingrich uses religion to promote his attack on the welfare state, even though he has never shown deep faith in anything. Lee Howell, his press secretary and speechwriter in 1974, remembers: "Newt had me take out all the references to God, because he was not very religious—and isn't very religious. He went to church in order to get a nap on Sunday morning. He became a deacon because of who he was, not what he believed. He did not like us to use God in his speeches; he didn't want people to think he was using God, because he said that would be hypocritical. He said, 'I'm not a very strong believer.'"[4]

But with some encouragement from the Religious Right, Gingrich suddenly discovered that his work was a mission from God to help Americans "to find honest self-government and to survive as a free people."[5] Gingrich found religion, politically speaking, about the same time the Religious Right found politics in the early 1980s. Paul Weyrich was one of his early contacts, and Weyrich recognized Gingrich's potential and his willingness to work with the religious conservatives. However, Weyrich always knew it was a marriage of political convenience, not religious faith, and he mocks "the New Age kind of Third Wave Alvin Toffler nonsense that Newt is very much caught up in."[6]

Gingrich soon established himself as one of the leaders in the fight for a Constitutional amendment to "allow" voluntary school prayer, a cause he continues to promote. Although voluntary prayer in public schools has never been prohibited, Gingrich supports a school prayer amendment because "It would block the state from prohibiting any student from engaging in prayer."[7] Gingrich saw the school prayer fight as "the beginning of a cultural battle" fought by those who "fear a theocracy, feel that somehow we will impose a state religion more than they fear cocaine, more than they fear drunk drivers, more than they fear the reality of the world around them."[8]

According to Gingrich, prayer in schools has remarkable, even magical, effects: "We can show you schools which are very poor, but pray. As a consequence, they have no problems with discipline, no problems with homework, and no problems with obedience. On the other hand, we can show you other schools which are very rich, but do not pray. Therefore, they have problems with violence, with people vandalizing the schools and with an absence of homework."[9] Not only did the "ban" on prayer destroy schools, but Gingrich also gave an ominous prediction: "somewhere in America, some day, a first grader will stand up and pray and be arrested" and even "sentenced to a Federal penitentiary for violating a U.S. Supreme Court decision. That is literally what could happen."[10]

Gingrich maintains his delusions about the prayer police to this day. Recently, Gingrich declared that "most people don't know it's illegal to pray. When they learn that a 10-year-old boy in St. Louis was put in detention for saying grace privately over his lunch, they think that's bizarre." But what's really bizarre is that Gingrich thinks this happens. In fact, school officials in St. Louis deny that anything like this ever occurred, and report that the child was disciplined for behavioral problems that had nothing to do with prayer.[11] But for Gingrich, God is a political tool to be used against liberalism, and a politically effective lie is better than telling the truth.

Although Gingrich used religion to sell himself, his biggest accomplishment was convincing the Christian Coalition to strongly support the Contract with America while keeping a low profile on other issues. By secretly helping the Christian Coalition, the National Rifle Association, and similar influential groups, he could push the Contract's goal of economic deregulation without distraction. Gingrich is waiting until Republicans solidify their political control—as Gingrich plans to do in the 1996 elections—to move forward on a conservative social agenda to ban abortion, impose mandatory prayers in public schools, and overturn gun control.

Chapter 13

Lunching on Block Grants: The Destruction of Public Education

When Newt Gingrich announced his plans to repeal the National School Lunch Act and cut billions from funding for school children's lunches, he was shocked at the harsh backlash he received. An indignant Gingrich claimed that the attacks were lies because the Republican plan would increase expenditures by 4.5% each year. But as the *New Republic* pointed out, "this is a phony number." It was Gingrich, not his critics, who tried to lie with statistics.

All denials to the contrary, the Republican plan would sharply cut the school food program. The current program cost $7.6 billion in 1995, and Republicans would have cut it back to $6.6 billion in 1996, and only then increased it by 4.5% each year to keep pace with inflation. Funding would not return to 1995 levels until the year 2000, when the existing program is estimated to require $10 billion. (One wonders how Gingrich would feel if his salary were cut by 13%, and then "increased" at the rate of inflation.) Block grants would save Republicans $2.15 billion annually by 2000 at the price of depriving students from low income families (who might not otherwise get a nutritious meal) of free or reduced-cost lunches.[1]

The school lunch fiasco taught Gingrich a lesson in tactics: never allow the Democrats to take the initiative, and always respond forcefully to any attacks. Gingrich was far more successful at manipulating the debate when he simply lied about the budget cuts than when he ignored the Democratic criticism.

But Gingrich failed to learn the deeper lesson of the school lunch controversy, which is the depth of the American people's opposition to his ideas. The school lunch program is one of the most popular around, and there is overwhelming support for other education programs like Head Start, funding to impoverished schools, and financial aid for college students. While polls show that education is the number one priority for Americans, Gingrich wants to cut all of these education programs. Believing that government is the source of all evil, Gingrich creates private charities which pay children to read books, instead of increasing funding for schools and libraries. If Gingrich can solidify his power in Congress, he will also follow the Christian Coalition's agenda to pass a school voucher plan that will harm public education by diverting resources to religious schools. An enormous gap exists between the desire of most Americans to improve education, and Gingrich's goal of undermining public schools.

Gingrich planned to use block grants to conceal the cuts in school lunches. But no extra money would be available if a recession were to increase the numbers of poor children who need discounted lunches. No federal nutrition standards will be imposed; as a result, states are likely to turn lunch programs over to cheaper and more popular fast-food companies which serve junk food. The era when ketchup was classified as a vegetable to meet nutrition requirements will be gone, replaced by a free market where schools no longer bother to serve vegetables at all.[2] Republican leader John Boehner (R-Ohio) has even attacked what he calls the Agriculture Department's "fat police" for trying to make school lunches more nutritious.[3] The school lunch program, a highly successful government project which has improved child nutrition, will be one more victim of the Contract with America.

Dumbing Us Down

Part of the hidden Contract with America was a decision by Gingrich to dramatically cut back government funding for education. The House planned to completely eliminate the Goals 2000 program aimed at setting nationwide standards and improving the quality of teaching; it cut Title I funding for public schools with large numbers of poor students (which usually have far fewer resources per student than public schools in rich areas) by 17%.

According to House majority leader Dick Armey, "even in our poorest neighborhoods we spend some $7,000 to $10,000 per student" per year in public schools.[4] Harsh budget cuts are not a surprising result when Republican leaders believe such nonsense. The truth is that the average spending for public schools in America is far less than $7,000 per student, and in most of our poorest neighborhoods, it is usually far below the average. Because the federal government spends so little on public education (providing about 6% of public school funding), most of the money must come from local property taxes, and as a result, educational disparities between rich and poor communities are enormous. The Republican plan to cut programs for poor students means that these large gaps between rich and poor will grow even larger.

Of course, there are a few major cities where spending on public schools reaches or even exceeds the average. But many of these schools deal with high operating costs from unionized workers, a central bureaucracy, older facilities, and a large number of disadvantaged and special education students who require greater help. Even with these problems, urban schools spend far less per student than suburban public schools, where students have all the advantages.

In the eyes of the Republicans, anything that helps the poor is a "welfare" program that needs to be cut or destroyed. Even the Head Start program would be cut by $137 million under the House plan. Head Start is already underfunded, and preschools enroll only 35% of low-income children. While President Clinton proposed increasing Head Start by $400 million, the Republicans want to cut Head Start's budget by 4%. Although some studies had questioned the long-term value of Head Start (no one doubts its positive short-term effects), a comprehensive study by the Packard Foundation's Center for the Future of Children determined that Head Start does benefit children, increasing high school graduation rates, and reducing the number of poor children who end up on welfare or in prison.[5] A small investment in Head Start and similar child care programs not only helps welfare mothers get jobs, but it saves a huge amount of money in the future by reducing welfare and criminal justice costs.

If Gingrich were truly concerned about an "opportunity society," he would try to narrow the education gap between rich and poor. Although 82% of children from high-income families attend preschool, only 45% of children from low-income families do.[6] Even if we ignore the moral obligation to help poor children improve their opportunities, one would think that conservatives would support a program that saves money in the long run, and in the past, Republicans like George Bush have been strong defenders of Head Start. But supporting an effective program like Head Start would be an admission that the federal government can help people. The reigning anti-government ideology of today's Republicans leads them to irrationally ignore the clear evidence of Head Start's success. The irony is that Gingrich is trying to destroy government education programs that he profited from long ago. He went to graduate school on a fellowship provided by the National Defense Education Act, and his daughter Kathy attended preschool for free thanks to the Head Start program which he is now undermining.[7]

Gingrich's attack on equal opportunities covers every level of education. In higher education, Gingrich wants to cut $20 billion over the next five years, depriving many poor students of the opportunity to get a college degree. The largest part of this cut is $12 billion from ending interest moratoriums on student loans. Instead of delaying interest on student debts until after graduation, interest on student loans will start accumulating immediately. The result will be to place poor students deeper and deeper in debt, another hidden tax on the poor inside the Contract.[8]

One study found that 89% of the American public supported maintaining federal aid to higher education. Yet the Republicans have targeted access to higher education for large cuts.[9] At a conference of college presidents in February 1995, Gingrich complained that the government "tolerates the expenditure of a great deal of money on people who are not getting the job done." Gingrich argued for eliminating the Pell grant program because students "are just getting it for being alive....I think that's wrong." Gingrich suggested that work-study programs for impoverished students replace Pell grants, apparently unaware that almost all of the poor students who get Pell grants already work their way through college because the grants are far too small; hypocritically, the Republican proposal will actually cut work-study programs. A further reason why students can no longer work their way through college and need financial assistance is the falling value of the minimum wage at a time when tuition costs have skyrocketed.[10]

Many of Gingrich's "education" policies have more to do with the interests of major banks than with the interests of students. Gingrich says he is "unalterably opposed" to direct lending of student loans on the grounds that the federal government "has failed miserably in almost everything that it has done." Yet direct lending is a perfect example of how the government is actually more efficient than the private sector. Instead of subsidizing banks with risk-free loans backed by the federal government, under direct lending the government provides the money directly, in a much faster period of time, with better means of ensuring repayment. Only Gingrich's obsessive hatred of government programs (and his desire to help out the wealthy bankers who contribute to Republican causes) can explain his opposition to an effective government program.

Bookscam: The Earning by Learning Program

The "Earning by Learning" program is one of Gingrich's favorite charities, and he donated thousands of dollars from royalties during his *To Renew America* book tour. Gingrich founded Earning by Learning with a $3,100 donation of his own in 1990; the money came from $67,491 he made in honoraria, of which $40,000 had to go to charities because of a House limit on accepting money for speeches. After 1990, when a new law banned members of Congress from pocketing any honoraria at all, Gingrich directed his speech money into the "Earning by Learning" program, gaining him an image as a charitable politician, and letting him "prove" that private charity can do a better job than government.

The rest of the money for "Earning by Learning" came from the right-wing Randolph Foundation, whose executive director is Heather Higgins, a close friend of Gingrich, and host of his cable TV show, "Progress Report with Newt Gingrich." Higgins herself gave $15,000 to GOPAC, and ordered her foundation to give $50,000 to Gingrich's "Renewing American Civilization" course. Since foundations are prohibited from giving money to candidates or political action committees, Gingrich's phony nonprofit groups were the only way

Higgins could reach into the deep pockets of the Randolph Foundation to help promote her friend.[11]

"Earning by Learning" pays children $2 for every book they read. Newt touts it as a symbol of what can be done without government: "The overhead is totally volunteer, the entire structure is totally volunteer. The only money goes to the kids. So if you have $1,000,—at $2 a book you can pay for 500 books. Whereas, in the welfare state model, if you have $1,000, you pay $850 of it for the bureaucracy."

But it turns out that this isn't true. Since 1992, Mel Steely—a friend of Gingrich's when he was at West Georgia College, his 1986 campaign manager, and the author of his authorized biography—has pocketed nearly half of the program's $62,000 in funding for consulting fees. In 1995, Steely and two other West Georgia professors took 86% of the $24,126 spent on "Earning by Learning"—far worse than the evil government bureaucracy Gingrich imagines. Earning $75 an hour, Steely and his friends must have been learning a lot about this "phenomenal" program.[12] Steely also learned how to mix politics and charity, since he used "Earning by Learning" money to pay for three trips to Gingrich's Saturday-morning class, and he submitted notes and requests for reimbursement on Gingrich campaign stationery that read "Re-elect Newt" and "Newt Is My Friend" at the top and "Paid for by Friends of Newt Gingrich" at the bottom. Steely also apparently spent some of his time on the "Earning by Learning" payroll planning for Gingrich's political future, since its files include his notes about how his friend might be affected by reapportionment: "Newt should be OK in Floyd County".[13]

However repugnant the grab of cash by advisors can be, Steely was no outside consultant. Gingrich was in effect supplementing Steely's salary as his administrative assistant by funneling money to him through the non-profit West Georgia College Foundation that ran the "Earning by Learning" program. This kind of payment is called "self-dealing" and is banned under House rules.

Steely wasn't the only Gingrich friend to profit from "Earning by Learning." In Denver, the program allocated 43% of the budget for one staff position, and planned for only 280 kids to be paid a total of $16,800 for reading books in the summer of 1996. In contrast, the Denver Public Library sponsors a summer program for 30,000 children, with librarians who volunteer their time and reward children with donated items. These programs help improve literacy much more than the symbolic gesture of Gingrich's pet project. The "Earning by Learning" program demonstrates that it is often private greed rather than government bureaucracy which leads to waste.

But the program is more than a means for the Speaker to pad the salaries of his friends and staff. "Earning by Learning" offers its sponsors yet another tax-free way to influence Gingrich and his policies. In Houston, "Earning by

Learning" is sponsored by the Houston Automobile Dealers Association, and co-founder Charles Smith recently had the opportunity to testify against the luxury tax before a House committee. Smith notes that the "Earning by Learning" program gave the dealers' association access to Gingrich "about industry-related issues, tax-related issues, government-related issues, you name it."[14] Perhaps the program might more honestly be called "Earning by Lobbying."

Gingrich claims, "We do everything we can to get our kids to read. The poorest children in America are having their futures stolen by illiteracy." But we—and especially Newt Gingrich—are not doing everything possible to get poor kids to read. We allow them to go to inadequately-funded schools. We allow them to live in areas with impoverished libraries and reading programs. In theory, Gingrich wants to end illiteracy, but he is not willing to overcome his prejudice against any and all government programs to do it.

The "Earning by Learning" program does little to address the real literacy problems of children in poverty. A *Wall Street Journal* article told the story of Cassandra Mozley, who earned $414 in six weeks by reading 207 books, but Mozley said she wasn't motivated by the money.[15] The program at the Douglas Village summer camp was never repeated because, unfortunately, the camp closed the next year due to lack of funding.

Shoveling out cash to students may be an effective program in certain circumstances, but it rarely helps students become self-motivated readers. In Gingrich's college course, he assigns an essay by Barbara Lawton, who observes, "When external rewards such as money, television, gold stars, are used to motivate children (or adults for that matter), we send the message that what they are doing is of less intrinsic value than the reward and not worth doing for its own sake. These practices rob our work of meaning and put at risk the very value system we are trying to create."[16] Unless there is a support system to help provide educational opportunities for children in poverty, throwing $2 bills at kids will do almost nothing except promote the political ambitions of Newt.[17]

Gingrich wants to cut education funding even as he hypocritically and constantly talks about "opportunity." According to Gingrich, "we want every person who is, you know, born without money to have an opportunity. We believe in the equality of opportunity...we don't believe in the equality of outcome."[18] But what equality of opportunity is there when one group of Americans has access to quality preschools, and another group does not? What kind of opportunity exists when one group of Americans attends well-funded public schools with high standards, and another group must, because of their poverty, go to much poorer, inadequate schools? What kind of opportunity is possible when government cutbacks in student aid make it difficult for many Americans to attend college and get a higher education? Gingrich means "opportunity" in the narrowest sense of something not forbidden by the government; the fact that the free market fails to provide equal opportunity is simply inevitable to Gingrich, not a problem for which government intervention is needed. True equality, and real educational opportunity, cannot be just a slogan used for political purposes. It requires a commitment to make sure that every American child has an equal chance to succeed—an idea which Gingrich is fundamentally opposed to.

Chapter 14

Dying for Tax Cuts: Gingrich's Dangerous Health Policy

The Contract with America makes an impossible promise: to balance the budget while protecting Social Security, and adding large increases to build prisons, enlarge the military, and cut taxes for the rich. Much like Reagan, who promised all of this while running up the largest federal debt in American history, Gingrich was lying to avoid the political consequences of confronting America's economic problems. Unfortunately for Gingrich, the American welfare state is so small that even the massive cuts in education, welfare, and environmental protection planned by the Republicans would be insufficient to finance Gingrich's defense programs and massive tax cuts.

Lies, Damn Lies—and Accounting

In order to get popular support for the Contract, Gingrich promised to momentarily spare Social Security (but added a tax cut for wealthy individuals on Social Security, which will weaken the financial condition of the program). However, he decided to sharply reduce Medicare, the program that subsidizes health care for the elderly, using a highly regressive plan to save $270 billion in which most of the added costs and cuts in care fall upon the poor and middle-classes. The Medicare cuts are the linchpin in the Contract's plan, since without them there is no possible way to balance the budget and finance a $245 billion tax cut for the wealthy.

Gingrich repeatedly claims that Republicans aren't cutting Medicare. In 1995, he declared, "I just want to make a couple of public commitments that you can absolutely count on. The first is that Medicare expenditures per senior citizen will go up every year over the next seven years, and it will ultimately go up from $4,800 a year, which is this year's number, to over $6,700 a year, per senior citizen. So, first of all, it will be an increase."[1] But by 2002, when the Republicans offer $6,700 per senior citizen, inflating health care costs will require $8,400 to match today's benefits. The difference will come out of the pockets of senior citizens or in reduced quality of medical care.

The cut alleged by critics and denied by Gingrich is, in fact, a cut. If the price of bread goes up by one dollar and you give someone an extra quarter for bread, is that really an "increase" in spending, as Gingrich claims? By failing to account for the cost of inflation and for demographic changes which will make many more people eligible for Medicare, Gingrich is deceiving the public by labeling a cut as an increase. Lying through accounting tricks is Gingrich's favorite way to deny that the Republicans are imposing severe cuts on social programs.

Gingrich never revealed how he would actually reduce the cost of medical care using the free market. On *Meet The Press*, Gingrich offered his model of Medicare reform: creating an 800 number for people to report Medicare abuse. But as Health and Human Services Secretary Donna Shalala noted, "we actually have on the books a law that allows Medicare beneficiaries to receive 10 to 30 percent of recoveries." The 800 number for Medicare fraud already exists, and the government has made over $240 million since 1988, with $25 million going to the whistleblowers.[2]

The Republicans plan to save $270 million by cutting Medicare over seven years. The Republicans can fund their plan only by raising premiums (which is the equivalent of raising taxes, since Americans must pay for the program) or by cutting payments to doctors and hospitals.

An Office of Management and Budget study found that $101 billion would come from reduced payments to medical providers. Doctors and hospitals are unlikely to reduce their profits and salaries in response to these cuts. Instead, they will cut services or pass the costs on to the entire medical system. Cutting services may be a good idea in some cases, where there is waste in the system and excessive expense, but the Republican plan to "save" Medicare doesn't distinguish between good cuts to save money and bad cuts that reduce the quality of health care. All cuts are the same, and all cuts are demanded by the Republicans regardless of medical effects.

However, most of the budget "savings" in Medicare will come from increased premiums in the Part B program for doctor's visits and other non-hospital medical services. Some of the possible ideas (which the Republicans have yet to detail publicly, but are designing in secret) include means-testing Medicare to increase the premiums for wealthy people. But it is doubtful that the Republicans will try to make the rich pay more; the most likely result is that everyone in Medicare will have to pay a higher deductible for doctor's visits and higher monthly premiums.[3]

Gingrich promised that "no senior citizen anywhere in America will be forced to drop the present system." In fact, Gingrich admitted that senior citizens who stay with the existing Medicare system would have to pay "a little bit" more.[4] Gingrich claimed that senior citizens would only have to pay about $7 more a month for Medicare Part B, which pays for doctors' visits, but Bruce

Vladek of the Health Care Financing Administration estimates that the actual increase will need to be $21.50 a month, amounting to a $250-a-year stealth "tax" on the elderly.[5]

Gingrich protected doctors' fees to get the endorsement of the American Medical Association, and stopped a proposal to raise co-payments and deductibles for those who stayed in the traditional Medicare plan, to satisfy the AARP.[6] But both groups are foolish to believe Gingrich's promises. As it becomes clear that the amount saved on Medicare by free-market devices doesn't come anywhere near the $270 billion needed by Gingrich to balance the budget, both doctors and senior citizens will become the victims of further budget cuts.

The health care cutbacks will be particularly brutal for the poor, given the Republican plans to cut $150 billion from Medicaid coverage for the most impoverished individuals. The poor cannot afford the massive increases in premiums, so the likely result will be a sharp cut in the quality of health care they receive.

The Republicans will simply cut the federal subsidy for medical care, making individuals (particularly the poor) bear the brunt of the cost. The effect on public health will be disastrous, since increasing co-payments will discourage visits to doctors, even though early and effective treatment is the best way to reduce medical costs. The Republicans have entirely abandoned the concept of preventive medicine, which is the only way to truly reduce medical costs without cutting access to quality care. Now, only money matters, and saving money (even when the cost is directly transferred to the public, and causes social harm) is their sole short-term goal.

The Republicans' destruction of Medicare and Medicaid is based on a fundamental misinterpretation of health care and the free market. Gingrich assumes that medicine can be run like any other business: the rich will get what they can afford, and the poor will get little or nothing. But this violates the basic principles of most doctors and hospitals: their job is (or should be) to save lives, not check insurance records.

Already, there is a growing gap in health care between the rich and poor in this country. With the Republican proposals, it will reach a crisis point. As managed care companies try to reduce costs, and Medicaid payments are made smaller and smaller, doctors and hospitals will be pressured to refuse poor people who come seeking care. There will be millions of people, many of them children, who will be unable to get medical treatment and will be left to suffer.

It is not certain that the Republicans in Congress will allow this to happen. But it is clear that if they intend to balance the budget and cut taxes for the rich by denying medical entitlements that poor children, disabled individuals, and impoverished elders will go without necessary care and medication.

The Republican budget for Medicare and Medicaid can only be achieved by this level of cruelty, and whether they (or the American people) have the compassion to stop it remains to be seen.

Science Fiction Health Care: Newt's Medical Ethics

"I believe in the 21st century," Gingrich told the American Medical Association in a 1995 speech.[7] For someone who claims to think about technology so much, he is remarkably ignorant of its effects on health care. He says medical technology "will cause a revolution and will lower the cost of health care" by tens of billions each year.[8] It is this fantasy that enables Gingrich to imagine cutting hundreds of billions of dollars from Medicare over the next seven years while promising that health care will not be made worse for people. But medicine is greatly different from other fields when it comes to technology. In addition to the high cost of medical research, a new treatment is often more expensive than the old one. And by extending the lives of people, medical expenses over a lifetime inevitably will rise. This is the most important reason why medical costs are rising so dramatically.

In *To Renew America*, Gingrich imagines futuristic scenarios for health care. When sick, "you sit in your diagnostic chair and communicate with the local health clinic." And, "if you face some rare or life-threatening disease, information systems will allow you to study the most advanced work around the world." Because there is so much information in the future, "health care has become more flexible and convenient—and less expensive."[9]

With a utopian vision this bizarre, it's no surprise that Gingrich's solutions to the health care crisis are completely inadequate. A "diagnostic chair" in every home would be an extraordinarily expensive and wasteful device. Most people don't have enough money to buy sophisticated medical technology and use it for furniture.

As for the information revolution, it will not lower medical costs. Even if you could find the latest medical research on the internet and understand it, the knowledge wouldn't cure you. Medical expenses are rising because of expensive technology and expertise, which won't be cured by an inexpensive magic pill available on the World Wide Web if only everyone would search for it. Neither the information revolution nor Gingrich's increase in medicare premiums will change the key reason for rapid growth in health care costs: the huge profits generated by hospitals, HMOs, doctors, and drug companies.

Gingrich imagines a future where waves of "medical tourists" come to America for top-notch medical treatment, and American doctors perform surgery in India via computer. This plan to save American medicine would not, however, do anything to help the poor who cannot afford similar treatment. Gingrich imagines that the free market will solve every problem, if government just gets out of the way. But the reality behind Gingrich's fairy tale of free enterprise is much more grim.

The goal of the Gingrich health care plan is not to improve efficiency, expand coverage, or merely control costs. Rather, Gingrich ultimately wants to eliminate the "socialist" flaw in our medical system, which gives care to poor people who cannot afford to pay. In its place will be the unfettered free market, where hospitals maximize their profits by catering to rich patients and ignoring the poor. A hospital, according to Gingrich's ideal, should be no different from any other business. After all, a pizzeria isn't obliged to give away pizza to people who can't pay for it, even if they're starving. Why should a hospital treat anyone if they can't afford the medical care? Why should hospitals be different from other businesses just because people will die without medical treatment?

Answering that question requires some sense of an ethical obligation to prevent the suffering and death of fellow human beings, a moral belief that it is wrong for the poor to be denied medical care. But in the amoral free market ethics of Newt Gingrich, there is no reason to care about the poor. Gingrich's health care program is determined not by compassion for the dying, but by a ruthless determination to cut budgets and help out the corporate leaders in health care whose donations have helped him rise to be Speaker of the House.

Selling Out Medicare: Medical Savings Accounts

The guiding force behind Gingrich's ideas for health care reform is the corporate leadership of Golden Rule Insurance. Chairman J. Patrick Rooney, along with president John Whelan, gave a total of over $150,000 to GOPAC. Golden Rule's executives and its PAC have given $42,500 to Gingrich's campaign. In 1993-94 they spent more than $1 million on Republican candidates and PACs in an intense drive to "privatize" Medicare and replace it with "Medical Savings Accounts," a kind of health care IRA. Gingrich has endorsed this plan to destroy Medicare, and in October 1995 he declared about Medicare, "We don't want to get rid of it in round one because we don't think it's politically smart. But we believe that it's going to wither on the vine," claiming that people are "going to leave it voluntarily."[10]

Gingrich's "wither-on-the-vine" strategy is to destroy the Medicare system by forcing the elderly into Medical Savings Accounts. The Republicans envision a system of triage that will control few costs and drain money away into the pockets of managed care companies, Medical Savings Account insurers, and healthier senior citizens, with dramatically worse health care for the sick and dying.

The regular Medicare system will quickly become the last refuge of the ill. As healthier and wealthier individuals move to managed care and Medical Savings Accounts with smaller premiums, the cost of the regular Medicare system will rise precipitously, since those left in the program will be the sick and the poor. To meet this rising expense, premiums will be increased repeatedly, driving more and more people out. Then, in triumph, Gingrich and his allies will point to the artificially high cost of regular Medicare (caused by the sicker pool of people) as evidence of its inefficiency, and cite the people driven to managed care by high premiums as evidence of the popularity of their program.

This process is known as "creaming," since it removes the healthiest people from the system without fundamentally improving medical care. Gingrich's claim that this will increase "choice" is pure fantasy. The only choice Americans will have is whether to pay astronomically high health care costs or submit to the Republican plan.

It is difficult to imagine an idea more destructive to the Medicare system than Medical Savings Accounts. The Republican plan is to substantially raise Medicare premiums, forcing people out into cheaper HMOs or Medical Savings Accounts. Companies who run these alternatives will be able to make large profits with a gatekeeping function: excluding the sickest senior citizens (who will remain in the Medicare program, if they can afford it) will allow the companies to save substantial amounts of money without improving the efficiency of America's health care system at all. According to an Urban Institute study, if 20% of the healthiest workers switched to MSAs, premiums would have to rise by 60% for those who stayed within the regular system.[11] As Medicare premiums are raised to pay for these lost resources, more of the healthy will shift to MSAs, leaving Medicare in an increasingly dire position. Even the Congressional Budget Office under the Republicans found that the plan for MSAs would increase the taxpayers' cost for Medicare by $4 billion over seven years.

Taxpayers will have to pay ever-increasing taxes to subsidize Medicare, since huge amounts of money will be drained out as profits to companies like Golden Rule Insurance. MSAs will exacerbate the health care crisis, not solve it, but because the advocates of MSAs are some of the biggest donors to Newt Gingrich and the Republican Party, he is willing to sell out the Medicare system.

In 1992, Rooney had one of the "power walks" with Gingrich which was a perk to major GOPAC donors. Rooney reports, "He took my ideas and ran with them." Gingrich praised Rooney in his "Renewing American Civilization" course and declared that Rooney's Medical Savings Accounts are "the most important new idea in health care."[12] Suzanne Katt, an assistant to Rooney, reports that Golden Rule's massive donations helped persuade Gingrich to support the idea: "To get access to just about any political figure, you've got to find a way to reach them." As usual, the way is money, since Katt says, "You pay to go to GOPAC."[13]

Rooney was not the only corporate executive to whom Gingrich gave special consideration on health care issues. Richard Scrushy, chief executive of HealthSouth, has been a regular donor to Gingrich. Scrushy raised $38,000 for Gingrich's 1994 campaign at a fundraiser held at a HealthSouth rehabilitation facility, and HealthSouth executives and employees have given Gingrich's campaign $42,700 in the past three years. After HealthSouth gave $15,000 to the Progress and Freedom Foundation that was used to broadcast his college course, Gingrich praised the company in a lecture to his students.

In repayment for his generous support, Gingrich named Scrushy as the head of a secret task force to reform workers' compensation, and appointed others to the task force, including Scrushy's vice-president for public relations and representatives of major business interests, who have a financial stake in changes to the law concerning on-the-job injuries.[14] The task force had seven members, four of whom—including Scrushy—were executives at HealthSouth, and two of the four outside advisors were top executives at HealthSouth's lobbying firm. The Scrushy task force consulted no experts in worker's compensation, nor did it consider the interests of workers and insurers. Not surprisingly, the secret task force recommended Medical Savings Accounts as the primary mechanism to help cut costs for employers.

After Scrushy's task force was sharply attacked for its incompetent and unworkable suggestions, Gingrich's office claimed that it was "not an official task force" and Gingrich had simply "empowered a private citizen" to look at the issues, not to propose legislation. The bipartisan American Legislative Exchange Council, a group of state legislators and private corporations, expressed "a great deal of skepticism" toward the task force's proposals to create Medical Savings Accounts, to allow companies to "opt out" of the state workers' compensation system, and to establish a "loser-pays" legal system to discourage worker lawsuits.[15] But even though the task force has been ridiculed for its incompetence, Gingrich will probably use many of their ideas to transform the process of determining who gets health care—and who pays for it.

The Rich and the Dead

Of course, Medicare does present a financial problem that needs to be dealt with, as does Social Security. But there is no crisis that requires enormous increases in premiums, which is the most regressive way to deal with the problem. A far better solution is to means-test Social Security and Medicare, so the wealthiest Americans do not receive an unnecessary government subsidy. Gingrich could also have chosen to save money from Medicare and Medicaid by going after the estimated $100 billion a year in health care fraud. But that would have disgruntled doctors and Health Maintenance Organizations, two groups which support Gingrich because he has promised to increase their influence.

Gingrich could have tried to reduce costs by targeting the expensive use of emergency room treatment by people who have no other access to health care. Emergency walk-ins are unnecessarily high because the same system that requires costs to be borne by the individual encourages people to wait until their health problems become acute, undercutting preventive care that would save millions. But addressing that, of course, would require the "socialism" of universal health care. The truth is that America already has universal health care, but we have a particularly limited and inefficient form of it. Anyone can enter an emergency room and receive care at a high price to taxpayers, but they can't get doctor's visits and far cheaper preventive care. The cost of these emergency room visits doesn't vanish—it gets passed on to all Americans.

It is an undeniable fact that the end result of the Republican "reforms" of medical care will be more dead poor people. And the horrifying truth is that, although Gingrich won't admit it for political reasons, he doesn't care if this happens. After all, the poor didn't put him in power. The poor didn't make contributions of thousands of dollars to his campaigns and projects. The poor didn't elect the Republicans who voted to make him their ruler. Helping the poor would be a bad business decision in the enterprise of politics, where Newt, Inc. seeks to be the largest and most powerful conglomerate. Passing laws to help the poor would be as irrational as hospitals treating people who couldn't pay. And unlike doctors, Newt Gingrich never took a Hippocratic Oath to help people; Gingrich, as the CEO of the House of Representatives, always expects to be paid back for his work. And, not surprisingly, the highest bidders for his services are the corporations who had bought his influence in previous years.

Chapter 15

De-Funding the Left: Gingrich's Attack on Culture

Perhaps the least publicized crusade of the House Republicans is destroying liberalism in America by undermining government institutions that promote cultural enrichment. Dick Armey's book, *The Freedom Revolution*, includes this chilling declaration: "One of the more perceptive bumper stickers I've ever spotted said simply, 'De-fund the Left!' Whoever came up with that motto is my kind of social philosopher."[1] Stephen Moore, an analyst at the libertarian Cato Institute, observes: "There is a movement in Congress to de-fund the left. They are secretive about it."[2] Gingrich wants to take money away from government projects like the National Endowment for the Arts, the National Endowment for the Humanities, and the Corporation for Public Broadcasting—all of which tend to be conservative institutions, but occasionally fund a dissenting voice. Gingrich and friends claim that the "currency of ideas" should rise and sink with the marketplace. But given the overwhelming influence of money on that so-called free market, termination of government funding for the arts will ultimately translate that hackneyed slogan into "money thinks." Gingrich is hoping that big business and wealthy conservatives will fund right-wing ideas exclusively. He is almost certainly right. The Republicans plan to start a revolution, not by the power of their ideas, but by their political and economic power to advance those ideas.

Armey took his argument directly to the private sphere, writing in April 1995 to 82 major corporations, warning them that "many companies are using their philanthropic budgets to support public-policy advocacy groups." Armey's letter targeted "liberal advocacy groups" such as the American Cancer Society and the Anti-Defamation League. The letter was a warning to these companies to start supporting conservative groups (perhaps including Gingrich's Progress and Freedom Foundation) or face retaliation when they sought favors from the Republican leaders.[3]

The Republicans also tried to de-fund the left by attacking charities that receive federal grants. Rep. Ernest Istook proposed a bill designed to silence Gingrich's critics. Congressional staffers report that momentum for the Istook bill grew after protesters from the Association of Community Organizations for Reform Now (ACORN) shouted at Gingrich during a speaking engagement.

Gingrich condemned ACORN as an example of "those who would extort money out of the taxpayer," even though ACORN doesn't directly receive federal funding at all. But ACORN's affiliate groups receive federal grants, which the Republicans would like to cut off.[4] It was ironic, to say the least, for Gingrich to try to punish legal non-profit groups for their activities while he ran illegal non-profits to promote his electoral ambitions.

In fact, Republicans want to punish all left-leaning non-profit groups so that for-profit corporations (who support the Republican agenda) will be able to dominate Congress with their influence. The Republicans resoundingly defeated an amendment to ban for-profit corporations from lobbying Congress if they get federal contracts. But the principle should be the same: people who get money from the government have a First Amendment right to petition and address their representatives.

Message to the Poor: Don't Go Away to Charities—Just Go Away!

Non-profit groups paid by the government are exactly the same as for-profit corporations: they provide services in exchange for money. The American Association of Retired Persons, for example, receives $140 million annually to run programs that help senior citizens find jobs. Catholic Charities gets $218 million a year to run social programs. The fact that Republicans are attempting to harm these groups even though they represent exactly what Gingrich supposedly stands for—privatizing social programs rather than leaving them in the hands of the federal bureaucracy—puts the lie to his "effective compassion" rhetoric.[5]

The Republicans would like to simply cut off government funding and rely on charity to support these programs. But private donations provide only 18% of funding for charities, while government aid supplies nearly twice as much. Non-profit groups are already regulated in their lobbying; they cannot use government money to do lobbying, and no more than 20% of their private donations can be used for lobbying.[6]

As Georgetown law professor David Cole observed, "The law's reporting requirements are perhaps its most draconian feature."[7] Every single nonprofit group with a federal grant would have to keep track of how much money they spend on "political advocacy." Any individuals or contractors who devoted more than 15% of their funding to political speech or activity would count as a political advocate and would need to be reported to the government. While the Republicans complain about overregulation of business, they want to mount a government-imposed ideological inquisition against non-profit groups who disagree with them. It's an ominous sign of the times when charities are defined as being on the left simply because they provide things like clothes and food to help the poor.

Another Istook Amendment was proposed in response to the massive protests against the Contract on more than 100 college campuses around the country in March 1995. These student protests, organized by coalitions of local progressive groups, provided the largest outcry on college campuses since the Persian Gulf War.

In an attempt to silence opposition like this, Istook proposed an amendment which would cut off all federal funds to any college or university that allowed money from student fees to support "any organization or group that is engaged in lobbying or seeking to influence public policy or political activity." Not only would this proposal censor liberal groups opposed to the Contract, but it would also threaten student governments and other groups who fought the Republicans' efforts to cut financial aid to the poor in college.

While neither of the Istook proposals were passed, the Republicans are pursuing their agenda to "de-fund the left" by reducing the budgets of agencies they deem too liberal. Any department that does not promote a conservative, pro-business agenda is vulnerable to attacks from the right.

The House Republicans, angry that a few decisions have been made in favor of labor, cut $52 million from the National Labor Relations Board's $175 million budget, and added riders to prevent the Board from prosecuting certain violations of labor law. Of course, the NLRB isn't a pro-union organization. But in an environment where the Republicans plan to hand all of the advantages to business, the last thing they want is an objective, fair agency to resolve disputes when business can win by crushing unions. The NLRB estimates that the budget cutbacks will quadruple the backlog of cases, showing that the Republican goal is a less productive government, not greater efficiency.[8]

The War on Culture and the Limitations of the "Free Market"

One of Gingrich's goals as Speaker is to control American culture. Gingrich condemns PBS as "an enclave of elite people that take care of each other" and he attacked the "enclaves of the left using your money to propagandize your children against your values." Yet at the same time, he pledged $2,000 a year to his local PBS station. It was a completely contradictory position: condemning PBS as left-wing elitist propaganda, and then offering a substantial amount of his own money to support it. But it made political sense, since it enabled Gingrich to claim that he was trying to privatize PBS, not to destroy it.

Other Republicans joined in the witchhunt against PBS. Sen. Larry Pressler (R-S.D.) sent a questionnaire to PBS, NPR, and other public broadcasters, asking about the content of its liberal programs, such as the "balance and objectivity" of *Frontline* and *P.O.V.* and the "profanity, nudity and indecency" of *American Playhouse*.[9]

The truth is that PBS isn't a left-wing elite network. It has a massive audience spread throughout the economic classes. The vast majority of its programs are non-political nature, music, and children's shows like Sesame Street. Although a few programs like the *P.O.V.* and *Frontline* documentaries have a liberal slant, many more present the establishment point of view (like the *News Hour with Jim Lehrer*, which a study by Fairness and Accuracy In Reporting found had predominantly white male government officials as guests) or aggressively conservative perspectives like *Firing Line* and the *McLaughlin Group*. In response to the attacks, PBS announced plans for yet another right-wing public affairs series, featuring exclusively conservative commentators like Fred Barnes, Morton Kondrake, Suzanne Garment, P.J. O'Rourke, and Juan Williams as correspondents.[10]

Gingrich argues that Big Bird and Barney don't need federal subsidies; the truth is, they don't get them—highly popular programs like Sesame Street actually subsidize the less popular ones that don't draw nearly as much in donations. But a program like Barney is unlikely to survive on commercial networks largely because it appeals to children so young that advertisers don't consider them to be consumers—and parents are reluctant to let them be brainwashed by commercials. Perhaps most importantly, no network would ever give a show like Barney the chance to succeed in the first place. What network executive would imagine that a big, annoying, singing purple dinosaur could have so much appeal? It is always easy to take a successful show and point out that commercial television could sustain it as a moneymaker. But one of the virtues of public television is that it takes a chance on programming that commercial TV is unwilling to try in the first place.

Of course, Gingrich is right about one thing: PBS can survive on its own—by becoming yet another commercial TV network, sustained by individual donations and corporate sponsorships that more and more resemble commercials. But in doing so, it will tend to sacrifice its independence from the restraints of the "free" market. PBS will need to appeal to a larger and larger audience to satisfy its corporate advertisers, making it less outstanding amid the squalor of network programming. It will discard its best viewing options, such as the educational programming (like WNET's programs for 100,000 viewers who are learning to read or are earning GEDs).[11] When PBS and NPR provide the only in-depth hour-long news broadcasting in America, and the only serious educational programs (like Ken Burns' *The Civil War)*, it seems strange to destroy them. Clearly, there are some things that the free market can't provide effectively, and educational programming is one of them. Educational cable networks like A & E are plainly inferior to PBS, and are also unavailable to those who can't afford cable television.

It is Gingrich who is the true elitist, in the worst sense of the word. He says, "I'm very much for increasing contributions to the Smithsonian and the

Library of Congress. You ought to have national institutions that are world class."[12] Gingrich doesn't object to elite cultural institutions, but to programs like the NEA, NEH, and PBS, which bring culture directly to the American public. (His support of the Smithsonian may also have something to do with the $5,000 replica of a *Tyrannosaurus rex* head in his office, made and loaned to Gingrich by the Smithsonian at his request.)

Gingrich's hatred of PBS funding is symbolic of his anti-government program. Even though the benefits of educational programming have been numerous, and a government-supported network poses no threat to the commercial networks, Gingrich believes that the free market must be worshiped, and not degraded by non-commercial values. To allow PBS to continue being funded with government money would suggest that there exists something that network television and the free market cannot provide.

Of course, this is exactly what Dole, Quayle, Gingrich, and other cultural conservatives have argued in their endless sermonizing about values. One would imagine, given their complaints about Murphy Brown, NYPD Blue, and similar shows, that they should be the strongest supporters of PBS, which is one of the few bulwarks against the stupidity of network TV. But the Right is not opposed to stupidity, only to liberalism, and they are angry that "social misfits" like gays and liberals are, on rare occasion, able to express themselves on PBS, since there is less pressure from advertisers to silence such programs.

Republicans like Gingrich and Dole, who complain about the lowly state of our culture and the supreme importance of values, turn around and destroy the few government-supported institutions that are working to preserve our culture. Their venomous hatred of government is so profound that they must eliminate an area of government funding that is useful and effective.

The fact that the arts and humanities will survive in the absence of government subsidies is hardly a reason for destroying the NEA and the NEH. It's akin to arguing that privately-funded libraries would exist without government support, or that private highways could take the place of federal transportation programs. Although true, such arguments fail to mention the enormous loss of public culture that will occur, particularly in poorer areas where the opportunities for private funding are smaller, if the NEA and NEH are terminated. Even today, budget cuts are eliminating arts programs from public schools.

What Gingrich envisions for television is a "free market" similar to the model of political campaigns, where the people with money determine the content of programming for the rest of us, who are only nominally in control. Hence, advertisers, not viewers (and contributors, not voters) are the ones with real power to decide what is shown. Gingrich's answer to the problems of the free market is to deny them: his response, in both cases, is to exacerbate the problem with more private money and the total exclusion of public involvement. Hatred of government is the closest thing Gingrich has to a real ideology. And it makes sense: it is the one area where his own conservative/libertarian tendencies directly match the interests of his major corporate donors.

When Robert Hughes wrote an essay in *Time* criticizing the severe cuts in the arts, Gingrich wrote a two-page response, perhaps the longest letter *Time* has ever printed.[13] Gingrich declared, "When we have a national debt of nearly $5 trillion, it is the height of arrogance to believe that anyone's pet programs should be sacred cows." Yet the arts and humanities are hardly sacred cows: they were cut by 40% in one year, while the corporate welfare supported by Gingrich's business allies was untouched.

Ironically, Gingrich wrote that "contributions to federal political campaigns are not tax deductible, because taxpayers should not have to subsidize the political activity of their fellow citizens." Yet this is exactly what Gingrich illegally forced taxpayers to do with the Progress and Freedom Foundation. Gingrich asks, "Why then should they be forced to pay for skillfully presented political statements masquerading as art?" Gingrich is the prince of hypocrisy: he illegally uses taxpayer money to help write and promote his books, he illegally uses taxpayer money to subsidize his self-promotion efforts via his "college course," and then he complains because a small amount of taxpayer money is used for art he doesn't like.

Gingrich attacked NEA-supported cultural institutions with invented anecdotes, such as his claim that Ron Athey was paid by the NEA for a performance that dripped AIDS-contaminated blood onto the audience. In reality, the blood wasn't HIV-positive, it wasn't dripping on the audience (the blood was staining paper towels hung over them), and the NEA never funded the performance. Rather, the NEA gave a general grant to the Walker Art Center in Minnesota, of which $150 was used to support the Athey performance. By Gingrich's logic, any cultural institution should be completely de-funded if it ever supports one performance which offends him. If the same principle were applied to the Library of Congress, one can imagine the long list of books he would want to burn.

According to Gingrich, "Republicans share the basic optimism of the American people and prefer to emphasize a positive vision of our nation's future." Gingrich promised that Republicans would favor "restructuring the tax system to create further incentives to contributing to the arts and other worthwhile charities."

But now Gingrich is plotting with Dick Armey to create a flat tax that will eliminate all deductions for charitable contributions, harming all non-profit arts groups and charities. Although Gingrich goes through the motions of pretending to support culture, his real aim is to get rid of cultural institutions which support a broad range of ideas and activities. Without them, the free market will reign, and whoever has the money can dictate what the people see and hear.

Chapter 16

Congressional Gay Bashing: Homophobia in the House

When it comes to homosexuality, Gingrich's moral depravity comes slinking out of the closet. Here is a man who stands without principles, willing to bend to whatever interest group can exert enough power against him. It matters little to Gingrich that his half-sister Candace is openly lesbian—Newt has never been one to let family values stand in the way of his political ambitions. Gingrich uses anti-gay rhetoric carefully and effectively, avoiding some of the bigoted extremes of his homophobic friends. He has no deep-seated hatred of gays and lesbians, only a pragmatic understanding of the political power which is exerted by the anti-gay right.

However, Gingrich has an ugly history of anti-gay remarks and votes. In 1990, Gingrich attacked liberals for opposing contact tracing of the AIDS virus. In 1992, Gingrich was one of nine House Republicans who denounced Republican official Robert Mosbacher for meeting with the National Gay and Lesbian Task Force at the request of Mosbacher's openly lesbian daughter. In 1994, Gingrich defended three representatives who said they would never hire a gay or lesbian.[1]

Karen Van Brocklin, one of Gingrich's top staffers, spread false rumors that Speaker Tom Foley was gay in an unsuccessful attempt to get the media to cover the story. Larry Sabato, author of *Feeding Frenzy*, observed that Van Brocklin was "particularly aggressive" in spreading the rumors. Van Brocklin told a *New York Daily News* columnist, "We hear it's little boys." The story finally came out when the Republican National Committee communications director, Mark Goodin, sent a memo to Republican leaders titled, "Tom Foley: Out of the Liberal Closet," and compared Foley's voting record to that of openly gay Congressman Barney Frank. The memo was leaked to reporters so that the rumors would appear on the day Foley became Speaker.[2]

Gingrich refused to fire Van Brocklin, who also did the research attacking Jim Wright's ethics. He claimed that she was merely asked by a reporter if there were stories around about Foley's personal life, "and she stupidly said yes." But the *Los Angeles Times* discovered that Gingrich was lying: several reporters said that Van Brocklin "had brought up the subject of Foley's alleged behavior with at least three news organizations and had tried to get them to publish stories on the subject by claiming other newspapers were about to do so."[3]

Gingrich on Gays: "An Orientation the Way Alcoholism Is An Orientation"

In 1994, according to the Human Rights Campaign Fund, Gingrich didn't cast one vote in favor of equal treatment of homosexuals. Gingrich declared, "it would be madness to pretend that families are anything other than heterosexual couples," and suggested that homosexuality was "an orientation in the way that alcoholism is an orientation."[4] Gingrich also supported a 1993 resolution by Cobb County, Georgia—located in his district—which called homosexuality "incompatible with the standards to which this community subscribes." When gay and lesbian critics urged the organizers of the 1996 Olympics to keep volleyball events out of Cobb County because of its bigotry, Gingrich condemned the request as "emotional blackmail." Gingrich said, "over time we want to have an explicit bias in favor of heterosexual marriage. If you look at the pathologies and weaknesses of America today, reestablishing the centrality of marriage and of the role of male and female in that relationship is a very central issue of the next two years."[5] Gingrich frequently uses the "family values" line to disguise a vicious attack on gays and lesbians.

In order to get the active support of the Religious Right during the 1994 elections, Gingrich promised Lou Sheldon, head of the Traditional Values Coalition, that he would hold hearings attacking public-funded AIDS prevention programs as part of the "Gay Rights Agenda." Sheldon has urged banning all federal funding of public schools that offer counseling on HIV/AIDS, anti-gay violence, or teen suicide. At a January 14, 1995 town meeting, Gingrich explained, "if we have a one-day hearing on whether or not taxpayer money is being spent to promote things that are literally grotesque, that that's a legitimate request."[6] Rather than question the obvious lies being spread by the anti-gay right, Gingrich said: "I think frankly you have had clearly what is in effect recruitment in so-called counseling programs. So I'm very cautious about the idea that you want to have active homosexuals in junior high school and high school explaining that they have all of these various wonderful options."[7] By spreading one of the sleaziest myths of the anti-gay movement ("active" homosexuals are "recruiting" young boys and girls to become their sexual partners), Gingrich showed that he has no principles or honesty, only a passionate desire for political gain.

In 1995, when a federal judge struck down Clinton's "don't ask, don't tell" policy as an unconstitutional form of discrimination against gay and lesbian soldiers, Gingrich promised that he would work to re-impose the even more restrictive policy that previously existed: "I expect Congress to take up that issue....We're going to probably go back to the rules that existed prior to President Clinton changing them." Even though Gingrich opposed an anti-gay amendment in 1993 to require the military to ask recruits about homosexuality, he has shifted toward the anti-gay far right in order to appease the most extreme elements of the Republican Party.[8]

In 1996, Magic Johnson urged Congress and the President to overturn the new Pentagon rule to discharge 1,049 healthy HIV-positive members of the military. Johnson wrote about the need to "stop ignorance, fear and prejudice from forcing them to 'retire' from the jobs they love and their importance to our country." But Gingrich lashed out against Johnson, declaring that "what Magic Johnson doesn't understand is the nature of being in the military and the danger of being in combat." According to Gingrich, "No one who has ever studied seriously how bad combat can get wants to have a person in your unit who's HIV-positive, because you have a very real danger of transferring blood. It is a totally irresponsible position for the administration to take. It's a sign of how little President Clinton understands combat and the difficulties of being able to deal with these kinds of dangers." In fact, it is Gingrich (who has never been in the military, having received family and student deferments during the Vietnam War) who doesn't understand military policy, which prohibited HIV-positive soldiers from serving in combat or going overseas.[9]

Gingrich does not hesitate to surround himself with bigots. Dick Armey, majority leader under Gingrich, noted in a 1994 radio interview, "I like peace and quiet and I don't need to listen to Barney Fag...Barney Frank haranguing in my ear because I made a few bucks off a book I worked on." Armey claimed that he was "stumbling over words" and has a problem "with alliteration." As Barney Frank noted, "people who start out to say 'Frank' rarely say 'fag' as a purely random act."[10] Armey has a perfect anti-gay voting record. In 1994, he supported a bill denying federal funds to any school that suggested in any way that homosexuality is "a positive lifestyle alternative."[11] After Gingrich's close friend Terry Kohler (who is also Gingrich's leading donor, having given over $715,457 to GOPAC), lost the 1982 governor's race in Wisconsin, he declared that his opponent "promised to appoint queers and he has," referring to an openly gay press secretary.[12] Gingrich has never criticized his friends and financial supporters for their homophobic views.

Gingrich claims, "I am against repression, and I'm against promotion. I believe in tolerance." In his 1984 book, *Window of Opportunity*, Gingrich reminisces about traditional values of old: "When I was a boy, the movie *The Moon Is Blue* was banned in Boston for using the word 'virgin.' A group in southern California was trying to keep Tarzan out of public libraries because Tarzan and Jane had not married....We prayed in school." Gingrich writes, "Most Americans now think that the pendulum has swung too far. While they don't want Tarzan banned from the library, they are not very pleased with sadomasochism or child pornography. While they don't favor control over what adults do in their private bedrooms, they generally don't believe homosexual couples should adopt children or teach in schools or that homosexuality is an acceptable alternative lifestyle."[13] This is Gingrich's idea of tolerance: not invading bedrooms, not policing bathrooms, but banning gays from teaching or adopting children.

Gingrich is firmly opposed to equal rights for gays and lesbians. When he was asked on *Meet the Press* if "a businessman should have the right not to hire a gay person," Gingrich replied, "Absolutely. Absolutely."[14] Not surprisingly, one of the major donors to Gingrich's "Renewing American Civilization" class was Cracker Barrel, a restaurant chain notorious for firing gay and lesbian employees.

Yet before he submitted completely to the agenda of the Religious Right, Gingrich was one of the few Republicans willing to criticize the Reagan Administration's mishandling of the AIDS crisis and ready to urge sensible advice to stop the spread of AIDS. In a 1986 position paper, Gingrich wrote that AIDS was "a real crisis which in our lifetime could affect virtually every family in America." Although Gingrich seemed concerned only with the spread of AIDS to heterosexual families, and not the epidemic of AIDS among gay men, his public policy solutions were excellent. He urged that "we need to communicate in clear, explicit terms how to avoid AIDS. We should talk openly about the use of condoms. We must explore public health education opportunities in both our schools and in the media."[15] Today, the newly-homophobic, right-wing Gingrich condemns all of these ideas he once promoted.

It is a sad commentary on the state of bigotry in America that by the standards of the anti-gay movement in America, Gingrich is a moderate. He has never had an intense hatred of homosexuality, but he understands the power of the Religious Right and the political effectiveness of his attacks on having "your tax money" go to "teach you effective methods of sadomasochistic interaction" or to "have first-graders being taught a set of values that, in fact, have no place in the first grade."[16] Like most of what Gingrich says, these "examples" of taxpayer guides to leather and first graders being taught how to be gay are pure invention. But they serve an important political purpose in appealing to the worst side of the American people.

Newt Gingrich is not a bigot in his heart. Unlike the Christian Coalition and his other allies, Gingrich hates gays out of political expediency, not personal hatred. But this makes him even more dangerous. In a country where bigotry against gays and lesbians has reached alarming levels, Gingrich is one of the politically-motivated Republican leaders promoting the homophobia of the Religious Right.

Part IV

The Pseudo-Intellectual

Chapter 17

Newt in Space:
America's Most Vacuous Intellectual

Of all the illusions Gingrich has created about himself, perhaps none is so absurd as Gingrich's claim to be a serious intellectual. Gingrich distinguishes himself from mundane politicians by pointing to his devotion to the realm of ideas. Gingrich excuses his political errors as the excesses of a brilliant professor who cannot restrain himself from expressing unique ideas in spite of the political harm his courage causes.

Behind the Cloak of Ideas: An Odyssey of Power

But buried beneath all of Gingrich's futurist rhetoric and warmed-over Reaganomics is a vapid thinker who uses clichés and harsh attacks on his opponents to disguise the superficiality of his ideas. Gingrich has no devotion to serious beliefs, only a megalomanical drive to make himself the constant subject of attention, even when his stupidity harms his own political ambitions in the process.

Gingrich is not an intellectual turned politician; instead, he is a master manipulator of partisan rhetoric who treats ideas like any other political tool, as powerful instruments for his personal advancement. He understands that a political revolution is not run on ideas, but on power. In his political career, Gingrich had never come up with an idea for legislation that anyone took seriously. But he was considered useful by many Republicans because, unlike the House leadership of the minority party, Gingrich was willing to stand up to the Democrats and viciously attack them. By making himself tactically useful to his fellow Republicans—but certainly not by showing any intellectual or legislative leadership—he rose within the ranks of the Republican Party. It was Gingrich's political leadership, and his remarkable political skills, that made him valuable to the Republican Party. He liked to think of himself as the Republican's intellectual leader, but no one—including his fellow Republicans—could ever figure out exactly what he really believed.

Gingrich's style is to serve up ideas in machine-gun manner, without much concern about whether they are politically viable or even whether they make any sense. His ideology is a fickle creature in constant flux, held stable only by the interests of his major corporate donors: lower taxes on the rich, and a smaller government less able to help most Americans. The Contract never had a coherent ideological framework behind it. Like so much else of his empire, it was a combination of vague promises and standard Republican policies designed to serve major corporations. The only principle that he truly believes in is power: his own.

The Thirst for Power

Gingrich's drive for control and incredible ambitions were apparent at an early age. A look at Gingrich's early years shows a young man desperately seeking power and attention at any cost. When Gingrich was a graduate student in the late 1960s, Tulane University administrators stopped the campus newspaper, the *Hullabaloo*, from printing two photos that they deemed "obscene." One photo showed a nude male arts instructor in front of a giant sculpture with enlarged sexual organs; another depicted a machine with sexual organs and other body parts around it.

Gingrich led a week-long demonstration against the university's censorship, including sit-ins, a march of 700 people to the university president's house, and boycotts of major businesses whose executives were Tulane trustees. Gingrich threatened to stop classes for weeks unless the University allowed the pictures to be printed. In a meeting with president Herbert Longenecker, Gingrich declared: "It is now a question of power. We are down to a clash of wills."[1] For Gingrich, the censorship controversy was an opportunity to experiment in political activism and direct action. In the end, the pictures were not printed, but students were promised greater participation in university governance.

However, Gingrich's true ambition was not to lead protests, but a political revolution. Gingrich was never a creature of ideology. As Bill Kristol, editor of the *Weekly Standard* and chief of staff under Vice President Dan Quayle, observes, "The notion that Gingrich is an ideologue is wrong."[2] Gingrich's friend Vin Weber notes that "many of the other leaders in the House today are far more conservative ideologically than Newt Gingrich."[3] His goal was never to shift the political system toward a particular belief system. Instead, what drove him was the desire to be a historic figure in American politics. Although he was always Republican by inclination, part of his decision to make the Republican Party his instrument of change was a conscious plan to take the minority party and lead them back into power. Joining the Democrats and rising through the system via seniority and obedience to the rules was not Gingrich's style. He wanted a more revolutionary change which would assure him a substantial place in history.

Gingrich's ideological mobility became clear early on. He started off on the liberal wing of the Republican Party; in 1968, he campaigned on behalf of Nelson Rockefeller and went to the Republican Convention as a Rockefeller supporter. His friend David Kramer reported that Gingrich was "really down on Nixon."[4]

But four years later, Gingrich was the Georgia head of the Nixon Committee to Re-Elect the President, (CREEP). A decade later, after Nixon's fall, Gingrich turned to him for advice in organizing like-minded conservatives in Congress. Gingrich was a political opportunist above all else, and he needed the support of influential Republicans to get into office and exert power from within Congress.

However, he needed to get elected first. When Gingrich started looking for a teaching job after receiving his Ph.D., he had a few concerns that were unusual for most graduate students seeking their first job. Instead of trying for a job at the most prestigious and high-paying college he could find, he sought out a good district where he felt the incumbent was vulnerable and he could be elected to Congress.

He chose a small institution called West Georgia College, and started teaching history. Gingrich was looking for a springboard into national politics, and he had an overwhelming desire for power. He sought almost immediately to become chairman of his department. When that failed, he made a rather pathetic bid to become president of the college. Eventually, he alienated most of his history colleagues and shifted over to the geography department.

Benjamin Kennedy, chair of the history department when Gingrich came to West Georgia College, resigned the chair after a year of Gingrich's criticisms: "His way of getting to the top is by destroying other people, building alliances behind the scenes, fighting just to advance himself, to make himself look good. He didn't do the sort of things that academics do. He didn't publish, he didn't do research, he wasn't collegial."[5] It was a style of politics that Gingrich would later hone into an art form in Congress: confrontational, self-serving, and power-hungry.

Gingrich's intense ambition meant that he was unsatisfied with merely academic politics. Although he was a popular teacher, Gingrich could never stick with an idea long enough to write an article about anything. But even more important, Gingrich never had the intellectual talents to be a solid thinker.

Gingrich earned a meagre 2.8 GPA in college, and got into a mediocre graduate program only because of a high score on the Graduate Record Exam at a time when admissions standards were low. He completed an unremarkable dissertation on education policy in the Congo, and never did any scholarly work again. The lure of politics proved far more alluring than the realm of ideas.[6]

It's not surprising that Gingrich was too incompetent to get tenure at a tiny college like West Georgia State; what is surprising is that by recycling a few mediocre ideas from outdated bestsellers like *Future Shock* and *The Third Wave*, he has fooled people into thinking of him as a serious intellectual.

A Short Biography of the Leopard's Spots

Gingrich's first campaign was in 1974, when he portrayed himself as a liberal populist, bashing his opponent as a "watchdog for big industry" and servant of the "special interests which dominate Congress," whom Gingrich accused of "exploiting the American people." He promised tax reform so that "everyone pays their own share" and said he would "start by closing loopholes which allow the very rich like Nelson Rockefeller and the giant corporations to avoid taxes."[7] In 1976, Gingrich played the class card again, calling himself the candidate for "working people," and declaring that "those of us who work for a living are being discriminated against. The tax laws favor the rich." Gingrich said he was "running because the special interests dominate our government and have come to believe that they own it." In the 1976 campaign, his Democratic incumbent opponent attacked Gingrich as too liberal, accusing him of being a "McGovern operative" who helped disrupt the 1972 Convention and declaring that his campaign director was a "former McGovern worker."[8]

Today, Gingrich has turned full circle. Instead of criticizing partisan politics for fear of gridlock, he is the one promoting it for political uses, even shutting down the government rather than compromise with the Democrats. Instead of being attacked as a "McGovern operative," he accuses President Clinton and his wife of being "McGoverniks." The candidate Gingrich, who railed against business interests and the wealthy, turned into Speaker Gingrich, the man who gave big business more de facto ownership of the government than they could ever dream of in 1976.

Of course, Gingrich was never really a liberal. He always played both sides of the fence, appealing to liberals and conservatives simultaneously, defending environmentalism while he took money from major polluters, attacking special interests and big corporations while he courted conservative businessmen with deep pockets. His success as a politician depended on his ability to avoid being pinned down on anything.

And Gingrich was a successful politician, despite losing his first two elections. Gingrich almost certainly would have won were it not for the boost given to Democrats by the Watergate scandal in 1974 and Jimmy Carter's sweep of Georgia in 1976. Gingrich was simply too skilled at the job of being a politician to be kept out of office for long.

But when he ran in 1978, it was as a conservative opponent of a liberal Democrat named Virginia Shapard, whom Gingrich attacked mercilessly for putting political ambitions ahead of her family. Gingrich had learned that right-wing rhetoric could get him more financial support than denunciations of special interest groups. The big money, Gingrich realized, was in conservative politics, where he could raise enormous amounts from the wealthy by defending their interests in Congress. It was then that Gingrich's pro-business, pro-free market, anti-government ideology actually began to develop. Gingrich had never run on a platform; he had never stood for anything other than the latest trick to get himself elected. But Gingrich understood the power of this deep flaw in democracy, which made the representatives of the people beholden to the wealthiest corporations rather than the needs of the many. Because the campaign finance system was so deeply corrupted, Gingrich knew that his best chance for political success would lie in appealing to these entrepreneurs, and so he embarked on a program of trying to lure these donors and doing a remarkable job, even by the corrupt standards of Congress, of serving his wealthy constituents—whether or not they actually lived in his district.

Gingrich had always regarded himself as a national politician. He cared little for the details of legislation, and did little to serve his district. Although Gingrich was, in theory, the representative of the people in his district, he soon became a national congressman, in the sense of seeking money from people around the country. A wealthy donor from Wisconsin would buy influence in the upper echelon of government, while Gingrich ignored the poor in his own district.

The Bulwark Against Slavery

Gingrich defines himself only as a "conservative futurist." Like most of Gingrich's labels, it obfuscates more than it reveals. What Gingrich really believes is in flux, depending on the latest idea to flash through his mind and the latest lobbyist to influence his thinking.

Gingrich begins his book, *Window of Opportunity*, with an embarrassing prediction that casts his powers as a futurist into serious doubt. According to the 1984 Gingrich, "We must expect the Soviet system to survive in its present brutish form for a very long time. There will be Soviet labor camps and Soviet torture chambers well into our great grandchildren's lives."[9] A year earlier, he had warned that unless the "liberal welfare state" was destroyed, "in the long run the forces of slavery may indeed win and we may enter a millennium of darkness such as we have not known for a long time."[10] Gingrich could not imagine that the Soviet Union, the worst villain of his world, was on the verge of collapse. When the Soviet Union fell apart under the forces of democracy and freedom, Gingrich and the other Cold Warriors of his generation lost the greatest enemy they had ever known.

Gingrich still doesn't realize the Cold War is over, considering his endorsement for increasing a massive military budget and implementing a "Star Wars" system that doesn't work and isn't needed. But the Cold War provides the background for many of Gingrich's beliefs about politics. According to Gingrich, politics is just another form of war, and he regularly assigned his staffers to read classic books on military strategy so that they could understand him.

Newt in Space: a Night at the Hilton

Many of Gingrich's ideas are literally out of this world. Gingrich imagines that technology is the solution to all of our problems, if only we would abandon all the regulations that restrain free enterprise. Gingrich urges "compassionate high-tech" for people with disabilities by sending paraplegics into space where they "can float as easily as anyone else."[11] Of course, floating in space doesn't help paraplegics move, and could be the most expensive physical therapy program ever imagined. Gingrich notes the "possible benefits of weightlessness to people currently restricted to wheelchairs," claiming that when he discusses it with paraplegics, they "begin asking questions in an enthusiastic tone."[12] Considering that Gingrich is currently trying to cut medical care and welfare for poor people with disabilities, it is hard to believe that he will pay to send the disabled into space.

Gingrich has always been an enthusiastic proponent of the space program. He never reconciled his hatred of government with this government program, although he once advocated giving an $8 billion reward to the first private company to build a space station, one of the largest acts of corporate welfare ever proposed.

But just as his cheerleading of the military industrial complex moves beyond the desire to transfer funds to wealthy corporations to the desire to have America rule the world, so it is with space. While his boosterism of space development helps corporations, it also fits his ideas of entrepreneurial heaven. Gingrich predicted about space travel: "As people grow wealthier and the cost of space transportation comes down, spending a week's vacation on a space station or a honeymoon on the moon may become commonplace. People aboard space shuttles—the DC-3's of the future—will fly out to the Hiltons and Marriotts of the solar system, and mankind will have permanently broken free of the planet."[13] For Gingrich, space is a vast frontier like the old Westerns he watched, a place where capitalism is certain to grow.

Gingrich also imagines a space-based anti-crime program: "A mirror system in space could provide the light equivalent of many full moons so that there would be no need for nighttime lighting of the highways" and would "reduce the current danger of criminals lurking in darkness."[14] Not only would such a plan be enormously expensive (costing far more than nighttime lighting), upset sleeping patterns, and destroy astronomy, but it obviously wouldn't eliminate crime. To paraphrase a favorite line of the NRA: darkness doesn't rob people, criminals rob people.

In his first term of Congress, Gingrich proposed a "Space Bill of Rights" to protect American freedoms in extraterrestrial colonies, and in the early 1980s he suggested in a speech on the House floor that we would have a working nuclear fusion energy source by 1990.[15] That Gingrich was ahead of his time is a bit of an understatement. His views about space show how science fiction, much more than science fact, inspires his ideas.

The Cookie Intellectual

Gingrich is often portrayed in the media as a thoughtful intellectual, despite the superficial (and often stupid) ideas he presents. As Barney Frank noted, "Gingrich does not have ideas, he has ideas about ideas. He keeps saying what a good idea it is to have ideas."[16] Frank continued, "Gingrich has no ideas. The quality of the thought is third-rate. Literally, there is no substantive issue on which anyone regards him as an authority."[17] Gingrich's former executive assistant, Dot Crews, observed about Gingrich: "He never had a philosophy, he always had an agenda: to get where he is right now."[18]

Even his conservative allies recognize the shallowness of Gingrich's ideas. Paul Weyrich observes that Gingrich "does not have a deeply-held philosophy." Weyrich cites an example of how Gingrich comes to beliefs: "He initially sided up on the pro-abortion side, at least tentatively, and then he encountered a radical feminist who backed him up against the wall and threatened him and so on and he said to me, 'If that is what they are about, then I'm with you.'"[19]

Gingrich is a human idea factory precisely because there is no fundamental ideology undergirding his thinking. Rep. Pat Schroeder observes that Gingrich's ideas "don't connect. He kind of just fire-hoses you with a whole range of issues and bits and pieces of information." Schroeder notes, "There's no way that it hangs together or fits as an ideology." What distinguishes his ideas from those of previous Speakers, Schroeder said, was that "they haven't been out trying to market them 24 hours a day."[20] As *Chicago Tribune* columnist Jon Margolis observes about Gingrich's intellectual ability, "Its absence overwhelms."[21]

Gingrich admits that one of his formative experiences as a child was being given cookies: "I was dramatically shaped by my grandmother and my aunts, because they convinced me there was always a cookie available. Deep down inside me, I'm four years old, and I wake up and I think, 'Out there, there's a cookie.' Every morning, I'm going, 'You know, it can either be baked or it's already been bought, but it's in a jar...somewhere....' And so that means when you open up the cupboard and the cookie isn't there, I don't say, 'Gee, there's no cookie.' I say, 'I wonder where it is.'"[22] Today, Gingrich gets his cookies from corporate donors who give him tens of thousands of dollars every day. His puerile optimism about life conceals his deep cynicism about government. If he gets his cookie, Gingrich reasons, why should he care about the children who don't have any cookies? Small wonder that the Republican attack on social programs he spearheads is as ideologically sophisticated as the selfishness of a four-year-old child.

Welcome to Newtopia: The Gingrich Wave

Best-selling author Alvin Toffler claims that Gingrich "smells the future."[23] But this is true only if money is the scent of the next century. Alvin and Heidi Toffler have been among the most powerful influences on his thinking. The Tofflers, a pair of futurists who have produced block-buster books about technological change, have never been taken seriously as intellectuals. Gingrich's speeches are full of ebullient enthusiasm for the future, with grand metaphors taking the place of concrete ideas. There is an enormous gap between the futurist rhetoric of Gingrich and the Second Wave kind of corrupt politician he is in reality. The Tofflers cannot conceive of such Second Wave political realities as influence peddling and ethics violations. They see only a "growing transfer of political power away from our formal political structures—the Congress, the White House, the government agencies and political parties—to electronically-linked grassroots groups and to the media."[24] They claim to be "neither Republicans nor Democrats"; they transcend politics.

Although the Tofflers pretend to be political opponents of Gingrich's conservatism, they strongly defend the deregulatory agenda of Gingrich and his corporate clients. In a book produced for Gingrich's Progress and Freedom Foundation, they write: "Republicans are basically right when they call for broad scale deregulation because businesses now need all the flexibility possible to survive global competition."[25] Government regulation is inherently evil: "again and again, new rules, new laws, regulations, plans and practices, all intended to solve our problems, boomerang and make them worse, adding to the helpless feeling that nothing works."[26] According to the Tofflers, all we need is freedom from government: "Liberation from all the old Second Wave rules, regulations, taxes and laws laid in place to serve the smokestack barons and bureaucrats of the past."[27] They offer no suggestions for preserving the freedom of individuals from the dominance of big business bureaucracies freed from the restraints of federal regulations.

"Diversity" in the eyes of the Tofflers takes place in the context of growing commercial monopolization and corporate control: "Computerized, customized production makes possible highly diverse life-styles. Just check the local Wal-Mart with its 110,000 different products, or check the wide choice of coffee now offered by Starbucks."[28] Marvel at the diversity in a Gingrichian Third Wave World! Every American walking down to the corner Starbucks and choosing a different kind of coffee! Meanwhile, the local coffeeshop goes out of business as pre-fabricated identical Starbucks sweep across the nation.

Gingrich makes a similar mistake in seeing a new "Wave" in every technological innovation. In Gingrich's introduction to the Tofflers' book, he writes: "In 1991 the world witnessed the first war between Third Wave military systems and an obsolete Second Wave military machine." Desert Storm, he claims, was won because "sophisticated Second Wave anti-aircraft systems were useless against Third Wave stealth aircraft."[29] In fact, the "Third Wave" technology—such as the Patriot anti-missile defense Gingrich sees as a model for his "Star Wars" program—turned out to be completely worthless. America won Desert Storm for old-fashioned Second Wave reasons: air superiority and overwhelming force against a demoralized foe.

The United States military spends $250 billion more per year than Iraq's military, which had a budget of only $8.6 billion. There was no "Third Wave," only bigger and better weaponry. If "Third Wave weaponry" means a faster, more powerful plane with better radar-evasion, then any technological advance can be hailed as a "Third Wave."

As Richard Brookhiser, senior editor of the right-wing *National Review*, observed about the Tofflers' three-wave theory, "It looks like history, but it is really trendology, or the game of threes: posit two eras, and predict a third."[30] The Toffler formula is to state the obvious, predict the inevitable, and evade the specific.

With roughly the same predictive abilities as tabloid psychics, the Tofflers write: "The mass media are de-massified in parallel with production, and giant TV networks shrivel as new channels proliferate."[31] Gingrich's book agrees that "the Information Revolution is breaking up" gigantic corporations and leading us back to 1830s America"—a curious fact considering that Gingrich's publisher is HarperCollins, a subsidiary of the huge Rupert Murdoch media empire; the book is primarily sold at huge chain super bookstores, in an industry becoming increasingly monopolized by a few giants. Media corporations are growing larger and larger to absorb the new communications technology, and Gingrich's telecommunications reform (supported by the Tofflers) will further ease what few rules limit media tycoons like Murdoch from controlling vast territories of the mass media, enabling them to gain a near-monopoly on ideas and information.

The Tofflers give us tautologies such as, "Massification gives way to demassification."[32] They imagine a utopian (or perhaps one could say Newtopian) future where everybody can be happy and prosperous: "Second Wave economic theories based on finite, exhaustible inputs are inapplicable to Third Wave economies."[33] They promise a "revolutionary new system for wealth creation on the planet."[34] The people will be so happy that the idea of work will disappear: "The super-symbolic economy makes obsolete not only our concepts of unemployment but our concepts of work as well."[35] Hearing this will certainly brighten the day of anyone who's been downsized recently.

Like all sleight-of-hand artists, the Tofflers use slick tricks based on the plan that if you can call everything "revolutionary" often enough, it makes you sound smart and insightful. "In the new economy," they tell us, "the customer adds value to capital"—a completely nonsensical notion leading to a breathless (but meaningless) conclusion: "Value results from a total effort rather than from one isolated step in the process." And, as always, progress comes from a "mighty convergence of Third Wave changes".[36]

In addition to the futurist mumbo-jumbo, the Tofflers make up historical nonsense, like: "the appearance of the computer and the new communications media in the mid-twentieth century smashed Moscow's control of the mind in the countries it ruled or held captive."[37] As every political scientist knows, the Soviets never had total control of the mind; instead, the Communists ruled with sheer military power and terrorism. Moscow's control fell almost entirely because of Gorbachev's decision to liberalize policies and end the reign of totalitarianism. The idea that computers, fax machines, and cellular phones—which were rare in the U.S.S.R, especially in the early 1980s, and almost never available for personal use—caused the fall of Communism is ridiculous. Many theories have been offered for the end of Communism—including American military spending and the failure of Communist economic policies—but no one until the Tofflers ever suggested that Eastern European computers brought about the downfall of a superpower.

The Tofflers declare in *Creating a New Civilization: The Politics of the Third Wave*, "We hope this book will help readers make the zero-base revaluation of their ideas that tomorrow's emergent civilization demands."[38] The advantage of futurist jargon like "zero-base revaluation" is that it can mean almost anything the reader wants it to mean. This is one reason why the Tofflers' work has so much appeal for Gingrich. It gives him the superficial appearance of belief in something, the facade of an ideology and impressive-sounding technical jargon, while allowing so much intellectual flexibility that he can fit almost any idea that benefits corporations into the framework of Third Wavism.

The Third Wave metaphor is broad enough to mean anything, and justify almost every Republican policy. Since change is the mantra, any sort of change—even when terribly destructive to lives, political freedom, and the social good—can be defended as necessary to undermine Second Wave institutions so that we can adapt ourselves to the Third Wave.

One remarkable document of Third Wave propaganda is a "Magna Carta" for the Third Wave world proposed by Gingrich's Progress and Freedom Foundation. The "Magna Carta" declares that big government of any kind is an evil remnant of the Second Wave status quo: "The reality is that a Third Wave government will be vastly smaller (perhaps by 50 percent or more) than the current one—this is an inevitable implication of the transition from the centralized power structures of the industrial age to the dispersed, decentralized institutions of the Third." Like Majority Leader Dick Armey, the Third Wavers see "cutting government in half" as a historically inevitable goal.[39] The Third Wave is used as a justification for the all the provisions of the Contract with America, to say that those who oppose the Gingrich agenda are not merely wrong, but futilely fighting against an historical moment.

The "Magna Carta" proposes a "future-friendly government" with these yardsticks to policy proposals: "Is it based on the factory model?" "Does it centralize control?" "Does it encourage geographic concentration?" "Is it based on the idea of mass culture?" The Third Wave, we are told, will "encourage uniqueness," "empower those closest to the decision," and "transform diversity." The fact that none of these yardsticks are politically meaningful only adds to their political power. Like Gingrich's Contract with America, the rhetoric of futurism only conceals a refusal to address social problems, since the mantra of "change" tells us they will disappear with the coming of the Third Wave. But Gingrich doesn't mention what his Third Wave of politics has brought to Washington: an increasingly dominant class of wealthy businesspeople who influence which proposed legislation becomes law and which gets quietly killed in the Speaker's office.

The Arrogance of Power

Gingrich has finally achieved the historic importance he alone has always seen in himself. Throughout his career, Gingrich tried to prove his importance to everyone else. He instructed his staffers to read a biography of Winston Churchill and told them, "you'll see a lot of me in that." When a staffer was confused by the assignment of Isaac Asimov's science fiction *Foundation* trilogy, Gingrich explained, "what I'm trying to convey to you is that I'm a figure who thinks in terms of 100-year increments and I think in terms of civilization's rising and falling over 500-year increments, and that's the level of thought and change that I would like you to get in sync with."[40] The *Foundation* stories are an epic tale about the future of civilization, in which brilliant "psychohistorians" manipulate events secretly in order to bring humanity out of the coming dark ages. Gingrich sees parallels between that universe and this one, and imagines himself as one of those psychohistorians. The psychohistorians do not follow the wishes of the people. Everything is done in secret according to a master plan of leading intellectuals, with misdirection used to deceive the masses. The *Foundation* trilogy is Gingrich's fantasy of political leadership, one where democracy and honesty take a backseat to power and manipulation.

But there is a darker side to this arrogance. His friend and top assistant Kip Carter reports that after finally winning the election in 1978, when

Gingrich flew back to his district, he yelled at Carter for walking up to the gate to greet him instead of waiting. When Carter warned Gingrich about losing touch with the people, Gingrich told him, "Fuck you guys. I don't need any of you anymore. I've got the money from the political action committees, I've got the power of the office, and I've got the Atlanta news right here in the palm of my hand. I don't need any of you anymore."[41]

Renewing Republican Civilization

The best glimpse into the mind of Newt Gingrich can be found in the readings for his college course, "Renewing American Civilization," embodied by Arianna Huffington, a vapid exponent of new-age Republicanism, and one of Gingrich's favorite "intellectuals." Huffington's claims to fame are a bad accent, the adoration of Republican leaders, and the great wealth of her husband, a failed candidate for the U.S. Senate in California. Yet Gingrich considers her thoughts so brilliant that he included one of her essays as the concluding assignment for his college course.

Huffington believes in something she calls "The Fourth Instinct." The first three instincts are biological survival, sexuality, and status and power, while the Fourth Instinct "strives for spiritual fulfillment, and seeks a context of meaning and purpose for 'ordinary human life'" and "reunites us with our true nature, and guides us by our true interest." In contrast to "the lie of political salvationism" (whatever that is), Huffington offers "a vision that emphasizes our interconnectedness with everyone else."[42]

Perhaps the most bizarre passage in Huffington's essay is this declaration: "Our evolution has always depended on the few preening forward from stage to stage. Any new principle of existence must first establish itself in the few and then, once a critical threshold is reached, it mysteriously and automatically spreads to the many."[43] Huffington's pseudo-scientific "evolution" is reminiscent of the old social Darwinists. For Huffington, Newt is a kind of Nietzschean Übermensch, superior to the masses which he must lead away from their own stupidity. Huffington is presumably one of those elite few with Gingrich who are "preening forward" to the next mystical stage of knowledge.

To Renew America

To Renew America is Gingrich's call for us to follow him to the ends of his anti-government ideology. In the acknowledgments, there is a line thanking "my co-writer" Bill Tucker, although the cover and title page omit Tucker—when you're pretending to be an intellectual, it doesn't look good to admit that you had a ghostwriter. And *To Renew America* bears all the obvious signs of being ghostwritten—and rather badly ghostwritten, to boot. One finds the usual clichés, the unproven assertions (the revolution will not be footnoted), the bland Perot-like lines ("without personal responsibility there cannot be freedom. It is just that simple.") and the dumbed-down ten-word sentences written so that any fifth-grader (or member of Congress) can read them.

Gingrich's enemy list is a familiar one: spineless liberals, anti-American academics and journalists, and the irresponsible poor who are jealous of the success of their betters. Although Gingrich often sees himself as a "populist," the truth is that the people hate him. Even the voters in his own district don't like him. Only a few years ago, Gingrich was fighting for his political life, winning re-election by the narrowest of margins. Gingrich is Speaker of the House by the will of the Republicans, not the people.

Gingrich's political plan has always been warmed-over Reaganomics: cut welfare, cut taxes on the rich, increase defense, and pretend that wealth will trickle down to everyone else by economic growth—which will balance the budget. The difference is that Reagan was a man beloved by the people who had trouble organizing the Republican Party to impose his agenda. By contrast, Gingrich is disliked by the people, but highly skilled at leading the Party. The Contract with America was a work of political genius—not for winning the 1994 elections, but for centralizing power after the elections. Gingrich came into office with a group of Republicans who promised to follow his leadership in lockstep to fulfill their contract with him. Gingrich reports, "Our freshman members went through scripting and practice before they were even sworn in."[44] Many of them had been trained and funded by GOPAC, the secret political action committee that Gingrich ran for nearly a decade before becoming Speaker of the House. Gingrich recognizes that party discipline, not popular approval, is the key to maintaining power.

According to Gingrich, "we need to revise welfare so that going to work never lowers your standard of living."[45] But Gingrich's Republicans are working to reduce the earned income tax credit, eliminate the minimum wage, and prevent health care reform that would cover the working poor. Instead of improving conditions for the working class, Gingrich wants to change incentives by getting rid of welfare benefits. He thinks we should repeal the welfare state and return to a traditional American philosophy: "If you don't work you won't eat."[46]

Gingrich says that we don't need to cut the budget, just control the spending outside of Social Security: a 17% increase over the next seven years. "Imagine your child had a ten-dollar allowance and you decided to increase it by two dollars a week. You announce a twelve-dollar-a-week allowance, thinking your child will be grateful. Instead, using the liberals' 'current services' logic, your child announces that he or she was automatically due an increase to twelve dollars and fifty cents, and you have 'cut' his or her allowance. Sounds nutty, doesn't it?"[47]

Actually, it sounds exactly right if you account for inflation. Keeping a child's allowance at ten dollars over seven years (when inflation will devalue the allowance by at least 25%) will be a "cut" in real terms if you only increase it by 20%. Gingrich's "gimmick" here is to disguise the fact that he is really cutting money for social programs. With such a tenuous grasp of economics, it would be surprising if Gingrich could ever balance the budget. Like all the past Republican claims to balance the budget, Gingrich is diverting attention from his plans to cut taxes for the rich and cut social programs for the poor.

Gingrich blames government for every problem. He believes, for example, that the worldwide information system was created by "unknown entrepreneurs" because "no government could have planned this system. In fact, an active government, in collaboration with the few older companies, probably would have done everything it could to put roadblocks in the way."[48] He seems totally unaware of the fact that the infrastructure of the internet is a product of the federal government, not any entrepreneur. Gingrich thinks that drug companies won't create drugs for "a rare genetic disease that affects only a few thousand people" because the sales could never "cover the costs of shepherding the drug through the FDA."[49] In fact, the FDA procedures are only a tiny cost compared to the price of research and development.

To Renew America features senseless lines like: "America is a series of romantic folktales that just happen to be true" and "America is a great country with good people living in it."[50] Gingrich's solutions to social problems are equally nonsensical. They include cutting payments to women on welfare to reduce abortions "since without the financial support of the government young people were less likely to engage in casual sex."[51] That's right: Teenagers have sex because the government pays them to do it. Later, Gingrich suggests that the real cause is that poor children are not taught standard English: "The final result is an angry young man who feels that violence is the only way he can express himself, or a young girl who thinks that the only great accomplishment she can achieve in life is to have a baby."[52] Gingrich imagines we will have a perfect world if only impoverished children are given more homework and are forced to diagram sentences.

In the words of Gingrich, "When people turn toward political leaders and government for help, all too often they encounter meaningless platitudes." But Gingrich's meaningless platitudes are far more dangerous, for they conceal a powerful political leader determined to tear out social programs and regulations, leaving government funding only for the tax exemptions, corporate welfare (which goes unmentioned), defense spending, and similar aid supported by the wealthy elite which has helped to fund Gingrich's rise to power. In the technology-filled world of the future, students will call up *To Renew America* on their computers with a keystroke and marvel at its stupidity and all the human misery its author caused.

Chapter 18

Don't Know Much About History: The World According to Newt

> "'But, darling, Germany and the United States are not at war. What harm is there if we share the occasional bit of…gossip? Surely you don't think that I, a loyal Swede…?' The question trailed off in a lethal pout as his beautiful and so very exotic mistress stretched languidly, mock-innocent appeal in her eyes."
>
> —the beginning of Newt Gingrich's novel, *1945*.

As a writer, Newt Gingrich is so very awful. That's not surprising when one remembers that his books have been written purely to profit himself, rather than out of a love for literature. His first attempt at writing a novel, *Window of Opportunity*, which he never finished, was a transparent bribery scheme to get money out of wealthy business friends. His first book in print was publicized with a $105,000 slush fund from major contributors. By the time he became Speaker, Gingrich's price had risen to $4.5 million, but his writing is still about as interesting as a "lethal pout." Gingrich always stretches the facts, with "mock-innocent appeal", hoping that the public will not see through the lies he tells.

Historian Garry Wills notes that Gingrich's dissertation on "Belgian Education Policy in the Congo, 1945-1960" was actually a defense of Belgian colonialism. Gingrich wrote, "Within the beliefs of twentieth century American liberalism, European colonialism is an unacceptable political policy, but what did it mean to the natives? Did the colonial powers perform a painful but positive function in disrupting traditional society and so paving the way for more rapid modernization?" Gingrich approved heartily of the Belgian attempt to "modernize a hitherto traditional society". He objected not to European imperialism, but to the "pathetically inadequate leadership cadre." It is only when Gingrich turns to America that he questions the role of government in leading social change. Gingrich's anti-government views are a very recent phenomenon acquired as he latched on to the movement for a smaller government.[1] He is drawn to *The Third Wave*, not because it has great insights on the future, but because its epic description of the rise and fall of civilizations appeals to his historic imagination about power.

Gingrich sees colonialism as the model for America ruling the world, which may explain why he is so strongly opposed to the idea of the United Nations: Third World nations might have a voice in world politics. In a 1995 speech to the American Medical Association, ostensibly about Medicare, Gingrich concluded: "we have to lead the planet. The fact is very simple: We are the only country large enough, complex enough, multiracial enough to reach out to the entire human race. When we fail to reach out, we get Bosnia and Chechnya, Somalia and Rwanda. And we're either going to lead the planet towards freedom and prosperity and safety, or, as we withdraw, it is going to become a dark and bloody planet for our children and our grandchildren."[2]

But beneath Gingrich's praise for a "multiracial" America is a deeper racism, a fear of non-white foreigners invading the United States. In his speech announcing the Conservative Opportunity Society in 1983, Gingrich expressed his fear that America would no longer serve as the disseminator of Western values throughout the world. "Without our leadership," he declared, "the Third World...will continue to arm, to rob, and to pillage its neighbors." Even worse, "the people of the Third World will continue to move to the United States"—undermining our (implicitly white) civilization. Gingrich expressed his support for immigration, and pointed out his "German background, with some Scotch, Irish, and English blood." But he feared that the United States will be overwhelmed with non-white immigrants, noting the "clear recipe for trouble" caused by the number of "18-year-old Mexican males there will be."[3]

While Gingrich's Cold War colonialism seems grotesque and out of date in today's world, his racist fear of immigration is a growing force in the Republican Party, spread more explicitly by leaders like Pat Buchanan. Although he is smart enough to avoid the extremism of Buchanan's racism, Gingrich sees the popular swell against immigration policies and is joining the Republican efforts to restrict immigration. Although Gingrich pretends to be a leader among Republicans in opening up the party to minorities, his racism is often only barely below the surface. In 1988, Gingrich opposed the Civil Rights Restoration law, claiming that anti-discrimination laws would support a "secular, left-wing value system."[4] Gingrich's obsession with "Renewing American Civilization" promotes his fear that America is losing its civilized, white foundation because of Mexican immigrants.

Newt Gingrich, A Hero in His Own Mind

What makes Newt Gingrich truly frightening is the way he views the world through a prism of absolute morality. "People like me are what stand between us and Auschwitz," he said two years ago. "I see evil around me every day."[5] This helps explain why, during 1994, Gingrich declared that people who were horrified by Susan Smith's drowning of her two children should vote Republican. Gingrich feels compelled to see his opponents in Washington as defenders of evil. To do otherwise would be an admission that he is merely a politician fighting a partisan battle for his special interests, and not a heroic leader in the eternal struggle between good and evil.

The good vs. evil mindset is most clearly evident in Gingrich's recent novel, *1945*. Although it is difficult to know whether Gingrich actually wrote any of it (sci-fi writer William Forstchen is listed as co-author, and Albert Hanser as "technical editor"), his values permeate it. Just as movies and fiction guide so much of Gingrich's thinking, his novel reveals a great deal about his delusions of grandeur and the militaristic ideals that guide his thinking.

As a piece of literature, *1945* is unadulterated garbage. Even by the lowly standards of derivative science fiction, the writing is bad to the point of being very funny. The President's Chief of Staff makes clever remarks like "Aw, hell, I don't want to...I wish I could just *divorce* Mrs. Little Goodie Two-Shoes!" This may be a subconscious reference to Gingrich's first wife, since Gingrich not only had sex with many mistresses but also fulfilled his own wishes by divorcing his wife. In the novel, the Nazi spy mistress tries to force the A-bomb secret out of the hapless Chief of Staff, torturing him with bad dialogue: "Suddenly the pouting sex kitten gave way to Diana the Huntress. 'Tell me,' she hissed."[6]

In between the hissing and the languid stretching, the plot is predictable: the Nazis plan a sneak attack on the Manhattan Project, stealing the A-bomb secrets, destroying the facility and killing the scientists. Our hero saves the day. Gingrich's glorification of the military is even more comical when one realizes that he, like Dan Quayle and so many other hawkish politicians, evaded service in the Vietnam War. Yet, having grown up as a military brat, Gingrich is obsessed with envisioning himself as an American hero.

The novel is full of dumb dialogue attacking liberal ideas like gun control. "The Federal government runs the facility and in a typically brilliant display of bureaucratic wisdom has decreed that no one living in Oak Ridge may own a firearm," says an evil Nazi. "If it wasn't for that, our job would be a lot more difficult."[7]

Gingrich is fond of alternative history because he is always living in a state of delusion, imagining an evil world around him that he must destroy. Once, the U.S.S.R. and its dictators provided an easy villain for Gingrich. The fall of the Soviet Union and the end of the Cold War only accelerated his drive for power: without Communism (that great symbol of evil) around anymore, Gingrich could turn his black-and-white, evil-and-good vision of the world against his true enemy—the Democrats. Just before the 1994 election, he declared on national television: "Democrats are the enemy of normal Americans." In 1989, Gingrich was even more explicit about the Democrats: "These people are sick. They are destructive of the values we believe in. They are so consumed by their own power, by a Mussolini-like ego, that their willingness to run over normal human beings and to destroy honest institutions is unending."[8]

Gingrich hopes to draw parallels between the fight against Nazism, which he never participated in, and the destruction of the "welfare state" which he wants to command. But like the plot of *1945*, Gingrich's crusade is a fantasy. Gingrich is a man who has seized tremendous political power and now must convince himself (and the world) that he is serving some noble goal beyond his own self-aggrandizement. It's a tough job.

Gingrich's dream is to become a leader with great power, benevolently leading the ignorant masses into the Third Wave. Gingrich considers *The Sands of Iwo Jima* to be "the formative movie of my childhood. It was about a Marine platoon sergeant who is essentially disliked by his men while he trains them. And does a series of things to them necessary for them to survive the battle. And who is killed in the last part of the movie as his troops begin to understand why he has been so tough."[9] Gingrich imagines himself as a similar hero, bravely sacrificing himself to save his country, even if it makes him unpopular in the process. The movie allows Gingrich to delude himself into thinking that his massive negative ratings are simply a sign that the American public dislikes the harsh training it needs to survive.

Gingrich is almost pathological in his lying, so obsessed with his own self-admiration that he often blurs the line between fiction and reality. Novels and movies form the core of his beliefs, as Gingrich is drawn to the simplistic world of a *Boy's Town*. What makes fiction so appealing to Gingrich is that he can manipulate it to serve his purposes. In the real world, you cannot solve a foreign policy problem by tough-minded posturing. You cannot eliminate human suffering by destroying welfare programs. You cannot create economic justice by cutting taxes on the rich. But in the fantasyland of Newt Gingrich, all of these fictions are possible.

Gingrich's History of the World

Throughout his career, Gingrich has never been satisfied with mere political success. He wants to be a historic figure. This is why he never followed the usual path to power: he wanted to be the leader of a revolution, not just the leader of a political party. Early on as a Congressman, Gingrich expressed this ambition to make history: he created an archive for himself at West Georgia College, and fined his staffers $200 if they failed to record every speech he made. But Gingrich also understands his own tenuous place in history: "I happen to be this year's version of a Teenage Ninja Turtle, or the Morphin Power Rangers. America operates with wave-like moments."[10]

Gingrich's interest in history has never been as an academic interested in learning the truth about the past. Instead, he uses history to provide models of civilizations and their downfalls, and models of the great figures of history who he hopes to imitate. His is an obsession with making history, not learning it.

In a 1983 speech, Gingrich asserted that we needed to change our school system because it was "designed for the smokestack industries of the past. It was designed for the assembly line. People arrived on time to the sound of a bell just as they would in a factory. They sat in a row in an organized way....they went to assembly-line courses that became assembly-line building blocks to get assembly-line degrees."[11] However, the modern school system evolved long before Henry Ford created the assembly line in 1903. Schools were not modeled on "smokestack industries," but on the church. The often-used metaphor comparing schooling to the assembly line is a cliché, but his invented history of it is completely inaccurate.

In Gingrich's world, history is re-written to serve today's conservative political agenda. Why did the Wright Brothers invent the airplane? "Because they had the after-tax income to do it," Gingrich told his students.[12] Of course, it is ridiculous to think that the airplane would not have been invented if there had been a progressive tax; in fact, government-sponsored research and development has almost certainly helped create more inventions than America's minimal government of a century ago did.

Gingrich's understanding of history is poor for someone who holds a Ph.D. in European history and who regularly announces his credentials. For a historian, Gingrich makes some remarkably stupid factual errors, such as his claim that "the centrality of God and religion" in the Jamestown Colony is "unmistakable."[13] In fact, Jamestown was the height of impiety.

In his first speech as Speaker, Gingrich told the American public that Benjamin Franklin had stopped the squabbling at the Constitutional Convention by urging them to pray together, and the Convention members "took a day off for fasting and prayer." Gingrich later devotes nearly a page of his book, *To Renew America*, to quoting Benjamin Franklin's motion for prayer at the Constitutional Convention. In the world of Gingrich, "the convention heeded Franklin's eloquent plea and shortly after was able to resolve its differences and complete the Constitution of the United States."[14] To argue that the Constitution would not exist without a prayer may be one of the silliest attempts to prove the power of religion. It's particularly ridiculous because the convention never "heeded Franklin's eloquent plea." They argued for a short time about the proposal, decided that they didn't want to pay a minister or risk making their divisions public, and then adjourned without voting on Franklin's proposal. In fact, James Madison reports that "After several unsuccessful attempts for silently postponing the matter by adjourning, the adjournment was at length carried, without any vote on the motion."[15] The Founders refused to have a prayer, and created a secular document without the benefit of divine intervention.

Gingrich praises Thomas Jefferson for facing "the scourge of slavery" as one of "those who argued that blacks could not legitimately be enslaved in a free country" and who "called again and again on the power of the Deity as a final witness to this judgment."[16] But Jefferson could not have been too scared of divine justice, since he kept slaves throughout his life (including some who were his relatives), and Jefferson probably had an affair with one of his slaves. Professor Gingrich also omits the fact that Jefferson took a razor blade to his Bible to excise the supernatural elements.

Historian David Samuels notes that Gingrich's version of history "is overtly partisan and sometimes bizarre." As a historian, Gingrich is a frequent failure, despite repeatedly reminding everyone that he once was a history professor. Gingrich told his students to go to Williamsburg and stand on the spot where Patrick Henry proclaimed, "give me liberty or give me death!" (but Henry said it in Richmond, not Williamsburg, and it is doubted that he ever used that phrase). Gingrich told students, "Thomas Jefferson originally wrote 'life, liberty, and the pursuit of property.'" Jefferson actually wrote "life, liberty, and the pursuit of happiness" in the Declaration of Independence. John Locke originally referred to "life, liberty, and property," but no one until Gingrich ever talked about the pursuit of property. Still, it's a reassuring delusion for someone like Gingrich who wants to put property rights in the pantheon of American mythology. The Contract repeats this same false history, claiming that the Constitution requires that property owners be paid for government regulations that may reduce the value of their land: "the Founding Fathers knew this to be a matter of liberty and simple fairness."[18] If they did, it is strange that not one of the Founding Fathers ever proposed that the right of property was so absolute that government could make no regulation of it whatsoever. Nor does Gingrich seem willing to respect the Fourth Amendment's protections against illegal searches and seizures, which the Founders considered far more dangerous than property regulations.

Gingrich can't even correctly cite the historians from whom he steals his limited understanding of history. In his college class, he calls Gordon Wood by the name Gordon Woods. In *Window of Opportunity*, Gingrich manages to misspell both the first and last name of Garry Wills, and mangles the title of his book *Inventing America* as "Discovering America."[19]

The Holocaust Historian and the Need for "Balance"

Gingrich's disregard for honest history is reflected in his decision to appoint Kennesaw State political scientist Christina Jeffrey to the post of House historian. Jeffrey reports that the job offer came when she and her husband Robert were in Washington in December 1994, following their old friend Gingrich around. According to Jeffrey, "Robert spoke with Newt about spending some time in Washington to work on a chronicle of the first 100 days. Newt immediately went to the phone to inquire whether the House historian was a job the speaker appoints. Getting an affirmative answer, he said, 'I'm sending down a couple of good friends; one of them may be the next House historian.' " Although Jeffrey was reluctant to take the job, Gingrich chose her over her husband: "Newt's argument for giving me the job rather than Robert was that it was to involve more public relations."

Clearly, Gingrich had radically re-conceived the idea of the House historian. Instead of protecting records for posterity and studying the history of Congress, Newt wanted the House historian to be a public relations expert promoting the work of the Republicans to the American people, and chronicling Gingrich's own place in history. Not surprisingly, he chose Jeffrey, who had no credentials as a historian, but a proven record as a Gingrich ally with skills in organizing distance learning programs and public relations. She had helped publicize Gingrich's course at Kennesaw State, and defended him when other professors criticized the fact that he was teaching such a partisan class.

Perhaps hoping to conceal his re-invention of the House historian post, Gingrich didn't announce Jeffrey's appointment. In fact, when former historian Ray Smock announced that Gingrich had disbanded the historian position, Gingrich's office mysteriously confirmed it. When Gingrich announced at the beginning of 1995 that Jeffrey would be the House historian, it took everyone by surprise.

But Gingrich had apparently forgotten about a national controversy involving Jeffrey in 1986, when she was widely condemned for criticizing a training program about the Holocaust called "Facing History and Ourselves," for high school teachers and students. Although her main criticism of the program was that it was too left-wing (she compared its educational techniques to the propaganda of Hitler, Goebbels, and Chairman Mao), she sparked outrage because she wrote: "The program gives no evidence of balance or objectivity. The Nazi point of view, however unpopular, is still a point of view and is not presented, nor is that of the Ku Klux Klan."[20]

Gingrich concluded that even if he wanted to defend Jeffrey, it would be too much of a distraction during the first days of working to pass the Contract. One week after taking office, Jeffrey was dismissed by Gingrich, and he even broke a promise to keep her on the government payroll until March 1.[21]

Jeffrey maintains that she was made a scapegoat by Education Department officials (who, she says, were "mishandling the grant review process") in an October 19, 1988 Congressional hearing. It is her contention that the hearing was used by supporters of the Holocaust education program to pressure Republicans who had refused to fund the program.[22]

Jeffrey admits, "I did not do a great job of expressing myself" and "I didn't know anything about the Holocaust." She blames her "unfortunate" mistake on "the value-free jargon of the social sciences."[23] But as Deborah Lipstadt pointed out, the "Facing History" curriculum Jeffrey reviewed had 16 quotes from Adolf Hitler as well as Nazi Party platforms and Third Reich textbooks. Lipstadt concluded, "The question to be asked is not whether Prof. Jeffrey is an anti-Semite or a Holocaust denier—I doubt she is either. The question is, 'Does she read?'"[24]

Yet the criticism of Gingrich about Jeffrey—quickly muted by his decisive action—revolved around this plainly false charge that he had appointed an anti-Semite to be House historian. Jeffrey was many things—not qualified for the job, a crony of Gingrich's, and an unknown right-wing academic who had shown poor judgment and shoddy work in the *Facing History* evaluation—but she was definitely not anti-Semitic. The accusation of anti-Semitism gave Gingrich an easy escape from an embarrassing situation, since he could claim that she never informed him or his staff about the *Facing History* incident (although Jeffrey actually discussed it with staff in early December).[25] Gingrich quickly put himself back in the good graces of Jewish groups by supporting the move of the American embassy in Israel from Tel Aviv to Jerusalem.

It is just as bad that no one pinned Gingrich down on the fact that he tried to misuse a House office for his own personal self-promotion and self-aggrandizement by appointing a friend to the scholarly post of House historian with the express purpose of turning that position into a patronage and public relations office. As he so often did, Gingrich saw history as something to be used for his own political gain.

He reminisces fondly about the good old days when "everyone absorbed a sense of how to be an American," even if it meant lying about history. For Gingrich, truth is a secondary consideration compared to the emotional power of a myth: "Even myths such as Washington cutting down the cherry tree and not being able to tell a lie had a larger truth."[26] The fact that this was, ironically enough, a lie told about Washington's life seems not to faze Gingrich in the least. He knows that what's important is the propaganda, not the reality. As a politician, Gingrich has spent his career twisting reality, giving people the impression that he is something which he is not: at times a great historian and forward-looking intellectual, at other times a heroic leader of his Republican soldiers, at still others a historic figure starting a grand revolution.

What Gingrich can never do is look beyond his own self-delusions and see himself clearly, see his true nature. He is a politician, a servant to whoever can give him enough money to buy his loyalties. The intellectualism, and the rhetoric of praising democracy and serving Americans, turns out only to be a smokescreen. Beneath the clever phrases is just another corrupt Washington careerist seeking power and fame, willing to sacrifice principles of democracy and anything else that stands in his way.

Conclusion

Taking Back Democracy

"With the world as it is, '96 will be a critical election," noted a prescient GOPAC staffer in a 1990 meeting, planning a Gingrich presidential run.[1] Although Gingrich proved to be far too extreme and unpopular to make a serious race for president, his power depends a great deal on maintaining control over Congress and having a Republican in the White House. At stake is not just another election, but the future of this country and success of the Republican Revolution.

Although the Contract with America has already had a destructive impact, its effects have been fairly small. One reason was the presence of Bill Clinton in the White House, vetoing budget plans that would decimate social programs and overturn environmental regulations; Gingrich's majority in the House is still not strong enough to overturn a presidential veto consistently.

But the primary obstacle to the Contract with America came, surprisingly enough, from Bob Dole in the Senate. Since the Senate elects only one-third of its members each year and is slow to change, the Republican Revolution never hit as strongly there; also, Democrats in the Senate exerted more power as a minority than they did in the House because of the ability to use the filibuster and other Senate rules. And there weren't any Republicans in the Senate organizing a farm team of activist candidates as Gingrich did with GOPAC in the House. Gingrich consciously kept Republican senators out of the group who signed the Contract with America, knowing that they might weaken its provisions or divide the coalition of Republicans he had formed to support it.

However, the barrier in the Senate was especially large because of the role of Bob Dole as majority leader. Dole and Gingrich have always enjoyed a hate-hate relationship. Gingrich once called Dole the "tax collector for the welfare state" and Dole has always regarded Gingrich as a bombthrower, not a statesman. Circumstances have put them together, but their interests do not coincide. However, they share the large donors who contribute vast amounts of money to the Republican Party and its campaigns, hoping that pro-business legislation will be the result.

Throughout the Revolution in the House, Dole was plotting his run for the presidency. The last thing Dole wanted was for the Contract with America to pass intact. Not only would such an effort in the Senate require an incredible amount of the energy that Dole would rather save for the campaign trail, but he also feared the political consequences of passing the Contract. Because many of the Contract's provisions were highly unpopular, Dole didn't want to run for president with the Contract as his campaign platform. Passage of the Contract could easily inspire a backlash against the Republican Revolution that would destroy Dole's last chance to become president.

Perhaps the ambition to be a figure in history was even more important than the political consequences. If Dole had pushed the Contract through the Senate, Gingrich would have gotten all the credit for inventing it. But by delaying the Contract until he could be elected president, Dole would be able to preside over the Republican Revolution as its leader rather than be seen as a follower.

If Dole can beat Clinton, and the Republicans can maintain control of the House and Senate, it will assure the passage of most of the Contract. With Dole out of the way, the Senate is more likely to approve the Contract, and though Dole is skeptical of many parts of the Contract, it is difficult to imagine him vetoing any of it.

In the 1996 Republican campaign, the Contract disappeared entirely. The Republicans proposed no new agenda to unify their party, knowing that if they revealed their plans it would virtually guarantee a disastrous loss. But the hidden agenda of the Contract is still the guiding force behind Gingrich and the Republicans. If Dole wins, Gingrich will become the *de facto* leader of the country. Gingrich will set the agenda in Congress, and Dole is unlikely to veto Republican legislation as president. Dole was one of the chief barriers to the Contract as majority leader of the Senate, fearing that, if passed intact, it would destroy any chance he had to get elected; Dole even resigned from the Senate in the middle of his campaign in order to avoid having to defend Republican proposals.

With Dole in the Oval Office, Gingrich's power will only increase. Dole doesn't have the political drive to create a radical legislative agenda. Gingrich does, and with Trent Lott running the Senate, Gingrich is certain to be the guiding force in a Republican-controlled Washington. Lott is much more conservative than Dole, and he has been a friend of Gingrich from the early 1980s, when Lott moved to strike Tip O'Neill's denunciation of Gingrich on the House floor from the Congressional Record. Gingrich called Lott the "godfather" of his Conservative Opportunity Society.[2]

Even today, few people understand the full extent of Gingrich's proposals in the Contract with America. Although most of them have been watered down, blocked in the Senate, or stopped by Clinton's veto, Gingrich promises to continue bringing them up in their original form until he is able to pass them. The Contract is too profitable to Gingrich's business allies for him to ignore.

The 1994 "revolution" was only a small hint of what will happen if

Republicans can take control of the White House, solidify their power in the Senate, and maintain their hold over the House. If this happens, 1996 will bring a true revolution never imagined by the American voters. The elections of 1994 were, in Gingrich's mind, only the beginning of the Revolution. He points to April 1997—100 days after a Republican president is inaugurated—as the coming of the true Revolution. As Republican guru Irving Kristol notes, "much depends on the '96 election. If we have a Republican President, [Gingrich] obviously will be very, very influential."[3]

The 1996 elections may be a true turning point in American politics. If Bob Dole wins, the Republicans will have the power to impose their agenda. Such is Gingrich's power within the Republican Party that a vote for Dole to be president is, in essence, a vote to make Gingrich the real ruler of the country.

The Cure for American Democracy

Although corruption is rampant in government, Gingrich is a landmark in American politics, a fundamentally new and dangerous brand of politician, a cancer on democracy. The only cure for the corrupt system that could create a politician like Gingrich is more democracy, more equality, more liberty, and more justice. The current system has been so distorted by official and unofficial bribery that the popular will has repeatedly been thwarted by lobbyists. This bias eroding American democracy must be ended.

Unfortunately, Republicans have resisted all efforts to increase voter participation, since they know that today's non-voters are more likely to support a Democratic agenda. When the Democrats managed to pass the "motor voter" law to make voter registration easier, Republicans filed suit against it and fought to stop its implementation. In California, Pete Wilson filed a lawsuit demanding money from the federal government to pay for the "unfunded mandate." In Illinois, the Republican governor refused to allow the "motor voter" law to cover state and local elections. The state spent more than $250,000 on outside counsel to challenge the law in court. Yet this law is one of the most successful efforts to expand the voting franchise. The League of Women Voters estimates that 20 million new voters have registered because of the law, a greater expansion of democracy than any other time in American history.

Democracy is a threat to the Republicans because so much of their agenda has been tied to the money funding their campaigns. Any candidate who wants to win a primary, not to mention a general election, must attract large donations. Not surprisingly, the people who have a lot of money tend to be more conservative than average when it comes to policies for helping the poor or giving tax breaks to the rich. And all campaign money is given as part of an implied exchange: if the candidate doesn't espouse the right policies, cash will not be forthcoming.

For decades, the balance of power in Washington had been maintained in favor of big business due to money. Because the natural constituency of the Democratic party (blacks, the poor, labor) represented the true majority of Americans, it needed to be controlled somehow. Corporate lobbyists realized that the Democrats could be swayed by big donations. Since Republicans voted for corporate interests anyway, lobbyists saw no reason to funnel large amounts of money to them. Thus, even though the Republicans were more strongly pro-business, Democrats got a majority of the campaign contributions, which enabled them to maintain their power.

But over the years, the Democratic Party became a corrupt empire. They protected the interests of big business for the sake of money, but lost the soul of their party in the process. Voters who had once been enthusiastic Democrats turned away from the party, away from voting altogether in many cases. Taking their dominance for granted, the Democrats never built an organization to bring new people into their party.

In 1994, a political revolution happened: the party of big business, the Republican party, was finally able to seize power from the corrupt and inept Democrats, who had alienated so many of their core group of voters—by betraying their own professed values—that they could not sustain a majority. At the same time, the delicate balance of corporate control dramatically shifted, and lobbyists began pouring money into Republican coffers, hoping to ride their bandwagon to power.

The questions now are whether corporate money will be able to sustain an unpopular Republican regime, whether the Democrats still have enough integrity to resist the temptation to play old-fashioned politics by serving big business interests, and whether it can become a genuine party of the people and cast off the corruption infecting Washington and American politics.

This money bias in American politics has fundamentally distorted our democracy to the point that "democracy" is no longer an accurate term to use. The shift to the right in American politics, within both the Democratic and Republican parties, was fueled by money, not voters. As the Democrats moved to the right in order to appease the business interests that provided most of their campaign money, they marginalized more and more of the traditional core of Democratic liberal voters. Yet the Democrats responded to the drop in interest among voters by moving further to the right, reasoning that they needed to attract more centrist voters to make up for the lost core of liberals.

The Democrats were digging their own political grave, going deeper and deeper toward the Republicans without realizing that their centrist agenda was leading to disillusioned voters who stayed away from polling places on election day. Meanwhile, the Democrats' wishy-washy incoherence failed to attract many centrist voters, who no longer trusted them.

Bill Clinton is often attacked by the right as someone who ran as a centrist for president in 1992, but governed as a liberal. In fact, the situation is much more complicated than this simple analysis suggests. Although Clinton's background was as a leader of the conservative Democratic Leadership Council, a key factor in his election was Clinton's espousal of liberal values, emphasizing government investment and reforming health care. As president, Clinton hurt his centrist credibility by pursuing (for a very short time) a few high-profile symbolic liberal issues like equal rights for gays and lesbians. But more damaging to Clinton were regular attempts to appear centrist by avoiding controversy (such as when he dismissed nominee Lani Guinier after she was smeared by the right) and to serve the corporate interests of major Democratic donors. Clinton followed the advice of Republican pollster Richard Morris, Nixon advisor David Gergen, and Federal Reserve Chairman Alan Greenspan. Today, most voters distrust Clinton, not because he is a liberal, but because they cannot be sure what he is.

The opposite is true of Newt Gingrich and the Republicans, who the public distrusts because it knows Gingrich is a politician defending the interests of the wealthy. But Gingrich at least offers solutions to our problems, however destructive and counterproductive they may be. Restoring democratic power in America means offering the people a program they can believe in, instead of avoiding anything controversial.

The Fall (and Rise) of Gingrich

Gingrich's numerous gaffes and embarrassing mistakes have led him to take a more covert route to completing the Republican Revolution. Although it is against his nature to shy away from publicity, Gingrich has chosen a far less prominent role recently than in the past. But this should not be taken as a sign that Gingrich no longer runs the show. It's only the election year tactic of a man who is still the most powerful force in Washington.

Reports of Gingirch's fall from power have been greatly exaggerated. Despite his incredible unpopularity among Americans and his relatively low profile in the media, Gingrich is still the guiding force behind the Republican Party. Among Republican activists, Gingrich is nearly worshipped. He is the most powerful fundraiser in American political history, and nearly all Republican members of Congress want his support—or at least his money.

In the House, Gingrich is still in full control. Although Gingrich has delegated much of the day-to-day details to loyal supporters like Majority Leader Dick Armey, he remains the ultimate authority over legislation in Washington. Nothing gets passed without Gingrich's approval, and he only allows laws he opposed (like the minimun wage increase) to go through in order to prevent them from becoming campaign issues that would hurt Republicans.

Gingrich's relative silence in the media is a tactic designed to protect his own power. Because so much of the opposition to Republican policies ended up targeting Gingrich, he wants to stay in the background, using the money he has raised to keep Republicans in power in the House.

Because the most radical social program cuts proposed by Gingrich were never enacted into law, the extent of the destruction planned by the Republicans has never been revealed to the American public. As a result, there has been no substantial political backlash against the Republican Revolution. Ironically enough, the Republicans may achieve their revolution in 1996 precisely because they failed to fulfill most of their legislative goals from the 1994 elections.

Gingrich argues that we should try an experiment with our government: erode our laws and regulations and let the invisible hand of the free market protect us from environmental degradation, unsafe food and water, untested drugs, and corporate monopolies. To experiment with human lives like this, with so little concern about what will happen to the victims, is unconscionable.

Why should we "experiment" with the failed policies of the Republican Revolution? We have tried de-regulation of business, and the result was the $500 billion S & L bailout disaster. We have tried letting industry police itself, and the result was a heavily polluted America that we are still trying to clean up. We have tried the free market without a social safety net and the result has always been dire poverty, higher infant mortality, and homelessness. We have tried to cut taxes, increase defense spending, and eliminate the deficit—and the result was the Reagan years, with the largest accumulation of debt in our history. We have tried cutting programs for the poor and cutting taxes for the rich, and the result has always been an increasing gap between rich and poor in this country.

A Contract for the American People

A real revolution in Washington would result in a government that serves the people rather than obeying the corporate lobbyists, a government that ensures equal opportunities for all Americans, a government that sees social justice as its goal. Achieving such a government will not be easy, given the preponderant influence of money on Capitol Hill. When both parties have so little credibility with the public, it is not enough to make promises of reform. Real action is needed.

The most important revolution, because it makes other reforms possible, is campaign financing. The current system is indefensible: it rewards politicians (like Gingrich) who promise to serve major corporate donors; it maintains the power of parties who unlike candidates are allowed to accept huge soft money-donations; and it inevitably corrupts the system in favor of the rich.

Although Gingrich has repeatedly promised election reform, he has always stood in the way of any action to clean up our corrupt campaign system. Gingrich's idea of campaign finance reform is to pass a bill that will fine members of Congress who file "frivolous" ethics complaints, charging their offices for the costs of investigation. Obviously, this retaliation is intended to discourage ethics complaints like those filed against Newt Gingrich.[4]

Gingrich calls the FEC "irrelevant and dangerous," and his minions have actually sought to punish it for investigating GOPAC. In 1995, Republicans cut $1.4 million from the money already allocated to the FEC, and they have frozen its budget at $26.5 million ever since, despite a 25% increase in campaign spending since 1992.[5]

If they can't destroy the FEC, Republicans hope to intimidate it into submission. In June 1996, a Republican-controlled House Appropriations subcommittee ordered the FEC to cut its press office (which handles 100 calls a day from reporters) from five workers to only two. House Appropriations Chairman Bob Livingston (R-LA) declared, "They don't need that many people," claiming that the Treasury Department only had two people to deal with the media. However, Livingston was wrong: the Treasury Department has seven full-time employees for the media, in addition to secretaries and assistants. Lisa Rosenberg, the director of the Center for Responsive Politics's FEC Watch, said it "is appalling that the Congress would attempt to stifle disclosure of information on campaign finance."[6]

Although there are logistical and legal problems with government financing of campaigns, this should be the ultimate goal of any campaign reform. However, a more immediate step can be taken which could have a dramatic impact on democracy: limit all donations to a maximum of $250 for any individual, and make all parties and PACs adhere to these limits. Currently, federal election law limits donations to individual campaigns to $1,000, but individuals can give $25,000 to the Republican Party or the Democratic Party. This "soft money" gets allocated to candidates, and artificially strengthens party control over candidates because parties have the only sources of large amounts of funding. Putting a severe limit on these donations would also end the now-common party practice of holding $100,000-a-plate fundraising dinners. When money is donated on this scale, the opportunity for corruption is immense—as the entire political career of Newt Gingrich shows. Limiting donations to $250 would solve many of the problems, and even those who evade the law (like Gingrich) would find it very difficult to raise tens of millions of dollars like they currently do.

The importance of public funding and strict spending limits in the race for president is commonly accepted. Why, if we regard the general presidential campaign as too important to permit bribery of this kind, do we not view Congress in the same way? The total amount of money involved in campaign financing is small considering the overall size of the US budget. Preventing the waste and pork barrel deals that result from large political donations would save taxpayers far more than the cost of paying for the campaigns. But neither party wants to lose the money that enables party leaders to control candidates and members of Congress.

It is not enough for progressives merely to challenge the attacks on government from the right. As Newt Gingrich recognized more than a decade ago, a political movement cannot be based upon "negativism"; it must stand for something. One of the reasons why the Republicans were able to energize some voters was the fact that they put forth an agenda, however deceptive it was about the true goals of the Contract with America. A progressive platform is needed to counter these ideas, stating a number of feasible programs that resist the corporate encroachment on democracy.

Gingrich thinks that the true role of government is to hold mass executions and build Star Wars toys. Anything beyond that is questionable in his mind. All social programs are dismissed as "socialism." In his drive to turn American democracy over to the corporate CEOs, Gingrich is clever enough to hide his true goals. He claims to be devoted to the environment while he undermines the Environmental Protection Agency. He claims to support education while he viciously cuts away educational programs. He claims to want to help the poor while he guts any efforts to give the poor a helping hand.

In his heart, Gingrich knows that the American people disagree with him, but he believes that if he can manipulate the debate with his rhetoric, he will be victorious. And if he can generate large enough donations from his corporate allies to spread this disinformation in Republican campaigns, popular opposition won't matter. Posing as the leader of a democratic movement, Gingrich is in fact the greatest enemy of democracy, undermining its core values, dividing America along class boundaries, ruling the House with near-total power.

The threat to democracy starts when Gingrich replaces the principle of political equality with a corrupt regime where money dominates the very laws that control our lives. But there is an even deeper corruption of democracy in his ideas. He repudiates the idea of a social contract in a democracy, where all of us share responsibility for assuring equal opportunities.

Taking back democracy requires that we design a welfare program reform in order to genuinely help the poor, not so that we can save money to reduce the deficit or cut taxes for millionaires. It requires that we create a system of education that provides the best possible public schools for the poor, instead of the worst. It requires that we clean up the environment instead of subsidizing corporations that clear-cut forests. It requires that we have an ethic of responsibility, instead of an ethical vacuum where every form of corruption is accepted as a normal part of politics.

If Gingrich succeeds in solidifying his power, which could occur by the election of 2000, not only will the full Contract with America be passed, but the hidden Contract with the right will be enacted—including overturning gun control, imposing school prayer, banning abortion, destroying social programs, and anything else demanded by his constituents in corporate America's boardrooms.

The true extent of the danger posed to American democracy by the Contract with America has not been recognized. The United States is one presidential election away from a Republican Revolution of enormous proportions. The first steps in the Gingrich takeover of Washington have only provided a hint of the dangers that face us. If the Republicans can gain full power over Congress *and* the Presidency, they will remake the country. The Republican Revolution has barely set out on its destructive path.

Endnotes

Introduction: The End of Democracy

Introductory quotation from Larry Sabato and Glenn Simpson, *Dirty Little Secrets: The Persistence of Corruption in American Politics* (New York: Times Books, 1996), 43.

1 Jan Crawford Greenburg, "Despite Plea, Rostenkowski says he really wasn't guilty," *Chicago Tribune*, 10 April 1996, 1.

2 "Internal Documents Indicate Gingrich's GOPAC Mixed Fund Raising with Federal Policy Issues," *Wall Street Journal*, 30 November 1995.

3 Nancy Gibbs and Karen Tumulty, "Master of the House," *Time*, 25 December 1995, 60.

4 *Time*, 25 December 1995, 95.

5 *Wall Street Journal*, 6 March 1995.

6 GOPAC memo, 7 August 1990.

7 Connie Bruck, "The Politics of Perception," *New Yorker*, 9 October 1995, 56.

8 *Washington Post*, 21 March 1995.

9 *Los Angeles Times*, 7 December 1995.

10 GOPAC memo, 10 May 1990.

11 Clarence Page, "How the GOP's pork escapes the rancid label," *Chicago Tribune*, 9 April 1995, 4:3; Phil Kuntz, "Gingrich, Critic of 'Business as Usual' Helps Out Special Interests Like 'Any Member of Congress,'" *Wall Street Journal*, 3 April 1995, A20.

12 http://www.mojones.com.

13 "Gifts tied to Gingrich's FDA requests," *Chicago Tribune*, 3 February 1995, 6; John Dickerson, "Newt Inc.," *Time*, 13 February 1995, 28.

14 *Mother Jones*, March/April 1996, 54; http://www.mojones.com; *Los Angeles Times*, 3 February 1995.

15 Federal Election Commission press release, 13 March 1996, corrected 28 March 1996.

16 David Moore, Lydia Saad, Leslie McAneny and Frank Newport, "Contract With America," *Gallup Poll Monthly*, November 1994, 19; Elizabeth Drew, *Showdown: The Struggle Between the Gingrich Congress and the Clinton White House* (New York: Simon & Schuster, 1996), 34.

17 "GOP pollster never measured popularity of 'Contract,' only slogans," *Chicago Tribune*, 12 November 1995.

18 "The Unpopular Revolution," *In These Times*, 20 March 1995, 2.

19 Moore et al., 22.

20 *Progress Report with Newt Gingrich*, 3 October 1995.

21 *The Statistical Abstract of the United States*, 1994, 76.

22 Mike Males, *The Scapegoat Generation* (Monroe, ME: Common Courage Press, 1996), 55.

23 Newt Gingrich, "Beyond the 100 Days," *New York Times*, 22 February 1995, A15.

24 Don Balz and Ronald Brownstein, *Storming the Gates: Protest Politics and the Republican Revival*, (Boston: Little, Brown & Co., 1996), 53.

25 *Dollars & Sense*, March/April 1995, 43.

26 "Voter Turnout Falls Sharply Among the Less Affluent," *New York Times*, 11 June 1995, 16.

27 Jeanne Cummings, "Georgia lawmaker provokes GOP anger," *Atlanta Constitution*, 2 April 1993, A4.

Part I: The Crimes of Newt Gingrich

Chapter 1: The Hypocrite of the House

1 Lois Romano, "Newt Gingrich, Maverick on the Hill; The New Right's Abrasive Point Man Talks of Changing His Tone and Tactics," *Washington Post*, 3 January 1985, B1.

2 Mark Hosenball and Vern Smith, "How 'Normal' Is Newt?" *Newsweek*, 7 November 1994, 34.

3 Judith Warner and Max Begley, *Newt Gingrich: Speaker to America* (New York: Signet, 1995), 92.

4 *Frontline*, "The Long March of Newt Gingrich", 16 January 1996, http://www2.pbs.org/wgbh/pages/frontline/newt

5 Steve Sternberg, "Housebreaker," *Atlantic Monthly*, June 1993, 27.

6 Al Hunt, *Wall Street Journal*, 26 January 1995.

7 *Congressional Record*, 3 November 1983, 30870-1, 30875.

8 Balz and Brownstein, 120.

9 *Congressional Record*, 15 May 1984, 12204.

10 *Congressional Record*, 15 May 1984, 12203.

11 *Congressional Record*, 15 May 1984, 12042-3.

12 *Congressional Record*, 15 May 1984, 12201

13 Balz and Brownstein, 121.

14 Romano, B1.

15 *Congressional Record*, 15 May 1984, 12298.

16 John Barry, "Anatomy of a Smear," *Esquire*, October 1989, 220.

17 Barry, 220.

18 Barry, 220.

19 Barry, 228.

20 Barry, 217.

21 Barry, 222.

22 Barry, 227.

23 Barry, 218.

24 *Washington Post*, 5 March 1995.

25 James Ledbetter, "Press Clips," *Village Voice*, May 1995, 7.

26 Katharine Seelye, "Gingrich Promoted Company That Hired His Wife," *New York Times*, 7 February 1995, C18.

27 David Beers, "Master of Disaster," *Mother Jones*, October 1989, 32.

28 Michael Hinkelman, "Newt's Patron Reaps Harvest," *Atlanta Business Chronicle*, 23 October 1989, 1A.

29 Hinkelman.

30 Warner and Begley, 60

31 Jeff Gerth and Stephen Labaton, "The Local Forces That Helped Shape Gingrich as a Foe of Regulation," *New York Times*, 12 February 1995.

32 Hinkelman.

33 Hinkelman.

34 Hinkelman.

35 Robert Wright, "Speaker's Corner," *New Republic*, 1 January 1996.

36 Warner and Begley, 126.

37 Beers, 43; Glenn Bunting and Alan Miller, "Documents Raise Questions on Gingrich's House Ethics,"*Los Angeles Times*, 20 March 1995, A1.

38 Katharine Seelye, "Democrats Out to Destroy Him, Speaker Says," *New York Times*, 20 January

1995.

39 "Gingrich defies ethics panel, signs for 2 books and promotion tour," *Chicago Tribune*, 26 May 1995, 6.

40 "Despite Blunt Warning From Ethics Panel, Gingrich Signs a New Book Deal," *New York Times*, 27 May 1995, 9.

41 Lars-Erik Nelson, "Poor Newt Just Can't Get It Write," *New York Newsday*, 19 March 1995, A34.

42 Katharine Seelye, "Aides Say Gingrich Met Murdoch Before Book Deal," *New York Times*, 13 January 1995.

43. "Murdoch Lobbyist at Gingrich Meeting," *Washington Times*, 15 January 1995, A2.

44 Dave Eisenstadt, "Notes Sought on Newt, Rupe's Meeting," *New York Daily News*, 18 July 1995.

45 James Stewart, *Blood Sport* (New York: Simon and Schuster, 1996), 391.

46 James Warren, "Murdoch plans conservative political weekly magazine," *Chicago Tribune*, 30 April 1995, 3.

47 Dave Eisenstadt, "Dems Hit Rupe Deal," *New York Daily News*, 2 April 1995.

48 Gail Sheehy, "The Inner Quest of Newt Gingrich," *Vanity Fair*, September 1995, 222.

49 Edmund Andrews, "Mr. Murdoch Goes to Washington," *New York Times*, 23 July 1995, 3:1.

50 Sheehy, 222.

51 Greg Pierce, "Inside Politics," *Washington Times*, 27 June 1995, A16.

52 Drew, 54; Melissa Healy, "Partisan Feud Erupts in House Over Gingrich Book," *Los Angeles Times*, 19 January 1995, A6.

53 Timothy Clifford and Dave Eisenstadt, "Wail of a Tale in Washington: News Is Banned for Cry of Newt," *New York Daily News*, 17 January 1995, 5.

Chapter 2: Newt, Inc.: The Gingrich Empire

1 Maureen Dowd, "Speaking for House Speaker and Enjoying the Trappings," *New York Times*, 5 January 1995, A1.

2. Osborne, 15.

3 *Frontline*, "The Long March of Newt Gingrich," 16 January 1996, http://www2.pbs.org/wgbh/pages/frontline/newt.

4 *Frontline*, "The Long March of Newt Gingrich," 16 January 1996.

5 *Wall Street Journal*, 11 September 1994.

6 Kathey Alexander and Jeanne Cummings, "Investigation Widening," *Atlanta Constitution*, 17 December 1995.

7 *New York Times*, 4 October 1995, A14.

8. Transcript, 27 August 1989 GOPAC meeting.

9 GOPAC internal memo, 25 February 1988.

10 Beers, 31.

11 GOPAC fundraising letter, 30 May 1989.

12 Michael Duffy, "Back to the Bench," *Time*, 12 November 1995, 47.

13 Glenn Bunting and David Willham, "Major GOPAC Donors Got Special Access, Files Show," *Los Angeles Times*, 17 December 1995.

14 "GOPAC Documents Link Gingrich's College Course to Partisan Aim," *Atlanta Journal and Constitution*, 6 December 1995.

15. Internal GOPAC memo, 25 February 1988.

16 *Roll Call*, 7 December 1995.

17 Glenn Simpson, "Hiding the Money," *Mother Jones*, July/August 1995, 40.

18 *Roll Call*, 22 February 1996.

19 *Roll Call*, 4 December 1995.

20 Democratic National Committee, *Newtgram*, 7 April 1995.

21 Beers, 32.

22 Tom Baxter, "Gingrich had to cheat, ex-foe says," *Atlanta Journal and Constitution*, 5 December 1995.

23 "'Newt Support' Stressed in Papers: FEC Cites Illegal Help by GOPAC," *Washington Times*, 30 November 1995; "Gingrich Political Unit Broke Rules, FEC Says." *Los Angeles Times*, 30 November 1995; "FEC Says GOPAC Aided Gingrich Race Despite Law," *Washington Post*, 30 November 1995; "Election Panel Says Gingrich Got Hidden Aid," *New York Times*, 30 November 1995.

24 Kathey Alexander and Jeanne Cummings, "Investigation Widening," *Atlanta Constitution*, 17 December 1995.

25 "Aggressive Strategy Landed GOPAC in Court: Federal Agency Claims that Funds Were Illegally Spent to Re-Elect Newt Gingrich, *Atlanta Journal-Constitution*, 3 December 1995. "FEC: Group Illegally Provided Gingrich Political Boost in '90," *Marietta Daily Journal*, 30 November 1995. For examples of GOPAC abuses in other states, see "GOPAC Hasn't Complied with State Law, Some Say," *Dallas Morning News*, 7 December 1995; "PAC Possibly Broke Ethics Law in Texas," *Dallas Morning News*, 5 December 1995; and "GOPAC Letters Appear to Mislead '90 Texas Candidates on Compliance With State Laws," *Roll Call*, 7 December 1995.

26 Kathey Alexander and Jeanne Cummings, "Investigation Widening," *Atlanta Constitution*, 17 December 1995.

27 Damon Chappie and Juliet Eilperin, "Gingrich Presidential Bid Plotted by GOPAC Officials Back in 1990," *Roll Call*, 4 December 1995.

28 *Washington Post*, November 30, 1995.

29 GOPAC memo, 7 August 1990.

30 "Internal Documents Indicate Gingrich's GOPAC Mixed Fund Raising With Federal Policy Issues," *Wall Street Journal*, 30 November 1995.

31 "Speaker's Press Secretary Failed to Disclose Travel Expenses Paid for by GOPAC in 1991," *Roll Call*, 4 December 1995.

32 Barton (R-Texas) was GOPAC's second-leading fundraiser. Damon Chappie and Juliet Eilperin, "Gingrich Presidential Bid Plotted by GOPAC Officials Back in 1990," *Roll Call*, 4 December 1995.

33 "Internal Documents Indicate Gingrich's GOPAC Mixed Fund Raising With Federal Policy Issues," *Wall Street Journal*, 30 November 1995.

34 Glenn Bunting and David Willham, "Major GOPAC Donors Got Special Access, Files Show," *Los Angeles Times*, 17 December 1995.

35 *Atlanta Journal and Constitution*, 7 July 1992.

36 *Roll Call*, 23 May 1994.

37 *Los Angeles Times*, 17 December 1995.

38 *Washington Post*, 30 November 1995.

39 *Los Angeles Times*, 17 December 1995; Phil Kuntz, "Gingrich, Critic of 'Business as Usual' Helps Out Special Interests Like 'Any Member of Congress,'" *Wall Street Journal*, 3 April 1995, A20.

40 James Bovard, "Dole, Gingrich and the Big Ethanol Boondoggle," *Wall Street Journal*, 2 November 1995.

41 *Roll Call*, 15 January 1996.

42 *Roll Call*, 21 December 1995.

43 Terry Kohler, memo to GOPAC donors, 13 October 1989.

44 Warner and Begley, 214.

45 *Roll Call*, 15 February 1996.

Chapter 3: Politics for Profit: The GOPAC Files

1 Damon Chappie, "Set Up to Help Kids, Group Aided GOPAC: Non-Profit's Funds Went to TV

Shows," *Roll Call*, 11 March 1996.

2 "GOPAC Used Foundation to Fund Cable TV Series," *Washington Post*, 12/12/95.

3 Chappie.

4 GOPAC meeting notes, 6 August 1990.

5 Chappie.

6 Damon Chappie and Juliet Eilperin, "Gingrich Presidential Bid Plotted by GOPAC Officials Back in 1990," *Roll Call*, 4 December 1995.

7 Memo, "A Legal Structure: Levels of Permissible Activity," prepared by Gordon Straus of Thompson, Hine and Flory.

8 Damon Chappie, "Set Up to Help Kids, Group Aided GOPAC Non-Profit's Funds Went to TV Shows," *Roll Call*, 11 March 1996.

9 Damon Chappie and Juliet Eilperin, "Gingrich Presidential Bid Plotted by GOPAC Officials Back in 1990," *Roll Call*, 4 December 1995.

10 *Roll Call*, 10 April 1995.

11 *Business Week*, 27 June 1995.

12 *Atlanta Constitution*, 20 June 1995.

13 John Dickerson, "Newt Inc.," *Time*, 13 February 1995, 28.

14 Glenn Simpson, "Hiding the Money," *Mother Jones*, July/August 1995, 41-42.

15 Serge F. Kovaleski and Charles R. Babcock, "Gingrich & Co. Fund a Megaphone for Ideas," *Washington Post*, 21 December 1994.

16 William Safire, "Newt's 100th," *New York Times*, 3 April 1995, A11.

17 Simpson, 42; Associated Press, 30 March 1995.

18 Newt Inc, 28.

19 Glenn Simpson, "Gingrich Attacks 'Baseless' Charges," *Roll Call*, March 30, 1995.

20 Simpson, *Roll Call*, March 30, 1995.

21 "Approval of Gingrich course traced," *Chicago Tribune*, 13 March 1995, 3.

22 Damon Chappie and Juliet Eilperin, "Ethics Spars Over Plan To Clear Rep. Shuster," *Roll Call*, 13 June 1996.

23 Peter Applebome, "Gingrich Plan for Satellite Lessons Arouses Critics," *New York Times*, 4 September 1993, 6.

24 "Rep. Gingrich's Outrageous Abuse," *St. Louis Post-Dispatch*, 13 September 1993, 6B.

25 Glenn Simpson, "In Professor Gingrich's Class, Money Talks," *Roll Call*, 15 September 1994, 41.

26 Simpson, 41; Newt Gingrich, "Introduction to Renewing American Civilization," in Jeffrey Eisenach and Albert Steven Hanser, eds., *Readings in Renewing American Civilization* (New York: McGraw-Hill Inc. College Custom Series, 1993), 11.

27 Simpson, 41.

28 Jeanne Cummings, "Donors to Gingrich Class Currying Favor?" *Atlanta Journal and Constitution*, 3 September 1993, F1.

29 Cummings, F1.

30 Phil Kuntz, "Gingrich, Critic of 'Business as Usual,' Helps Out Special Interests Like 'Any Member of Congress,'" *Wall Street Journal*, 3 April 1995, A20.

31 Charles Babcock, "PAC Ties to Gingrich Class Questioned," *Washington Post*, 3 September 1993, A1.

32 Doug Cumming, "Newt Gingrich at Kennesaw State," *Atlanta Journal and Constitution*, 19 September 1993, F8; *ABC World News Tonight*, 23 February 1995.

33. Glenn Bunting, "Gingrich's Politics Got Boost from Nonprofits, Foundations," *Los Angeles Times*, 25 June 1996.

34. Bunting.

35 U.S. Tax Court ruling, 15 December 1987.

36 *ABC World News Tonight*, 23 February 1995.

37 Damon Chappie, "The IRS's 'Story of M' May Affect '96 Politics," *Roll Call*, 15 April 1996.

38 Douglas Frantz, "Populist Candidate Has Sophisticated and Lucrative Political Apparatus," *New York Times*, 4 March 1996, A13.

39 Benjamin Sheffner, "Foundations Still Popular in Senate," *Roll Call*, 22 June 1995.

40 "Lean times over, Republican Party rolling in political contributions," *Chicago Tribune*, 7 June 1995, 18.

41 Gay Hart Gaines, "GOPAC as a target of opportunity," *Washington Times*, 14 July 1995, A21; R.H. Melton, "GOPAC Donations Rise to Nearly $1.1 Million in First Half of 1995," *Washington Post*, 15 July 1995, A10.

42 "The Speaker's Secret Money," *New York Times*, 25 April 1995, A14; "Mr. Gingrich's Partial Disclosure," *New York Times*, 20 January 1995, A14.

43 "Mr. Gingrich Still Owes an Accounting," *New York Times*, 10 May 1995, A18.

44 Garry Wills, "Newt Gets Plenty of Loyal Support," *Chicago Sun-Times*, 6 December 1995.

45 Katharine Seelye, "Democrat Files a New Charge Against Gingrich," *New York Times*, 9 March 1995, A9.

46 Stephen Labaton, "Gingrich Asks For Dismissal of Complaints," *New York Times*, 29 March 1995, A12.

47 "Trouble Ahead for the Speaker," *Wall Street Journal*, 10 August 1995, A11.

48 Richard Phelan, "Do Unto Gingrich," *New York Times*, 3 January 1995, A11.

49 Albert Hunt, "Gingrich and an Outside Counsel: Do Unto Others..." *Wall Street Journal*, 26 January 1995, A19.

50 Warner and Begley, 121.

51 Drew, 53.

52 Glenn Simpson, "He's Really Got a Hold on Her," *Mother Jones*, July/August 1995, 39.

53 *Time*, 25 December 1995, 85.

54 Katharine Seelye, "Gingrich Makes It Fully Clear He's Not in Presidential Race," *New York Times*, 13 June 1995, C19.

55 *Washington Times*, 27 April 1995.

56 *Washington Times*, 28 March 1995.

57 Weston Kosova, "Jam Session," *New Republic*, 12 June 1995, 20.

58 *Atlanta Constitution*, 28 July 1995.

59 *Hartford Courant*, 25 July 1995.

60 *Manchester Journal-Inquirer*, 27 July 1995.

61 *Atlanta Constitution*, 28 July 1995.

62 *The Hill*, 3 May 1995.

63 Al Hunt, *Wall Street Journal*, 10 August 1995.

64 Damon Chappie, "FEC, Divided on Party Lines, Votes Against Appeal in GOPAC Lawsuit," *Roll Call*, 21 March 1996.

Chapter 4: The Authoritarian Speaker: The Corruption of Congress

1 Phil Kuntz and David Rogers, "How Gingrich Grabbed Power and Attention—And His New Risks," *Wall Street Journal*, 19 January 1995, A1.

2 Drew, 37.

3 Albert Hunt, "Special Interests Are Feasting at the Congressional Trough," *Wall Street Journal*, 27 July 1995, A11.

4 Connie Bruck, "The Politics of Perception," *New Yorker*, 9 October 1995, 66.

5 Drew, 256.

6 Juliet Eilperin, "House Bills Bypass Committee Process; GOP Leaders Circumvent Own Panel Chairs," *Roll Call*, 18 March 1996.

7 Bruck, 72.
8 Weston Kosova, "The G-Men," *New Republic*, 20 February 1995, 22.
9 *Time*, 25 December 1995, 99.
10 *Chicago Tribune*, 22 February 1995.
11 Bruck, 71.
12 James Warren, "Feeling the wrath of Newt," *Chicago Tribune*, 26 February 1995, 5:2.
13 Bruck, 71.
14 *Frontline*, "The Long March of Newt Gingrich," 16 January 1996, http://www2.pbs.org/wgbh/pages/frontline/newt.
15 Kathey Alexander and Jeanne Cummings, "Investigation Widening," *Atlanta Constitution*, 17 December 1995.
16 *New York Times*, 10 April 1995, A14.
17 *Business Week*, 12 June 1995.
18 Robin Toner, "Clinton Renews Pledge on Overhauling Welfare and Urges Senators to Seek Consensus Bill," *New York Times*, 11 August 1995.
19 Balz and Brownstein, 335.
20 Albert Hunt, "Special Interests Are Feasting at the Congressional Trough," *Wall Street Journal*, 27 July 1995, A11.
21 *Business Week*, 10 July 1995; *Washington Times*, 12 July 1995.
22 *Utne Reader*, March-April 1995.
23 "Lean times over, Republican Party rolling in political contributions," *Chicago Tribune*, 7 June 1995, 18.
24 Federal Election Commission press release, 13 March 1996, corrected 28 March 1996; Benjamin Sheffner, "GOP Shatters Money Record For 1996 Races," *Roll Call*, 14 March 1996.
25 Frontline, "The Long March of Newt Gingrich", 16 January 1996.
26 "Women's Group Backs Tax Checkoff Plan," *New York Times*, 23 May 1995, C19.
27 *New York Times*, 19 May 1995, A11.
28 Dickerson, 28.
29 Joel Bleifuss, "You Get What You Pay For," *In These Times*, 17 April 1995.
30 Balz and Brownstein, 49.
31 Jacob Weisberg, "He's Back!" *New York*, 23 January 1995, 22.
32 Amy Waldman, "Newt's Minions," *Washington Monthly*, March 1995, 21.
33 Stephen Engelberg, "100 Days of Dreams Come True for Lobbyists," *New York Times*, 14 April 1995, A8.
34 Weisberg, 24.
35 Weisberg, 22.
36 *Time*, 25 December 1995, 66.
37 Phil Kuntz, "Gingrich Backer Had Unusual Access As a Volunteer in the Speaker's Office," *Wall Street Journal*, November 10, 1995; *Roll Call*, 26 February 1996.
38 Robert A. Jordan, "Conflict of Interest Cloud Looms Over Gingrich," *Boston Globe*, 15 October 1995.
39 "Talk of the Town," *New Yorker*, 7 August 1995.
40 Kuntz.
41 Damon Chappie and Juliet Eilperin, "Gingrich Reveals New Evidence About Jones Case," *Roll Call*, 4 April 1996. In October 1995, Cyberstar abandoned the New Zealand project, saying it posed "too much risk."
42 "Klug's Trip to New Zealand," *Capital Times*, 29 April 1996, 2C.
43 Sarah Pekkanen, "Gingrich ally's deal may pose ethics conflict," *The Hill*, 1 May 1996, 1.
44 "Mr. Gingrich and His Volunteer," *New York Times*, 24 April 1996.

45 Congressional Accountability Project, 22 April 1996 complaint. For more information on the Don Jones connection to Gingrich, see http://www.donwatch.com.

46 Congressional Accountability Project, 22 April 1996 complaint.

47 Damon Chappie and Juliet Eilperin, "Jones Offered Gingrich Campaign Giver's View on Internet Regulation," *Roll Call*, 22 April 1996.

48 John E. Yang and Mike Mills, "Gingrich's Use of Adviser Raises Conflict Questions," *Washington Post*, 11 November 1995.

49 Damon Chappie and Juliet Eilperin, "Gingrich Reveals New Evidence About Jones Case," *Roll Call*, 4 April 1996.

50 Congressional Accountability Project, 22 April 1996 complaint.

51 "Wrist slapping," *Roll Call*, 4 April 1996.

52 "Mr. Gingrich and His Volunteer," *New York Times*, 24 April 1996.

53 Jerry Gray, "Move to Reopen Ethics Inquiry on Gingrich," *New York Times*, 23 April 1996, A17.

54 Drew, 52.

Chapter 5: Manipulating the Media

1 Romano, 1985.

2 *U.S. News and World Report*, 16 January 1996, 28.

3 *Business Week*, 12 June 1995.

4 *Extra! Update*, February 1995, 3.

5 *New York Times*, 11 June 1995, 16.

6 Don West and Kim McAvey, "Newt Gingrich: the great liberator for cybercom," *Broadcasting and Cable*, 20 March 1995.

7 "Gingrich Denounces Editorial 'Socialists,'" *New York Times*, 9 March 1995; speech to Newspaper Association of America, 26 April 1995.

8 James McCartney, "Newt Abused," *American Journalism Review*, April 1995, 38.

9 McCartney, 37.

10 Gingrich, 3 November 1995 speech; Richard Reeves, "The View from Newt's Head," *Buffalo News*, 24 November 1995, 30.

11 *Nightline*, 6 December 1995.

12 *Media Daily*, 6 November 1995.

13 *New York Times*, 21 January 1995.

14 *Washington Post*, 21 December 1994.

15 Clarence Page, "News media shown to have a bias against solutions," *Chicago Tribune*, 21 April 1996.

16 Howard Kurtz, "Gingrich Criticizes 'Nit-Picking' Media; Speaker to Take Break From Sunday," *Washington Post*, 10 January 1995, A7.

17 *Wall Street Journal*, 9 June 1995.

18 "Newt signs on," *Mother Jones*, September/October 1995, 8.

19 Leah Garchik, "Knee Slappers of 1995," *San Francisco Chronicle*, 12 March 1996.

20 William Glaberson, *New York Times*, 23 January 1995.

21 Mike Mills, "Meeting of the Media Giants," *Washington Post*, 21 January 1995, C1.

Part II: The "Contract with America"

Chapter 6: The "Contract with America" and the Attack on Democracy

1 Newt Gingrich et al., *Contract with America* (New York: Times Books, 1994), 22.
2 *Contract with America*, 14.
3 Bob Herbert, "Good Works? Bah!" *New York Times*, 24 May 1995, A15.
4 Drew, 28.
5 Damon Chappie and Juliet Eilperin, "Gingrich Presidential Bid Plotted by GOPAC Officials Back in 1990," *Roll Call*, 4 December 1995.
6 *Contract with America*, 4, 6.
7 *Contract with America*, 6.
8 Drew, 33.
9 Katharine Seelye, "House Debating Measure That Would Cut New Police," *New York Times*, 14 February 1995, A8.
10 Michael Kramer, "Newt's Believe It or Not," *Time*, 19 December 1994, 43.
11 Robert Frank, "No Quick Fix," *Wall Street Journal*, 1 May 1995, A1.
12 *Dollars & Sense*, March/April 1995, 4.
13 Paul Offner, "GOP Welfare Scam," *New Republic*, 29 May 1995, 11.
14 Drew, 101.
15 *Contract with America*, 8.
16 *The Hill*, 5 May 1995.
17 "House Protocol Director Post Sparks Mixed Reaction," *National Journal Congress Daily*, July 26 1995.
18 *Contract with America*, 23.
19 *New Republic*, 30 January 1995, 9.
20 Reuters, 9 November 1995.
21 Gingrich speech, 7 April 1995.
22 *New York Times*, 9 February 1995, A10.
23 David Moberg, "Class axe," *In These Times*, 20 February 1995, 14.
24 *Washington Post*, 31 March 1995.
25 Albert Hunt, "GOP's No Innocent Victim of the Class War," *Wall Street Journal*, 13 April 1995, A15.
26 Richard Armey, *The Freedom Revolution* (Washington, D.C.: Regnery, 1995), 38.
27 Paul Krugman, "The Wealth Gap Is Real and It's Growing," *New York Times*, 21 August 1995, A15.
28 Keith Bradsher, "Gap in Wealth in U.S. Called Widest in West," *New York Times*, 17 April 1995.
29 Clarence Page, "The Republicans and the race card," *Chicago Tribune*, 16 July 1995.
30 Keith Bradsher, "Low Ranking for Poor American Children," *New York Times*, 14 August 1995, A7.
31 Armey, *The Freedom Revolution*, 285.
32 Press conference, Bob Dole, Newt Gingrich, and Jack Kemp, 3 April 1995.
33 Robert Eisner, "Make Taxes Fair, Not Flat," *Wall Street Journal*, 11 April 1995.
34 *New York Newsday*, 6 March 1995.
35 Michael Kilian, "Attempt to end tobacco subsidies rekindled," *Chicago Tribune*, 16 July 1995, 2:2.
36 *Washington Post*, November 27, 1995; "Never Say Die: How the Cigarette Companies Keep on

Winning," ABC News special, 27 June 1996.

37 Michael Wines, "F.D.A. Gets Some White House Backing," *New York Times*, 14 July 1995, A9.

38 Bob Herbert, "Checking Out the House," *New York Times*, 10 May 1996.

39 George Will, *Restoration* (New York: Free Press, 1992), 97-101.

40 *Atlanta Constitution*, 24 February 1995.

Chapter 7: Let Them Eat Orphanages: The War on Welfare

1 Newt Gingrich, *To Renew America* (New York: HarperCollins, 1995), 39.

2 *Contract with America*, 65.

3 Charles Derber, "The Politics of Triage," *Tikkun*, Vol. 10, No. 3, 38-39.

4 Peter Gabel, *Tikkun*, Vol. 10, No. 2, 13.

5 James Krohe, *Illinois Issues*, March 1995.

6 Megan McLaughlin, "Orphanages are not the solution," *USA Today*, November 1995.

7 McLaughlin.

8 Mickey Kaus, "The G.O.P.'s Welfare Squeeze," *New York Times*, 6 April 1995.

9 Henry Rose, "Kids would be victims of AFDC cut," *Chicago Tribune*, 1 September 1995.

10 Mike Males, *The Scapegoat Generation*, 9.

11 *New York Times*, 28 February 1995.

12 Interview with Gingrich, *Washington Times*, 4 January 1995.

13 "Speaker Gingrich Lashing Out, in His Own Words," *New York Times*, 17 December 1995.

14 Drew, 343.

15 Lars Erik-Nelson, "Gingrich Is Hot On Wrong Trail," *New York Newsday*, 23 March 1995.

16 "Speaker Gingrich Lashing Out, in His Own Words," *New York Times*, 17 December 1995.

17 *Washington Times*, 4 January 1995.

18 Kramer, 43.

19 Males, 79.

20 *New York Times*, 21 April 1995.

21 "Teen pregnancies: High rates, higher costs," *U.S. News and World Report*, 15 April 1995.

22 Charles Murray, "Does welfare bring more babies?" Spring 1994, *Public Interest* 20, 23; see Males, 79.

23 Males, 80.

24 Gingrich speech, 7 April 1995

25 Julie Sandorf, "Building Homelessness, Not Housing," *New York Times*, 13 March 1995, A15.

26 Tamara Kerrill, "Cuts Threaten Transit System," *Chicago Sun-Times*, 14 August 1995, 6.

27 Males, 76.

28 Males, 90.

29 *Contract with America*, 67.

30 *Time*, 25 December 1995, 95.

31 *Time*, 25 December 1995, 84.

32 Warner and Begley, 25.

33 Sheehy, 154.

34 Sheehy, 154.

35 Osborne, 18.

36 Peter Osterlund, "A Capitol Chameleon," *Los Angeles Times*, 25 August 1991.

37 Osborne, 19.

38 Sheehy, 210.

39 Warner and Begley, 72.

40 Osborne, 19.
41 Gingrich, *To Renew America*, 78.
42 *Washington Monthly*, March 1995, 19.
43 Warner and Begley, 34.
44 Warner and Begley, 70.
45 Kim Masters, "Wedded to Politics," *Washington Post*, March 13, 1995.
46 Kim Masters, "Wedded to Politics," *Washington Post*, March 13, 1995.
47 "Prof. Gingrich puts men in their place: Ditches," *Chicago Tribune*, 19 January 1995.
48 *This Week With David Brinkley*, 2 April 1995; Democratic National Committee, *Newtgram*, 5 May 1995.
49 George Will, "Serious People Flinch...," *Washington Post*, 26 August 1992, A23.

Chapter 8: Dirty Politics: Gingrich's Betrayal of Environmentalism

1 Warner and Begley, 10-12.
2 Jeff Gerth and Stephen Labaton, "The Local Forces That Helped Shape Gingrich as a Foe of Regulation," *New York Times*, 12 February 1995.
3 http://www.lcv.org.
4 Gerth and Labaton.
5 Gerth and Labaton.
6 Sabato and Simpson, 93; Warner and Begley, 127.
7 Gerth and Labaton.
8 Warner and Begley, 96.
9 *Atlanta Journal*, July 9, 1995.
10 Will Nixon, "Jurassic Planet," *In These Times*, 17 April 1995, 23.
11 Nixon, 23.
12 Richard Blow, "10 Ways the Republicans Will Change Your Life," *Mother Jones*, March 1995.
13 Eric Alterman, "Voodoo Science," *Nation*, 5 February 1996.
14 David Helvarg, "Congress Plans an American Clearcut," *Nation*, 4 December 1995, 700; Nixon, 23; *New York Times*, 17 May 1995.
15 Tony Sanny, "Utah 5.7 Mil Wild!", *University of Chicago Free Press*, January 1996, 9.
16 Helvarg, 700.
17 Francis Clines, "Gingrich: Speaker, Author—But King of the Jungle?" *New York Times*, 14 July 1995.
18 William Welch, "Meat inspection plan faces delay," *USA Today*, 11 July 1995, 6A.
19 Marian Burros, "Congress Moving To Revamp Rules On Food Safety," *New York Times*, 3 July 1995, A1.
20 John Cushman Jr., "Narrow Defeat for a Measure on Bad Meat," *New York Times*, 13 July 1995.
21 "Compromise Reached on Meat-Safety Regulations," *New York Times*, 20 July 1995.
22 David Frum, "The GOP's 'Takings' Sell-Out," *Wall Street Journal*, 16 March 1995.
23 Jon Margolis, "Speaking of cowards, what about those conservatives?" *Chicago Tribune*, 13 March 1995.
24 Joel Bleifuss, "With Science on Their Side," *In These Times*, 30 October 1995, 12.
25 James Kunen, "Rats," *New Yorker*, 1995, 8.
26 Timothy Egan, "Industry Reshapes Endangered Species Act," *New York Times*, 13 April 1995, A9.
27 Stephen Engelberg, "Business Leaves the Lobby And Sits at Congress's Table," *New York Times*, 31 March 1995, A1.
28 George Miller, "Authors of the Law," *New York Times*, 24 May 1995, A15.
29 Bleifuss, *In These Times*, 17 April 1995, 12.

30 Ken Silverstein, "Newt for Sale," *Progressive*, April 1995, 28.
31 Joel Bleifuss, "Nightmare Soil," *In These Times*, 16 October 1995, 12-16.
32 Silverstein.
33 Ralph Nader, "Beware the History Books," *Progressive*, April 1995, 26.
34 Silverstein.
35 "Econotes," *Environmental Action Magazine*, 22 June 1995.
36 *USA Today*, 26 April 1995; *Washington Post*, 26 April 1995; "Meet the Press," 4 December 1994; *off our backs*, April 1995, 3.
37 James DeLong, "It's My Land, Isn't It?" *New York Times*, 15 March 1995.
38 Government Accounting Office, "The California Fire and the Endangered Species Act," 8 July 1994, GAO/RCED-94-224.
39 John Cushman, "Tales from the 104th: Watch Out, or the Regulators Will Get You!" *New York Times*, 28 February 1995.
40 Timothy Noah, "Cost-Benefits Bill, Passed By House, Would Curb Federal Regulation, Ease Burden on Business," *Wall Street Journal*, 1 March 1995.
41 Sandra Blakeslee, "Babbitt Sees 'Book Burning' in G.O.P. Moves," *New York Times*, 16 February 1995.
42 John Cushman, "Scientists Reject Criteria for Wetlands Bill," *New York Times*, 10 May 1995, A13.
43 Gregg Easterbrook, "The Good Earth Looks Better," *New York Times*, 21 April 1995, A15.
44 Jerry Gray, "Gingrich Plays the Dealmaker on Budget Bills," *New York Times*, 27 July 1995, A1.
45 Michael Kilian, "Hastert, Ewing wrestle with gender issue," *Chicago Tribune*, 16 April 1995, 2:2.
46 "Timber Salvage Bill Was Clear-Cut Bait 'n' Switch," *Seattle Times*, 28 February 1996.
47 "Forest Service reportedly allowed illegal timber harvest," *Chicago Tribune*, 26 March 1996, 6.
48 Brock Evans, "A Time of Crisis," *Vital Speeches of the Day*, July 16, 1995 speech, 691-692.
49 John Cushman, "G.O.P. Backing Off From Tough Stand Over Environment," *New York Times*, 26 January 1996, A1.
50 Phillip Hilts, "Fine Pollutants in Air Cause Many Deaths, Study Suggests," *New York Times*, 9 May 1996.
51 John Leo, "Want to take a dip in some sewage?" *U.S. News and World Report*, 29 May 1995, 23.
52 Will Nixon, "The forest for the trees," *In These Times*, 24 July 1995.
53 *New York Times*, 26 January 1996.

Chapter 9: Senseless Legal Reform: Defending Corporate Criminals

1 Richard Schmitt, "Truth Is First Casualty of Tort-Reform Debate," *Wall Street Journal*, 7 March 1995, B1.
2 Ralph Nader, "Easy money," *In These Times*, 19 February 1996, 15.
3 "Injustice for Consumers," *New York Times*, 8 March 1995, A14.
4 Philip Howard, "Put the Judges Back in Justice," *New York Times*, 3 April 1995.
5 Howard.
6 George Pring and Penelope Canan, "Slapp-Happy Companies," *New York Times*, 29 March 1996.
7 Steven Stycos, "Revoking Legal Services," *Progressive*, April 1996, 29-31.
8 Anthony Lewis, "Thumb on the Scales," *New York Times*, 29 March 1996.
9 Stephen Labaton, "Back From the Brink, the Legal Services Corporation Discovers It's in Danger Again," *New York Times*, 31 March 1995, B13.
10 Jan Crawford Greenburg, "Legal aid faces halt to federal funding," *Chicago Tribune*, 1 August 1995.

Chapter 10: Criminals in Politics: the NRA's Crime Bill

1 Gingrich speech, 7 April 1995.

2 Charlie Rose, 6 July 1995.

3 Bruce Alpert, "House Takes Swipe at 'Reckless' IRS," *New Orleans Times-Picayune*, 17 April 1996, A12.

4 Katharine Seelye, "House Debating Measure That Would Cut New Police," *New York Times*, 14 February 1995, A8; *Contract with America*, 50.

5 "Newt's Fryathon," *Progressive*, October 1995, 9.

6 Bob Herbert, "Gingrich Mugs the Crime Bill," *New York Times*, 17 August 1994, A15.

7 "Gingrich on Drug Dealers," *New York Times*, 15 July 1995.

8 Nat Hentoff, "The Murder of the Fourth Amendment," *Village Voice*, 28 February 1995, 23.

9 Hentoff, 23.

10 *Nightline*, 5 February 1995.

11 http://www.whatsnewt.com.

12 Lis Wiehl, "Program for Death-Row Appeals Facing Its Own Demise," *New York Times*, 11 August 1995, A13; Anthony Lewis, "Cruel and Reckless," *New York Times*, 11 August 1995.

13 Bob Herbert, "Guns For Everyone!" *New York Times*, 1 April 1995, 15.

14 Drew, 100.

15 Michael Kilian, "Simon, Durbin bill fight felon gun rights," *Chicago Tribune*, 13 August 1995, 2:2.

16 "Guns in the House," *Boston Globe*, 4 August 1995, 18.

17 Albert Hunt, *Wall Street Journal*, 27 April 1995.

18 Kilian.

19 David Johnston, "Republican Attacks Use of N.R.A. Consultant in Raid Case," *New York Times*, 19 July 1995, A10.

20 Frank Rich, "Shotgun Hearings," *New York Times*, 19 July 1995, A15.

21 Neil Lewis, "N.R.A. Takes Aim at Study of Guns as Public Health Risk," *New York Times*, 26 August 1995.

Chapter 11: Welfare for Bombmakers: Gingrich's Military-Industrial Complex

1 Gingrich speech, 7 April 1995.

2 Steve Tidrick, "The Budget Inferno," *New Republic*, 29 May 1995.

3 Common Cause, letter, March 1996.

4 Eric Schmitt, "Military Budget Would See Gains Under G.O.P. Plan," *New York Times*, 5 July 1995, A1.

5 Tim Weiner, "B-2, After 14 Years, Is Still Failing Basic Tests," *New York Times*, 15 July 1995, 1.

6 Peter Passell, "Getting by without the Energy Department could be hard to do," *New York Times*, 6 July 1995, C2.

7 David Moore, Lydia Saad, Leslie McAneny and Frank Newport, "Contract With America," *Gallup Poll Monthly*, November 1994, 26.

8 Robert Borosage, "$1.5 trillion for Defense Isn't Enough?" *Los Angeles Times*, 6 December 1994.

9 *Congressional Record*, 15 May 1984, 12302.

10 Elaine Sciolino, "The Schooling of Gingrich, The Foreign Policy Novice," *New York Times*, 18 July 1995, A1.

11 David Corn, "Newt's Blown Cover," *Nation*, 26 February 1996, 3-4.

12 Reuters, 26 January 1996.

13 Sciolino, A1.

14 *In These Times*, 17 April 1995, 28.

15 Adam Clymer, "Ethics Panel Will Not Act In Oath Case," *New York Times*, 13 July 1995.

16 Steve Daley, "GOP-led House votes to limit U.S. role in UN peacekeeping," *Chicago Tribune*, 17

February 1995, 4.

17 *New York Times*, 11 June 1995, 16.

18 Sciolino.

19 Garry Wills, *New York Review of Books*, 25 March 1995.

20 Arthur Schlesinger, Jr., "New Isolationists Weaken America," *New York Times*, 11 June 1995, E15.

Part III:
Fine Print: The Hidden Contract With the Far Right

Chapter 12: Praying for Power: The Deal with the Christian Coalition

1 Richard Berke, "Christian Coalition Unveils 'Suggestions'," *New York Times*, 18 May 1995, A11.

2 David Moore, Lydia Saad, Leslie McAneny and Frank Newport, "Contract With America," *Gallup Poll Monthly*, November 1994, 27.

3 Jerry Gray, "Gingrich Plays the Dealmaker on Budget Bills," *New York Times*, 27 July 1995, A1.

4 Osborne, 17.

5 Peter Boyer, "Good Newt, Bad Newt," *Vanity Fair*, July 1989.

6 *Frontline*, "The Long March of Newt Gingrich," 16 January 1996, http://www2.pbs.org/wgbh/pages/frontline/newt.

7 *Washington Times*, 4 January 1995.

8 *Congressional Record*, 7 February 1984, 2033, 2036.

9 *Congressional Record*, 7 February 1984, 2033.

10 *Congressional Record*, 7 February 1984, 2037; *Congressional Record*, 5 March 1984, 4472.

11 Kramer, 43.

Chapter 13: Lunching on Block Grants: The Destruction of Public Education

1 Vincent Schodolski, "GOP targets program that's working," *Chicago Tribune*, 13 March 1995, 1.

2 "No Free Lunch," *New Republic*, 10 April 1995, 7.

3 Lars Erik-Nelson, "Gingrich Is Hot On Wrong Trail," *New York Newsday*, 23 March 1995.

4 Armey, *The Freedom Revolution*, 38.

5 *New York Times*, 21 February 1996, B8.

6 "No Time to Cut Head Start," *New York Times*, 10 February 1996.

7 Warner and Begley, 34.

8 Lynda Richardson, "Anxious Families Await News on Cuts in Financial Aid for College Students," *New York Times*, 8 May 1995, C11; "Filling a hole by digging it deeper," *Chicago Tribune*, 25 June 1995.

9 Bob Hohler, "Gingrich is assailed on plans by GOP to trim student aid," *Boston Globe*, 3 February 1995, 21.

10 Jim Zook, "The Speaker's Drawing Board," *Chronicle of Higher Education*, 10 February 1995, A29.

11 Bill Osinski and Jeanne Cummings, "Gingrich charity probed; Democrats calling for outside counsel," *Atlanta Journal*, 26 June 1996.

12 Phil Kuntz, "Gingrich Pal Earns Over $30,000 in Fees From Reading Plan," *Wall Street Journal*, 17 July 1995.

13 Glenn Bunting, "Gingrich's Politics Got Boost from Nonprofits, Foundations," *Los Angeles Times*, 25 June 1996.

14 Michelle Dally Johnston, "Reading between the lines," *Mother Jones*, November/December 1995, 21.

15 Rochelle Sharpe, "Book Case-Study: Cassandra Mozley Is An Inspired Reader," *Wall Street Journal*, 17 July 1995, A1.

16 *Renewing American Civilization*, 118.

17 Sharpe.

18 Clarence Page, "The Republicans and the race card," *Chicago Tribune*, 16 July 1995.

Chapter 14: Dying for Tax Cuts: Gingrich's Dangerous Health Policy

1 Dole/Gingrich news conference on the Medicare Trust Fund, 3 August 1995.

2 *Washington Post*, 10 May 1995.

3 Alison Mitchell, "Budget Office Warns of Cost of G.O.P. Medicare Plan," *New York Times*, 9 August 1995, A7.

4 Adam Clymer, "As Demonstrators Gather, Gingrich Delays a Speech," *New York Times*, 8 August 1995, A8.

5 *Washington Post*, 11 September 1995; *Washington Post*, 12 September 1995; *New York Times*, 15 September 1995.

6 *Time*, 25 December 1995.

7 Gingrich speech to American Medical Association, 16 June 1995.

8 Henry Aaron, "Better Care, Yes. Cheaper, No Way," *New York Times*, 18 February 1995, 15.

9 Gingrich, *To Renew America*.

10 Robert Dunham, "Look Who's Talking to Newt," *Business Week*, 26 June 1995.

11 Robert Samuelson, "Getting sidetracked by symbols," *Chicago Tribune*, 10 May 1996, 31.

12 *St. Petersburg Times*, 26 February 1995.

13 Robert Dreyfuss and Peter Stone, "Medikill," *Mother Jones*, January/February 1996, 80.

14 *Roll Call*, January 25, 1996.

15 Meg Fletcher, "Comp Reform Ideas Please Few; Gingrich Distancing Self from Workers Comp Task Force," *Business Insurance*, 18 March 1996.

Chapter 15: De-Funding the Left: Gingrich's Attack on Culture

1 Armey, 269.

2 Christopher Georges, "Republicans Take Aim at Left-Leaning Groups That Get Federal Grants for Assistance Programs," *Wall Street Journal*, 17 May 1995.

3 "A Lesson in Charity," *Harper's*, September 1995, 12.

4 Jeff Shear, "The Ax Files," *National Journal*, 15 April 1995.

5 Georges.

6 Georges.

7 David Cole, "Shhh!", *Nation*, 30 October 1995, 489.

8 "The NLRB gets a potent message," *Chicago Tribune*, 13 August 1995.

9 "Sen. Pressler's PBS Inquest," *Extra! Update*, April 1995, 4.

10 *Extra! Update*, April 1995, 4.

11 Anthony Lewis, "Dumb and Dumber," *New York Times*, 13 February 1995.

12 *Washington Times*, 4 January 1995.

13 Newt Gingrich, "Cutting Cultural Funding: A Reply," *Time*, 21 August 1995, 70-71.

Chapter 16: Congressional Gay Bashing: Homophobia in the House

1 Weston Kosova, "Frank Incensed," *New Republic*, 6 March 1995, 19.

2 Larry Sabato, "The Smearing of Tom Foley," *Roll Call*, 21 July 1991.

3 Josh Getlin, "Gingrich, Right's Bad Boy, Target of Angry Democrats," *Los Angeles Times*, 11 June 1989.

4 *Washington Blade*, 25 November 1994.

5 Chris Bull, "Family Matters," *Advocate*, 7 March 1995, 28.

6 Town meeting, Lost Mountain Middle School, Kennesaw, GA, quoted in *Outlines*, December 1995, 12.

7 *Washington Post*, 17 March 1995.

8 Associated Press, 4 April 1995.

9 Reuters, 14 February 1996.

10 *Outlines*, December 1994, 12; *New York Times*, 30 January 1995.

11 Robert Bernstein, "Ugly times for ugly words," *Chicago Tribune*, 3 March 1995, 31.

12 *Mother Jones*, March/April 1996, 52.

13 Newt Gingrich (with David Drake and Marianne Gingrich), *Window of Opportunity: A Blueprint for the Future* (Tor, 1984), 205-206.

14 *Meet the Press*, 4 December 1995.

15 Warner and Begley, 170.

16 Town meeting, Kennesaw, Georgia, 14 January 1995. Robert Scheer, "Military Policy, Gay Epithets—No Big Deal," Los Angeles Times, 5 February 1995.

Part IV: The Pseudo-Intellectual

Chapter 17: Newt in Space: America's Most Vacuous Intellectual

1 Mark Hosenball, "How 'Normal' Is Gingrich?," *Newsweek*, 7 November 1994.

2 Bill Kristol, speech, University of Chicago, 24 April 1996.

3 *Frontline*, "The Long March of Newt Gingrich," 16 January 1996, http://www2.pbs.org/wgbh/pages/frontline/newt.

4 Warner and Begley, 36.

5 Frontline, "The Long March of Newt Gingrich."

6 Dick Williams, *Newt: Leader of the Second American Revolution* (Marietta, GA: Longstreet Press, 1995), 78.

7 Warner and Begley, 52.

8 Warner and Begley, 57.

9 Newt Gingrich, *Window of Opportunity*, 221.

10 *Congressional Record*, 3 November 1983, 30877.

11 Gingrich, *Window of Opportunity*, 9.

12 Robert Wright, "The $4 million mind," *New Republic*, 23 January 1995, 6.

13 *Futurist*, June 1985.

14 Robert Wright, *New Republic*, 23 January 1995.

15 Warner and Begley, 104.

16 Wills, 7.

17 Weston Kosova, "Frank Incensed," *New Republic*, 6 March 1995, 19.

18 Beers, 43.

19 *Frontline*, "The Long March of Newt Gingrich."

20 *Frontline*, "The Long March of Newt Gingrich."

21 Jon Margolis, "New Age advisers taking our leaders down a foolish road," *Chicago Tribune*, 16

January 1995.
22 *Esquire*, April 1995; see also Gingrich, *To Renew America*, 245.
23 *All Things Considered*, 29 December 1994, quoted in *Utne Reader*, March-April 1995.
24 Alvin and Heidi Toffler, *Creating a New Civilization: The Politics of the Third Wave* (Atlanta: Turner, 1995), 8.
25 Toffler, 76.
26 Toffler, 72.
27 Toffler, 79.
28 Toffler, 84.
29 Toffler, 15.
30 Richard Brookhiser, "Tout Newt," *National Review*, 20 March 1995, 68.
31 Toffler, 31.
32 Toffler, 32.
33 Toffler, 42.
34 Toffler, 61.
35 Toffler, 54.
36 Toffler, 61.
37 Toffler, 62.
38 Toffler, 111.
39 Armey, 288.
40 Interview with Frank Gregorsky, *Frontline*, "The Long March of Newt Gingrich."
41 Osborne, 19.
42 Arianna Huffington, "Twelve Steps to Cultural Renewal," in Jeffrey Eisenach and Albert Steven Hanser, eds., *Readings in Renewing American Civilization* (New York: McGraw-Hill, 1993) 219, 220.
43 Huffington, "Twelve Steps to Cultural Renewal," 220.
44 Gingrich, *To Renew America*, 124.
45 Gingrich, *To Renew America*, 79.
46 Gingrich, *To Renew America*, 39.
47 Gingrich, *To Renew America*, 98.
48 Gingrich, *To Renew America*, 48.
49 Gingrich, *To Renew America*, 173.
50 Gingrich, *To Renew America*, 34, 6.
51 Gingrich, *To Renew America*, 132.
52 Gingrich, *To Renew America* , 160.

Chapter 18: Don't Know Much About History: The World According to Newt

1 Garry Wills, *New York Review of Books*, 25 March 1995, 6.
2 Speech, American Medical Association, 16 June 1995.
3 *Congressional Record*, 3 November 1983, 30872.
4 Warner and Begley, 193.
5 Jeanne Cummings, "Gingrich Seeks Top GOP Positions," *Atlanta Journal and Constitution*, 12 September 1993, B1.
6 Newt Gingrich and William Forstchen, *1945* (New York: Baen Books, 1995), 1-2.
7 Gingrich and Forstchen, *1945*, 92.
8 Robert Scheer, "Let's Look at the Real Newt Gingrich," *Los Angeles Times*, 27 November 1994.
9 *Washington Times*, 4 January 1995.

10 *Washington Times*, 4 January 1995.
11 *Congressional Record*, 3 November 1983, 30875.
12 Samuels, 36.
13 Gingrich, *To Renew America*, 34.
14 Gingrich, *To Renew America*, 34.
15 Robert Alley, letter, *New York Times*, 9 January 1995, A10.
16. Gingrich, *To Renew America*, 35.
17. Samuels, 36.
18 *Contract with America*, 141.
19 Gingrich, *Window of Opportunity*.
20 *New York Times*, 10 January 1995, A1.
21 "Dropped from Payroll," *Washington Times*, 31 January 1995.
22 Christina Jeffrey, "In Washington, it's hard to distinguish between friends and foes," *Atlanta Journal and Constitution*, 9 February 1995.
23 Letter, *Washington Post*, 24 January 1995.
24 Letter, *Washington Post*, 5 February 1995.
25 "Gingrich real target, says ex-historian," *Chicago Tribune*, 11 January 1995, 11.
26 *U.S. News and World Report*, 16 January 1996, 28.

Conclusion: Taking Back Democracy

1 Notes of 9 August 1990 GOPAC meeting.
2 Williams, 99.
3 *Time*, 25 December 1995, 99.
4 Stephen Glass, "The Hall Monitor," *New Republic*, 1 July 1996, 11.
5 David Sands, "GOP ax hangs over FEC," *Washington Times*, 11 June 1996.
6 Damon Chappie, "FEC Ordered to Slash Staff in Its Press Office," *Roll Call*, 20 June 1996..

INDEX

D

E

F

G

H

I

J

K

L

M

N

O

P

R

S

T

U

V

W

Y

About the Author

John K. Wilson is a graduate student in the Committee on Social Thought at the University of Chicago. He is the author of *The Myth of Political Correctness: The Conservative Attack on Higher Education* (Duke University Press, 1995) and has written for the *Chronicle of Higher Education*, the *Chicago Sun-Times*, *In These Times*, and *Z Magazine*. He is also the editor of *Democratic Culture*, the journal of Teachers for a Democratic Culture, an organization of 1,700 left-liberal teachers and students devoted to countering the conservative attacks on academia, and co-editor of the *University of Chicago Free Press*, an alternative monthly student newspaper. He received B.A'.s in political science, philosophy, and history from the University of Illinois at Urbana-Champaign.